495

THE HOPE OF THE WORLD

Other Books

by

HARRY EMERSON FOSDICK

o

The Second **Mile**
The Assurance of Immortality
The Manhood of the Master
The Meaning of Prayer
The Meaning of Faith
The Meaning of Service
Christianity and Progress
Twelve Tests of Character
The Modern Use of the Bible
Adventurous Religion
A Pilgrimage to Palestine
As I See Religion

o

The Hope
of the World

*Twenty-five Sermons
on Christianity Today*

By

HARRY EMERSON FOSDICK

PUBLISHERS
HARPER & BROTHERS
NEW YORK AND LONDON 1933

Contents

CONTENTS

Foreword

WHILE many occasionally printed sermons of mine have appeared in pamphlet or parish paper to meet a local need, this, after thirty years in the ministry, is the first volume of sermons I have published. I release it with some misgiving, for the essential nature of a sermon as an intimate, conversational message from soul to soul makes it impossible for printing to reproduce preaching, and, unlike the traditional child, sermons should be heard and not seen.

These discourses were delivered first in the pulpit, taken down stenographically, and afterward given as addresses over the air. I send them out especially to my friends of the Riverside Church, New York, and of the National Vespers across the continent, who may find in them not only what the eye now sees but what the ear once heard. To them in an intimate sense the book belongs, for the audience as well as the preacher makes the sermon and friendly listeners draw out the message as well as take it in. True as it always is, it is especially true of the preacher that no man is the whole of himself—his friends are the rest of him.

HARRY EMERSON FOSDICK

September 1, 1933

THE HOPE OF THE WORLD

The Hope of the World
in Its Minorities

ONE of the most arresting statements recently made
by a public man was made by Mr. Einstein when he
said that if two per cent of our population should
take a personal, resolute stand against the sanction and support of another war, that would end war. Whether or not
this estimate of Mr. Einstein's is as accurate as his cosmic
mathematics, I presume no one of us can say, but there is no
doubt about the historical evidence on which the principle
of his judgment rests.

The creative ideas destined to remake society have always
been the possession of the minority. History has depended,
not on the ninety-eight per cent, but on the two per cent. Far
from being a matter of sociological and political interest
alone, this principle gave Christianity its start. When the
Master in Palestine began calling out his first disciples from
the mass of their countrymen, he was interested not in quantity but in quality—in seed, though but a few kernels, which,
if carefully sown, might multiply itself. He was thinking not
primarily of the ninety-eight per cent but of a germinal two
per cent. To use his own figure in the thirteenth chapter of
Matthew's Gospel: "The kingdom of heaven is like unto
leaven, which a woman took, and hid in three measures of
meal, till it was all leavened." Quantitatively small, vitally
active leaven—that is a true simile of the method of Christianity's transformation of the world.

But is Christianity working like that now? Take the measure of our American churches. Are we the germinal two
per cent on which the future of mankind depends? Are we
the little group of forward-looking men and women on
whom, as on the first disciples of our Lord, has fallen the
vision of a new world-order so that we are custodians of
prophetic principles that shall remake society? Are we the

minority ready to sacrifice fame or fortune or life itself for those ideas which shall some day permeate mankind with their healing and their truth?

You see, we do not answer to that description. Too frequently forgetting the mission that the Master left us and the way of working he committed to us, we have become a majority movement standing for the status quo, so that many are even startled when they hear a man like Mr. Einstein say that if two per cent should take a personal, resolute stand against war it would mean the end of war. What if, however, something like that is true? What if the future of mankind is in the hands of a minority? What if a little leaven hid in three measures of meal can leaven the whole?

There is no need of elaborating the historical evidence regarding this matter. In every realm the pathfinders have been few and the truths that at last triumphed were at first the possession of a minority. We all know that, but in our thought and life are certain factors which frequently prevent the full force of it from reaching us.

For one thing, we live in a democracy, where the only way of carrying on public business is to accept the voice of the majority. In consequence, the notion naturally prevails that the majority in the end probably is right and that, anyway, the majority rules. But neither of those ideas is true. The majority is almost certain to be wrong on any matter of fine taste or sound judgment, and, whether or not the majority is right, it certainly does not rule. The dominant influence in every situation is a militant minority. The decision of public policy in this country now is largely determined by resolute, militant, compact, closely organized minorities that want something and get it.

Look at this city. Is Tammany Hall a majority? Upon the contrary, it is a self-seeking, highly organized minority and it runs the metropolis. The majority are apathetic, careless, attending to their own business, not the city's, with no very strong convictions one way or the other, and that gives a resolute minority its chance. There is no use fooling ourselves that the majority rules. The United States today is ruled by organized minorities.

If, therefore, at first some were inclined to think that the doctrine of the two per cent is impractical idealism, let us disabuse our minds of that supposition. The serious truth is that the controlling power of the minority, so far from being impractical idealism, is most practical politics. Even in a democracy the minority rules.

The full force of this truth which Jesus put into his figure of the meal and the leaven is deflected from many modern minds also by our inveterate habit of romanticizing history. When we start in to glorify our ancestors for some outstanding achievement, such as, for example, the winning of the American Revolution, we make a thorough job of it and glorify all our ancestors. What a splendid outpouring of co-operative and unanimous zeal it was, we think, that all those colonists put their lives, their fortunes, their sacred honor at the disposal of the cause! That sounds splendid but there is not a word of truth in it. There were probably more Tories than Revolutionists among the colonists and more than either were the men who see-sawed back and forth, who stood first on one side, then on the other, who had no strong convictions either way, and only hoped they were betting right on who was going to win. I venture that more than one family is represented here this morning who wanted to join the Sons or Daughters of the Revolution and so looked up their ancestors—and have kept still about it ever since.

The Revolutionary War was won, the government established, and the Constitution put in force by a compact, highly intelligent, loyal minority. Do you remember John Adams' apostrophe to his posterity? "Posterity! you will never know how much it cost the present generation to preserve your freedom! I hope you will make a good use of it. If you do not, I shall repent it in heaven that I ever took half the pains to preserve it."

Such is the situation with every gain humanity ever made. It was the two per cent who fought for popular education, for religious liberty, for freedom of scientific research, against the majority. Always the majority has been dough, the few have been leaven; so that out of history there rises an admonition—in any cause that concerns the progress of mankind, put your faith in the creative minorities!

Again, this truth of Jesus is deflected from many modern minds because of our worship of bigness. One of my friends calls it "Jumboism." Especially in this country many people are impressed by nothing that is not big—big cities, big buildings, big corporations. We all are tempted to worship size. But size is an utterly fallacious standard when we are trying to estimate power. Could any one, at the height of Rome's colossal power, have thought of anything much smaller than Paul in a Roman prison writing his few letters? But the result! Whoever would have dreamed that that little man with his brief epistles would dig down so deeply, take hold so strongly, penetrate so powerfully the thoughts and motives of men? The things that are big are utterly misleading as to the location of the ideas that are powerful.

We have in our modern time a vivid illustration of this truth. Whatever else we may think about it, there are few more dramatic incidents in mankind's history than Gandhi confronting the British Empire. The greatest empire in history stands over against one man trying to make terms with him, while he will not fight with outward weapons, is ready to die if his followers use violence, and employs nothing but the ideas of a minority and a certain quality of soul to set them aflame. There are few things that we American Christians need much more to learn than the lesson of that. Bigness is not power. Power is in the ideas to which the future belongs, and they always have been the possession, not of the ninety-eight per cent, but of the two per cent.

Looked at from one angle, this truth is encouraging. When one thinks of the causes that are on our hearts today,—peace rather than war, industrial welfare rather than this desperate situation we are in, better education for the nation's children, or whatever it may be,—we should welcome the good news that we do not have to wait for the majority. Wherever a true idea is born and a creative minority rallies around it, there is the beginning of victory. That is encouraging and it is true. It is not, however, a truth to go to sleep on. We Christians were intended to be that minority. We were to be the salt of the earth, said Jesus. We were to be the light of the world. We were to be the leaven in the lump of the race. There is no possibility of misunderstanding his meaning, my friends. When a man becomes a real Christian he is supposed to move over into that small, creative, sacrificial minority seized upon by visions of a better world and standing for them until they shall permeate mankind with their truth. That does make being a Christian serious business! That is more than believing in a creed. That is more than partaking of the sacraments. That is more than the comfort of worship or the use of beauty as a road to God. That is joining the real church in the original Greek meaning of the word "church," *ecclesia*—called out—a minority selected from the majority to be leaven.

Only as we succeed in getting more Christians like that will power return to the Christian movement. When was Christianity most powerful? Shall we select some scene like that at Canossa, when the Pope bestrode Europe with his rule and even an emperor waited three days in the snow at his doorsill begging for audience and pardon? That seems powerful, yet even a scene like that, when time has worn its meaning off, loses its glamour. There was a time, however, when Christianity was very powerful. Little groups of men and women were scattered through the Roman Empire —"not many mighty," said Paul, "not many noble." They were far less than two per cent and the heel of persecution was often on them, but they flamed with a conviction that they represented truths to which the future belonged.

Do you remember what Paul called them in his letter to the Philippians? "We are a colony of heaven," he said. The Philippian Christians would understand that figure, for their city of Philippi was a Roman colony. When Rome wanted to Romanize a new province, it took Roman people and planted them as a colony in the midst of it. There, as a powerful minority, they stood for Roman law, Roman justice, Roman

[5]

faith, and Roman custom, leaven in the lump of the province, until the whole province was leavened. Rome understood the art of government. When, therefore, Paul said to that little group of Philippian Christians, "We are a colony of heaven," they understood. They were a minority thrown out, as pioneers, in the midst of an unchristian world to represent the ideals, faiths, and way of living of a nobler realm until the earth should be the Lord's and the fulness thereof.

In those days Christianity was very powerful. It stopped ancient curses like infanticide. It put an end to the bloody shambles of the gladiatorial shows. It laid hold on an old polytheism that had been glorified in literature, extolled in art, established in custom, and supported by government, and ended it in the interests of one God revealed in Christ. Then Christianity was very powerful. It was a minority movement with nothing to lose, with everything to gain, joining which a man pledged his very life as a forfeit. At last it became so powerful that it captured the Empire, entrenched itself in wealth and worldly prestige, stopped challenging the world, began compromising with the world, went on to defend the status quo of the world, and never again, I fear, on so vast a scale has exhibited such creative, superhuman power.

Let us, therefore, for our own sakes and for the sake of our generation, see if we can recover even a little the meaning of that saying of Jesus, "The kingdom of heaven is like unto leaven, which a woman took, and hid in three measures of meal, till it was all leavened."

In the first place, this clearly applies to our churches themselves. Not infrequently one is asked in these days whether or not one believes in the church. Just what is meant by the "church" in that question? These sectarian organizations that carry over from old political quarrels and theological debates denominational divisions that have no pertinency to modern life—are they the church? These sects so often splitting and overlapping their labor in our American communities, absorbed in their self-maintenance until they hardly think of the real issues on which the future of mankind depends, so that the best citizens often feel that they must pull up the church rather than be pulled up by it—are they the church? And by having faith in the church does one mean that he stakes his hope of the future of the race upon this inherited network of denominational organizations? Then let an honest answer be given: How can a man believe in the church?

My own faith is not in these formal organizations. Personally, I think most of them will have to die. Their lines of division and their points of emphasis have no just claim upon contemporaneous interest even, much less on permanency. My faith is in the church within the churches, the two per cent, the spiritual leaven, the inner group of men and women who have been genuinely kindled by Christ's spirit and are today living and thinking above the average and ahead of the time. Always the real church has been not the dough of the mass but the leaven of the few.

As for these formal organizations, let not the lesson of Russia be forgotten. The Greek Church in Russia allied itself with the status quo. It surrendered its prophetic mission and became the religious right arm of the most despotic government on earth and, becoming thus the defender and ally of a political and social régime that could not last, it went out with the system it was tied to. Religion is not dead in Russia. It will not die. Though it seems to die, it will have its resurrection day. But the church as a whole could not save it. Once more in Russia history will have to repeat itself —a little leaven beginning again to work in three measures of meal. My friends, whether by violence or by slow starvation, that is the fate of every ecclesiastical organization that allies itself with a dying order. Church of Christ in America, with all your wealth and your prestige, beware! Could Paul say of you, "Ye are a colony of heaven"?

If some one protests that the real church, then, must forever be standing for new ideas only and never for old ones, so that in consequence the real church becomes merely a radical, iconoclastic group, I am glad to answer that protest as a constructive contribution to our thought. Being a saving

[7]

minority is a much deeper matter than that protest understands.

Vital experience of God, for example, as a living force in daily life, has always been the possession of a minority. The faith of most men in God has been inherited, picked up from superficial education, assumed as a plausible explanation of the universe. But that inner flame of spiritual life which burns upon the high altar of a man's soul because of himself he can say, "O God, thou art my God," always has belonged to the few. The many have occasionally borrowed it.

So, too, a living faith in Christ, which enables one in some deep sense to say, "I live; yet not I, but Christ liveth in me," has always belonged to a minority. The majority have worshiped Christ, indeed, have recited resounding creeds about him and made obeisance at his altars, but to live Christ in private quality, in social life, in sacrificial devotion, has that belonged even to the two per cent?

This matter, therefore, of being a saving minority is not cheap and superficial; it goes deep. Indeed, in the Bible there are two kinds of religious minorities: first, Paul's "colony" thrown out as pioneers in an unchristian world, and, second, Isaiah's "remnant," the little group of the true Israel which, in a time that is surrendering old sanctities, clings to them and despite the pressure of an alien generation preserves them for children yet unborn. How much we do need both—minorities that pioneer and minorities that keep the high values of the faith amid a time that popularly surrenders them!

My friends, I am jealous for the church. So much of our Christianity is dough; I want the church to be leaven.

Our truth applies also to social problems. Men today, making their characteristic reactions to the social, economic, international difficulties which beset us, fall into three classes: first, those below the average—lawless, criminal, anti-social; second, those on the average, who play the game according to the rules with a fine sense of honor for observing them; and, third, those above the average, who question the rules. Are the rules themselves fair? Is the game itself equitable? Does it not minister to the advantage of the few against the many, and cannot the rules be altered so that the game itself will be more just? The hope of the world depends upon that third class.

The truth of this classification can be clearly seen when it is applied to a social problem of the past like slavery. In the days when slavery was in power there were: first, the dishonorable slaveholders, the Simon Legrees, below the average; second, the honorable slaveholders who accepted slavery and the rules of slavery's game and played it like gentlemen, caring for their slaves, ministering solicitously to their physical and spiritual welfare; but, third, both north and south, the people who questioned the whole game of slavery. The rules themselves were not right. The game itself was wrong. High-minded and honorable as the second class was, the future depended upon that third two per cent.

Often in these trying days, as your preacher, I think of you business men. You face heavy burdens, practically complicated and ethically difficult. The more I know of you the better I appreciate the fine code of honor with which you handle your responsibilities. Yet, after all, with you as with me, the final test of a social attitude is at this point to which our thought has brought us. Not for all the world would you run your business in lawless disregard of the rules. You have a careful sense of honor about observing them. But are you dedicating your brains—and the best brains of America are in the business world—to this third matter: Cannot the rules be improved? Cannot the whole game be made more just?

Only the other day I was talking with my friend, a representative of a great corporation. This spring that corporation is casting off into unemployment, absolutely unprovided for, thousands of its men. My friend told me that the corporation had built up a surplus of many millions of dollars to protect the stockholders against emergency. The stockholders are safe against crisis for years to come but not one cent of financial responsibility has that corporation taken for its employees, now cast off into unemployment. The only hope I found in the situation was that my friend himself belonged to the two per cent. He saw that that policy would never do, that it did not fit this new industrial order into which the machine has introduced us, that business must take financial responsibility against emergency, not simply for investors of money but for investors of life and labor.

This test of social attitude is the same in my realm as it is in yours. Suppose I should accept the present situation in the churches, settle down in my churchmanship to make myself as comfortable as I could, get what I might for myself out of it, and be undisturbed by it; you know that for me that would be a betrayal of trust. The least that a minister of Christ, if he is in earnest, can do today is to stand above the alliance of the church with this dying order and try to help bring forth that new church in which the spiritual life of the future can find its home.

That same test applies to all of us. Wanted in church, business, statesmanship, and international relationships men and women who are not simply playing the game according to the rules but who are trying to better the rules and make the game more just!

Of course, the fact that a man happens to be a member of a minority is no guarantee that he is right. There are all sorts of minorities, good, bad, and indifferent, and not simply every saving idea but every foolish fad can be a minority. That fact, however, argues not against but for our plea. Just because today there are so many uninformed, irresponsible, even violent minorities, let the forward-looking and responsible citizens the more assume their obligations!

As for being Christian, I suppose that, reduced to simplest terms, it means answering Christ's two-worded appeal, "Follow me." Where do we think it takes a man when he does follow him? Never into a majority. I wonder where you and I are this morning—three measures of meal or leaven?

Christianity at Home
in Chaos

MANY people feel that this is an exceedingly difficult time for Christianity. Even under fortunate circumstances, they say, it is not easy to hold Christian ideas about the love of God, the value of the human soul, and a new society of goodwill among men, but in distracted days like these how can such unworldly faiths seem true?

That mood comes to all of us. The unpromising qualities of human nature, dismay at wide-spread destitution, collapse of confidence, and the confusion of world affairs frown down upon the fragile, unearthly, idealistic faiths of Christianity. Nevertheless, if we look at history we shall find that the eras when Christianity was most certainly believed and sacrificially supported, when it made its great advances and won its resounding victories, were not prosperous times but chaotic days like these.

So, in the familiar story, Brer Rabbit persuades his enemy, Brer Fox, to throw him into a brier-patch on the supposition that that would be the worst thing which could befall him, but now, thrown into it, Brer Rabbit runs happily away, saying, "Bred en bawn in a brier-patch, Brer Fox—bred en bawn in a brier-patch!"

Similarly Christianity, far from feeling strange in a troubled time, was born and bred in a brier-patch like this. It started with a cross. The first Christian from Nazareth lived through difficult days. The early Christian community won its amazing victory against the opposition of a pagan world and the first church established itself amid the ruins of a collapsed empire and a wrecked civilization. We children of the Reformation would better not forget the travail out of which we were born, with Calvin crying about the people of his time: "Their wickedness has, however, reached such a pitch, that I hardly hope to be able any longer to retain any kind of position for the Church, especially under my ministry. My influence is gone, believe me, unless God stretch forth His hand." Especially we American Christians display a strange forgetfulness of our history with its struggle to plant the gospel in the wilderness of this new continent, if we accept a weak picture of a fragile, unearthly, idealistic Christian faith unfitted to deal with trouble. It ought to be wholesome to say to ourselves today that Christianity was born and bred in a brier-patch.

Indeed, it would be strange if I were not now speaking to some one who is persuaded that Christian faith is only an idealistic dream. It is beautiful and comforting, you think, if one can believe it, but it fails to take account of the tragic nature of the world. It turns its eyes away from the dark, cruel aspects of life, you say, to center its regard on what is cheering and comfortable, and so constructs theories of God and man and the possibilities of a new society incredible to one who honestly grapples with the terrific facts of human life. When you see a disbeliever like Bertrand Russell saying that there is no God, no unity or purpose in the universe, no human hope except temporary ameliorations of our earthly fate, and that at last on man "and all his race the slow, sure doom falls pitiless and dark," there, you say, is one who candidly faces the ruthless processes of nature and the essential tragedy of life.

My friend, we are not debating the whole question between theism and atheism, but this surely is certain: whatever else one may say about the historic Christian faith, one may not thus claim that it has failed to grapple with tragedy. The symbol of Christianity is the cross. Christianity started with tragedy, took tragedy for its very password and countersign. Open the New Testament anywhere and you will find, I think, not so much idealistic dreamers as men and women who, as the Epistle to the Hebrews says, were stoned, sawn asunder, tempted, slain with the sword, going about in sheepskins and goatskins, destitute, afflicted, ill-treated, of whom the world was not worthy. Look at Chris-

tian history anywhere and you find Christianity grappling
with tragedy, sometimes causing tragedy, often suffering
tragedy, and, at its best, learning lessons from tragedy,
changing the situations which produced it, and getting a new
grasp on the meaning of faith because of it.

"In the world ye have tribulation," said Jesus to his disciples that last night before he died. That does not sound as
though he were blinking difficulty. "In the world ye have
tribulation: but be of good cheer; I have overcome the
world."

Consider, then, some of the ways in which the historic
Christian faith has faced difficult eras—ways that in these
times we might well emulate and reproduce.

For one thing, repeatedly in desperate, dangerous times
Christians have caught a new vision of the value and indispensableness of Christ's moral principles. Why does moral
character in individuals and society find the test of long-
continued material prosperity so difficult? We all know what
poverty does to people, how it can shut doors of opportunity, wreck families, and leave bedraggled and distressed
countless lives that might have been radiant and happy.
Poverty is one of the major curses of mankind and we must
wage tireless war against it. Nevertheless, it is also true that
one of the severest tests which moral character in individuals
and societies ever faces is the long continuance of material
prosperity. Said Andrew Carnegie, "As a rule the 'almighty
dollar' bequeathed to sons or daughters by millions proves an
almighty curse."

That is not simply true about individuals but about generations. In Jewish history, out of which our Christian faith
emerged, where shall we look for the outstanding eras of
moral and religious insight? In Solomon's time? Judah was
prosperous then but we seek in vain for great spiritual truths
discovered or moral ventures undertaken. The outstanding
eras of moral and religious insight were times like the Exile.
Torn from their native land, impinged upon by the brilliant
paganism of Babylonia, stabbed every day by antagonistic
faiths and morals, shaken by an international earthquake

which made the slumberous soul impossible, those Jews saw new things and spoke new words which Judaism had never seen or heard before. Strange,—is it not?—out of what places the notable advances of the race's faith and character have come! Born and bred in a brier-patch!

What, then, do we think about our situation? Do we still believe that those post-war years which led up to 1929 were, as we called them, good times? Upon the contrary, history will write them down as bad times—bad for everything that makes for moral stamina in a nation. It will be many a year before we shall altogether escape from the wild gambling, the loose living, the decay of citizenship, the collapse of personal integrity, the growth of selfish cynicism, the desertion of religious faith, that marked those post-war years. And did some one come here this morning complaining that *these* days are bad for Christianity? Rather, this is the kind of weather in which Christianity habitually has achieved its strongest growth.

Let me say personally that in trying to present to you the principles of Jesus I find a clear contrast between the atmosphere of 1929 and today. Then, when we rode high, when our acquisitive society seemed all success, when, no matter what we did, the wealth of the world poured in to us, the moral principles of Jesus did seem idealistic. In Thackeray's Vanity Fair, Becky Sharp says that she thinks she might be a good woman on five thousand pounds a year. Such was our mood, and that mood always makes the moral principles of Jesus seem idealistic. Do they seem so to you now?

"Inasmuch as ye did it unto one of these my brethren, even these least, ye did it unto me"—that is not idealistic; that is basic. Any man must see that the crux of our problem today is what is happening to the common man. Look at him even with the economist's eye only—he is the ultimate consumer. Only if he can buy will business thrive. Only if he have confidence can the economic life go on. If he is poor, everybody will be poor. If he is panicky, the wheels of business must stop. We cannot see into the heart of our present catastrophe and the way out unless we see deeply the meaning of those ancient words, "Inasmuch as ye did it unto one of these my brethren, even these least."

"Whosoever would be first among you, shall be servant of all"—that is not idealistic; that is basic. When, in his inaugural address, President Roosevelt spoke with indignation about the unscrupulous misuse of economic power regardless of the welfare of all the people, he was voicing—was he not?—a wide-spread, deep-seated, dangerous indignation in the American people. Half blind though we the people are and ourselves involved in all the mistakes our scapegoats have made, nevertheless we do see, as we never in prosperous days saw half so well, that business cannot be merely an acquisitive game, every man for himself; business must be the loyal servant of the common interests of all the people, and, no matter how radical the changes required to incarnate that and make it real in our economic system, we must be prepared to face them. For a bank to sell bonds to the people and make millions out of them when the bank knows that those bonds are worse than dubious is not good business—not for the people; as it turns out, not for the bank; as we all see now, not for the nation. Whosoever would be first among you, shall be servant of all.

So one could run the gamut of the ethical teachings of Jesus. "Blessed are the peacemakers"—that is absolutely basic. And as for what he said about integrity of personal character, "Let your speech be, Yea, yea; Nay, nay,"—that is to say, Let your word be as good as your bond,—we are lost without that.

This is not a bad time for Christian morals. Christian morals were born and bred in a brier-patch like this. This is a bad time for anything except Christian morals, bad for selfishness and cynicism, bad for lapses of integrity and poor citizenship. These are even times when I, for one, a modernist, look on a shaken generation and out of the New Testament hear with fresh meaning and authority those words about Christ, "There is none other name under heaven given among men, whereby we must be saved."

Again, more than once in Christian history, in difficult and shaken times Christians have caught a fresh vision of the meaning and indispensableness of their faith in God and the eternal values of personality.

Why is it that religious faith never reaches its depth until it is faced with tragedy? Suppose a man who had met only the musical-comedy aspect of life, and we know at once, however correct the forms of his faith, his religion would be shallow and superficial. Some modern doubters persist in saying that religious faith is an idealistic dream because it never has grappled with tragedy. I say, upon the contrary, that no great religious faith in all history has ever even come into existence without grappling with tragedy. Did not Gautama Buddha's faith begin that day when he issued from the soft protection of his father's palace and for the first time looked on human misery demanding explanation and cure? Did not the Hebrew religion begin with a man concerning whom the Scripture says, "When Moses was grown up, . . . he went out unto his brethren, and looked on their burdens"? Did not the Hebrew religion take its decisive turn upward in the character and ministry of Jeremiah, whose very name is a symbol of tragedy? The great faiths that have gone ahead of the race like pillars of cloud by day and fire by night have been born out of tribulation. As for *our* faith, no cross, no Christianity!

Nor is it difficult to see why this should be so. When a man faces tragedy, he discovers the utter unlivableness of irreligion. When we are comfortable, stimulated and sustained by favoring circumstance, we can get on without thinking deeply about the human problem and often without conscious need of God. But when tragedy befalls and we are stripped of the cushioning of circumstance and in a dark hour the soul stands lonely and quivering before the eternal mystery, then there appears the utter unlivableness of irreligion—no spiritual source behind life, no eternal purpose running through it, no goal ahead of it, no sense in it. In dark hours like that the human soul at its best has risen up with an authentic surety that there is more to be said about human life than that. Out of such hours have come the creative faiths of the human race. Without some such hour no man has ever yet plumbed the depths of an invincible faith in God. A man must sometimes have faced an experience of deep and difficult need where he looked into what Carlyle called the "Everlasting Nay" of irreligion, if he is to understand the full meaning of the "Everlasting Yea" of religious faith.

What can we mean, then, by supposing that these days are an alien time for Christian faith? The only basis for so shallow a judgment is the identification, commonly made, of Christian faith with easy-going optimism. Now, Christian faith is optimistic but only in the sense of Jesus' saying, "In the world ye have tribulation: but be of good cheer; I have overcome the world." That is to say, Christian faith is an optimism that comes from facing pessimism. As one of our wise contemporaries has put it, "Religion is the hope that grows out of despair. It is the ultimate optimism which follows in the wake of a thorough pessimism. One reason why our generation is not religious is that it has been too sentimental to be thoroughly pessimistic." Walk around that for a moment and you will find truth in it. The greatest Christian faith in history is always like a Rembrandt portrait—an illuminated face shining out of a dark background.

The other day I ran upon some sentences from a once-famous portrait painter, William Morris Hunt. He says: "I tell you it's no joke to paint a portrait! . . . Into the painting of every picture that is worth anything, there comes, sometime, this period of despair!" That is true to experience, is it not? The greatest musical compositions were never written, no worth-while sermon, I think, was ever preached, no supreme monument of architecture ever was built, without the creative artist's facing at one point despair about his work. No more has religious faith been easily won, as so many people think.

How many of you would say today what I say, that there have been hours when I thought I saw into the profound depths of a triumphant Christian faith and they were not hours in the lecture room of a theological seminary but when

I went down into the valley to keep a rendezvous with tragedy, and when against the Everlasting Nay I saw the Everlasting Yea victoriously rise up?

That experience has sometimes been entered into on a large scale by a whole generation. The eighteenth century, for example, with its French Revolution, its collapse of an old social order, its appalling economic maladjustment and poverty, its rampant immorality and atheism, such that men said they were taking the "not" from the Commandments and putting it into the creed, was more like our generation than any other period in history. Christians were in despair. Did not their enemies say that Christianity already had one foot in the grave and needed only decent obsequies to complete its history?

My friends, when any generation backs Christian faith into a corner like that, a recoil is imminent. Then came the Wesleys to light a fire that broke into such a conflagration of triumphant faith and humanitarian endeavor as the English-speaking world never had known before. Once more came an authentic outburst of spiritual life, hope born out of despair, the Everlasting Yea rising as though in desperation to overcome the Everlasting Nay.

If we Christians were worth our salt we could reproduce that now. Did some one come here today saying, This is no time for Christian faith! I tell you this is no time for atheism. This is no time to tell men that there is no God, no eternal purpose through life, no goal ahead of it, no sense in it. This is no time for cynicism and skepticism and materialism. Such things we can stand a little of in prosperity. I ask you, What are you going to do with them now? This is a time to see again the deep meanings of the Christian faith.

Once more in many a generation like this, Christians have laid fresh hold upon their social hopes.

It is a strange thing—is it not?—that we should so commonly say that a discouraging time is the time when people really are discouraged. The fact is that if we wish to see outstanding examples of courage we must always look in a discouraging time to find them. In consequence, out of discouraging times have come the main forward movements of the race's social hope.

It is not difficult to see why this is true. Hope is not, as we commonly think, merely the denial of despair. Hope springs out of despair. Again and again in history, personal and social, despair has been the womb out of which hope has been born. Out of the despair of the Egyptian bondage came the hope of a free Hebrew people. Out of the despair of the Exile came the hope of a reconstituted Jewish state. Out of the despair of a falling Roman Empire came the hope of a universal church. Out of the despair of tyrannical monarchy was born the hope of democracy. And today out of the disheartening tragedy of war has risen the hope of peace, and out of the sickness of an acquisitive society springs strong the hope of a more humane, coöperative, economic life. Some of you are ready, as you never have been before, to agree to wide-spread, deep-seated, radical changes in economic life on behalf of the welfare of all the people. It is precisely out of days like these that the great social hopes of the race have sprung.

Some of you may be tempted to discouragement about Christianity even more than about the economic crisis. Christian principles, faiths, and institutions face, you think, a disheartening day. I wish I could change your tune. I think you are playing Brer Fox over again. You see Christianity thrown into a brier-patch and you think that is likely to finish it. "Bred en bawn in a brier-patch, Brer Fox."

That is true even of the church itself. The Jewish synagogue was born out of the need for spiritual fellowship in the Exile. The church was born out of the difficult situation of the early Christian brotherhood in the Roman Empire. The Protestant churches were born out of the terrific collapse of old Europe, and if we have in us anything like the spirit of our sires we will build in these days a better kind of church, freer in mind, more inclusive in hospitality, more communal in service, in a generation when men and women need spiritual sustenance and fellowship as seldom before.

As for our own interior, spiritual life, we know well that

[19]

we never tap the deepest levels of power until we face something hard, where we crucially need it. No man ever gets his second wind save in a long race. It is only when we have something for which we need power that power can come. We say that Jesus had inner power with which to face the cross. Turn it around. It was the facing of the cross that called out the power. O my soul, grasp that philosophy! Make your hardships develop your resources. Make your tasks call out your reserves. Face the tragedies of life like a veritable pessimist: "In the world—tribulation." Never blink that fact. But make tribulation release the deeper levels of divine resource, so that you too may say, "Good cheer; I have overcome the world."

Christianity's Stake in the Social Situation

A FEW days ago I saw a man, long unemployed, who had just received a letter calling him back to his old position. One who deals intimately with human life grows accustomed to seeing a mysterious light in the eyes of happy people,—little children when they are glad, brides and grooms, families that welcome back to life some one who has been close to death,—but accustomed as I am to seeing this, I think I never shall forget the eyes of that man with the letter in his hand, called back to work again.

That man may well symbolize for us a truth which, as much as any other, I suspect, needs now to be urged on the Christian conscience: we cannot separate the spiritual interests of individual souls from the social situation. Some seem to think we can. Recently a prominent citizen of this community asked me to recommend a minister to the pulpit of his church, but the kind of minister, he took pains to insist, who would preach what he called "the simple Gospel" and not talk about social questions. Recently, also, a clergyman in this city vehemently deplored a thoughtful statement of the Federal Council of the Churches of Christ because, so he seemed to think, Christianity deals only with individual souls.

Since we shall seriously differ with laymen and clergymen who so suppose that we can separate the spiritual interests of individual souls from the social situation, let us start by doing them justice.

For one thing, if they mean that a Christian minister is often poorly equipped to handle social questions, and that when he talks about economics and international relationships he commonly displays more energy than sound sense and information, we had better agree with that. There is a good deal to be said for a shoemaker's sticking to his last

[21]

and a clergyman's confining his remarks to areas where he has taken pains to be informed.

Or again, if they mean that when people come to church on Sunday, having lived another week in the hurly-burly of the world, their ears tired with boisterous debate, they are seeking something other than a continuance of the secular dispute, we had better agree with that. The church has lost its function which forgets how deeply men, one by one, need spiritual renewal.

Or again, if they mean that there are two major realms in public influence, the domain of persuasion and the domain of coercion, and that the church belongs in the domain of persuasion, as far away as possible from the domain of coercion, we had better agree with that. One basic trouble in the whole affair of prohibition has been that the church moved over from the realm of persuasion into the realm of coercion, using political power to enforce laws which it had not yet persuaded the people to obey. The testimony of all history is that that is about the most dangerous business in which the church ever can indulge. We had better agree with that.

Let all exponents of the social gospel in the churches, then, take notice! They do sometimes talk too much without informing themselves adequately; they do sometimes continue on Sunday the secular debate which the newspapers conduct a great deal better through the week; they do sometimes forget that when they cease to be persuasive and try to be coercive they are off their beat. Nevertheless, there is that man with the letter in his hand and the light in his eyes, his very soul saved from a hell of anxious fear by a chance to work again! Let a Christian minister, therefore, profoundly persuaded, as I am, that to talk about the Christian gospel as merely individual and not social is dangerous nonsense, speak to this point.

It is a point of first-rate importance to the minister himself. He is expected to help men, one by one, to nobler living, but constantly he finds consciences calloused, ears deafened, souls crushed, and fine resolutions thwarted by a maladjusted and cruel society. That, indeed, is an ancient story. Listen to it as the Book of Exodus tells the tale of Hebrew slavery in Egypt three thousand years ago: "And Moses spake so unto the children of Israel: but they hearkened not unto Moses for anguish of spirit, and for cruel bondage." That story is not finished yet: messengers of God trying to persuade people to a better life, baffled and thwarted not alone by individual sin but by social situations that bring to wide areas of the people anguish of spirit and cruel bondage. Let us, then, try to clarify our thought about this inextricable entanglement of the individual spiritual life with the social situation.

In the first place, any one who begins by feeling that the initial responsibility of the Christian church is to the individual soul, must inevitably include in his thought of that matter the pride of Christianity, its converted and renovated characters. No man need stay the way he is; he can be transformed by the renewing of his mind—that is the Christian gospel. Go to, then, some one says, be about *that* business and let the Christian church supply us with transformed individual lives.

To be sure, if we were not doing that we should be failing utterly, but, my friends, when any one seriously works for transformation of individual character, he is led not away from social questions but straight into them. Consider, for example, that all modern hospitals have social workers—no good hospital today would be without them—who follow individual cases out of the hospital to see in what social conditions of home and neighborhood and economic security the patients live. We cannot cure men and women even physically if for anguish of spirit and cruel bondage they do not respond to what the physician does. If a hospital cannot be individualistic, how can a church be?

We are having an exciting time now with foreign missions, and I suspect we shall have a still more exciting time before we are through with this admirably frank and thorough report of the Laymen's Inquiry. Now, no more important testimony to our truth could be given than has been given by foreign missions. The first missionaries were intensely individualistic. They went out to save souls, one by one, from hell. They did tremendously care about the individual lives of their people. See, then, what happened. They could not bring the gospel to the individual without the Bible, so they became the translators of the world; they have put the Book into over six hundred different languages. What is the use, however, of translating the Bible in countries where ninety to ninety-five per cent of the people cannot read? So the missionaries became educators and in many lands the methods of the best schools go back to the missionaries. But what is the use of educating people who needlessly die for lack of scientific medicine and sanitation? So the missionaries became physicians, and medical missions constitute one of the finest areas of human history. But what is the use of merely curing people when they must return to economic devastation and penury? At a conservative estimate, thirty million people go to bed hungry every night in India alone. So, many of the missionaries have become agriculturists, economists, engineers, trying to build a better social order. And the lesson of all this is clear: when any one anywhere starts seriously to care for the souls of people, he is compelled to go on to care about the social situation.

Can we think that the United States is so different from China and India that the case is radically altered? Too many people are unemployed and in penury in this nation now to make that plausible.

Indeed, in Russia the communists, starting out to destroy the Christian churches, issued orders that no social work should be done by them. They knew, able strategists that they have proved themselves, that if they could force the churches to be individualistic, with no social sympathy translated into action, no message of social betterment emerging from them, that would be disastrous to religion. It has been. The astonishing thing is that one still finds so many people in this country who suppose themselves to be friends of the churches—like that citizen who wanted his minister to ignore social questions—but who are doing to some of our churches precisely what the communists did to theirs when they wanted to destroy them. I plead instead for a church that shall be a fountainhead of a better social order. Any church that pretends to care for the souls of people but is not interested in the slums that damn them, the city government that corrupts them, the economic order that cripples them, and international relationships that, leading to peace or war, determine the spiritual destiny of innumerable souls—that kind of church, I think, would hear again the Master's withering words: "Scribes and Pharisees, hypocrites!"

Again, any man who begins by feeling that the central obligation of the Christian church is to individual souls, would inevitably include in that the religious training of the children. That is the function of the church, one says. Take our children, imbue them with the ideals of Jesus, open to them, one by one, the resources of spiritual power by which they can live nobly for the commonweal. To be sure, that is a plain case. If we were not doing that we should be failing. But the religious training of the children leads not away from social questions but straight into them.

For example, in the public schools of this city we teach the children civics, beautiful civics, all about democracy and the orderly processes of constitutional government as written in the law. Then the children, thus instructed in formal civics, go out into the city's real life only to discover that it is not run by democracy at all, that even when a mayor is to be chosen the reporters wait outside a doorsill behind which four bosses are deciding who it is to be; that, far from being run by constitutional processes, the city is run by a corrupt machine, not even mentioned in the constitution but in whose hands effective power is concentrated and to whose coffers flows an endless stream of graft. I can imagine a teacher of civics in the schools who takes his task as mere routine, draws his salary check, and lets the world wag, but any genuine teacher who seriously cares about his children's civic thinking and future citizenship must feel at times a very agony of soul about the futility of what he teaches, when so much of it at last will be driven out of mind, made ridiculous, or stamped upon and dishonored, by a shameful social situation. Can any intelligent person expect that a Christian church will be interested to teach the children the ideals of Jesus and not care about the social order into which the children must go?

Consider international relationships, for example. At first, with their vast and complicated problems, they seem a long way from our instruction of your son in the church school in the principles of Jesus. But if we do not achieve disarmament we will have another war and your son, let us say, will go. After the last war one father was bitterly annoyed at his boy because he would not tell him what had happened over there, and the father, being thrilled about the war, wanted to know. One day, then, that son exploded: "Just one thing I will tell you. One night I was on patrol in No Man's Land, and suddenly I came face to face with a German about my own age. It was a question of his life or mine. We fought like wild beasts. When I came back that night I was covered from head to foot with the blood and brains of that German. We had nothing personally against each other. He did not want to kill me any more than I wanted to kill him. That is war. I did my duty in it, but for God's sake do not ask me to talk about it! I want to forget it." Well, that is war. Do you mean that an intelligent church can be interested in teaching children the ideals of Jesus and not care whether at the last the social order will bring them to *that*?

Or come closer home. We want our children to grow up with such respect for their own personalities that sensuality will have no part in their lives. We would like them to be continent before marriage and faithful afterwards, but, surely, one cannot mean that we are interested so to teach our children in home and church and then care nothing about the economic system. Do we know these young people, multitudes of whom have had jobs and now have lost them, multitudes of whom never have been able to get any work at all, many of them youths and maidens who love each other to the breaking of their hearts, as you and I loved when we were young, and yet who cannot marry—no! nor see any chance of it? Sometimes I go home at night heavy at heart from having seen people on the edge of starvation. That is terrific. But sometimes I go home at night in very agony of spirit for something worse: young people who were taught right, young people who wanted to choose right, young people who had desperately tried to live right, but who now will not listen to any Moses for anguish of spirit and cruel bondage.

I do not mean that it is simply those who fall on the under side of the economic situation and are crushed into destitution who are hurt. Our economic order sometimes seems to me almost as bad for the people who profit by it as for the people who are ruined. All our lives we have been taught to sympathize with those Hebrew slaves in Egypt and to hate Pharaoh. I beg of you, spare a little sympathy for Pharaoh, also. He, too, was caught in a social system. He, too, found himself in the toils of an unjust and inhuman order, and, discovering himself by chance upon the upper side of it, he found himself driven with terrific compulsion to play the game according to the set-up which he had inherited. Any social order that involves slavery, as Lincoln said, is about as bad for the master class as it is for the slave class—"It debauches even our greatest men." Any social order that crushes anybody is bad for the character of everybody.

We do care about the spiritual lives of our children more than we care for almost anything beside, but what will happen to the spiritual lives of our children depends, more than one likes to think, upon what happens to our economic life and to our international relationships.

Once more, any one starting with the idea that the immediate, initial obligation of the Christian church is to individual spiritual life, would surely include in that the duty to persuade people about God. That is the function of the church, some one says; give people a sustaining faith in God. To be sure it is, but, as with renovated character and the religious training of children, that leads not away from social questions but straight into them. The major destroyer of faith in

God in this nation now is not atheistic argument but anguish of spirit and cruel bondage.

Did you read in the newspaper the story of that family, formerly able to support themselves but now long unemployed and destitute, who had a little child die in one of the public hospitals and only by desperate efforts succeeded in finding twenty-one cents to pay for the collect telegram that told them of it? My friends, if I were preaching in this pulpit about the goodness of God, the presence of that family in the congregation would bother me more than all the arguments of the atheists. I can answer the arguments, but what could I say to that father and mother?

It is not often that a Christian preacher feels called upon to quote Karl Marx, but Karl Marx said one thing so true that, ever since I read it, it has haunted me: "Philosophers have only interpreted the world differently, but the point is to change it." Just so! And that applies to preachers as well as to philosophers. We too often try to explain the world, harmonize its evil with our faith in God, concoct clever interpretations so that we say that its outrageous wrongs are but the shadows cast by ultimate good, and devious evasions such as that, and now by a stern situation we are being called back to another way altogether—Christ's way, mark it! He did not try mainly to explain the world. He tried to change it. When he wanted a man to believe in God he did not argue with him. He loved him, served him, lifted him out of his trouble, gave him such an exhibition, in practical experience, of the power and beauty of a divine spirit that the man had to believe, at least, in that. And around this personal service the Master lifted up a social gospel, forgetting which, the church would be irreparably doomed: "Thy kingdom come. Thy will be done, as in heaven, so on earth." That does belong to the essence of the gospel and only as we are true to that will any arguments for God amount to much.

Multitudes of people in this land doubt God, want to believe in him and cannot, rise at times into a temporary faith in him and are crushed out of it by anguish of spirit and cruel bondage.

I call you to witness that we have not talked about things on which we are ill informed, that we have not continued the newspapers' secular debate, that we have not moved over from the realm of persuasion into the realm of coercion. This thing for which we have been pleading is at the heart of the church's business. We never can separate the spiritual interests of individual souls from the social situation.

See that man with the letter in his hand and the light in his eyes, called back to work again, and remember that last night many a person in this country dreamed that that man was himself, only to awake this morning in despair to find the dream untrue.

Let no Christian dare to forget such!

Through the Social Gospel into Personal Religion

LAST Sunday we faced the impossibility of separating the spiritual interests of individual souls from the social situation. We said that if we start by caring about people's faith in God, we commonly discover that it is some cruel social condition that crushes faith in God; that if we start by caring about the religious training of our children, we commonly find that the loveliest results we expect from that are likely to be ruined by some social condition like unemployment; that if we start thinking that the conversion of individual character is the basic matter, we commonly discover that, from the slums of cities to war between nations, it is social situations that bedevil character. Wherever we begin caring about the spiritual interests of individual souls, we find ourselves constrained to go further and face a social problem.

This morning we intend going through that same tunnel from the other end. Today we start not with the exponents of personal religion but with the exponents of social reform who never have been interested in personal religion but who care about stopping war, building a better economic order, and cleaning up our political corruption. And to them we propose saying that if we do seriously begin with care about social reform and go clear through with it we come to personal religion.

I am convinced of that. If we can go through the Hudson Tunnel from New York to New Jersey we can go through the Hudson Tunnel from New Jersey to New York, and by the same sign, if starting with personal religion we are constrained to go through to the problems of society, so, starting with the problems of society, we are constrained to go through to personal religion. Be sure that I am not moved to this sermon by any mere motives of logical completeness.

I am thinking about real people, especially young people. I know them on our college campuses, the best of them sincerely concerned about economic affairs and international relationships. They often pooh-pooh personal religion, have no use for the church, think that preachers belong to the era of kerosene lamps and one-horse shays, and in general are dubious about God and condescending toward prayer, but they do care about the world's social problems.

Let us start with them and see where we come out. We might put the starting point in three brief propositions: First, much that we care for most, whether as persons or as families, depends upon what happens to two social problems, the organization of our economic life and that of our international relationships. Second, there is no relief from the evils of the world in those two fields without changing the world. Just as our fathers had to change their world from feudalism to monarchy and from monarchy to democracy, so deep-seated and far-reaching social changes will be required of us and of our children. And third, so far as the method is concerned, we have a choice between reform and revolution, so that I should suppose that any man in his senses would work sacrificially for reform if only to avoid the tragedy of revolution.

Start with such propositions. You will find them commonly in the minds of thoughtful youth, but often along with them neglect of, disbelief in, sometimes scorn about personal religion. Will some of you tentatively accept me for a guide for a few moments this morning? I think I see a path plainly marked from social reform to personal religion. At least I should like to try to point it out to you.

So far as history is concerned, that path is plainly there and has been often traveled. We have just sung Whittier's hymn, "Dear Lord and Father of mankind, forgive our feverish ways." To be sure, some one says, he was a Quaker and a mystic and, of course, he believed in personal religion. But that is not the whole story. Whittier was a social reformer and he never ceased being one. The conflict with slavery aroused Whittier. Once in his young manhood the abolition headquarters in Philadelphia were raided by a mob and only by disguising himself did he escape. In his old age he said once to a youth, "My lad, if thou wouldst win success, join thyself to some unpopular but noble cause." Nobody understands Whittier unless he sees him traveling that path from personal religion to social reform and from social reform to personal religion.

If you wish an exhibition of this same truth from the Bible, consider this from Jeremiah, "O Lord, my strength, and my fortress, and my refuge in the day of affliction." That is personal religion. But Jeremiah did not start there. He was a social prophet concerned with statesmanship, economics, international relationships. He was the wisest seer in public affairs among his people, but be sure that he never would have stood his ground, as he did, for forty years through national and international catastrophe, a very tower of public strength, a fearless and indomitable conscience to his people, if he had not deepened his experience through social reform into personal religion. And this is the gist of the matter, now as then, that the saving of society depends on things that only a vital, intelligent, effective, personal religion can supply.

In the first place, when we have said with all the earnestness at our command, as we did say last week, that social situations often do terrific things to individual souls, we need also to say that individual souls wield tremendous influence over social situations. The social conditions in Labrador are much better than they used to be, but that public transformation goes back to the young medical student, Wilfred Grenfell, who wandered into a religious meeting where something Dwight L. Moody said captured his imagination for a Christlike life. Social conditions among the natives of South Africa are incalculably better than once they were. A typical contribution to that, however, goes back to a Scotch home where a mother brooded over a growing boy and a Scotch church where a minister who thought his work a failure profoundly stirred the ambition of the lad for Christian service. Out of that home and church came Robert Moffat.

All social transformation goes back to somebody's sensitized conscience. Indeed it does! And when we have said our worst about the appalling failures of organized Christianity, the religion of Jesus has produced that. You who are social workers, what are your special interests? Prison reform? John Howard and Elizabeth Fry, their consciences made sensitive by a high religion, started your movement. Settlement houses? Canon Barnett of Toynbee Hall pioneered your movement. Care for the insane? It was a Quaker named William Tuke who started the first hospital for the insane in human history. We cannot trace social care for underprivileged children without coming to a great soul like Lord Shaftesbury, or our conscience about slums without coming to General William Booth.

All social advance starts with somebody's sensitized conscience. To be sure, some one may protest that much of our actual religion, so far from being socially useful, is socially ruinous. Granted that! Religion is one of the most dangerous things in the world. When it goes wrong it is disastrous. As Shakespeare said:

> "For sweetest things turn sourest by their deeds;
> Lilies that fester smell far worse than weeds."

So an unintelligent and unethical religion has held up social progress, blessed social abominations like slavery and war, preached a soft contentment with shameful present conditions in hope of a future heaven, or satisfied itself with relieving distresses caused by an inhuman social order without changing the social order itself. Say the worst you will about the anti-social effects of bad religion and we will agree with you, but the answer seems plain. The only power on earth by which we ever can overcome bad religion is good religion. We never will overcome bad religion with irreligion. We can win the victory over bad religion only by good religion and so, even on the basis of your own argument, we do need more of that.

Last week, for example, we said with deep feeling that futility often afflicts the teaching of a boy in the ideals of

Jesus when he goes out into a social order which will use him soon as cannon fodder on a battlefield. The war system, we said, is ruinous to the spiritual interests of individual souls. That is true, but it is also true that the war system itself comes out of individual souls. Here in this university area only a little while ago one student from abroad said to a personal friend of mine, "I can hardly wait to get back home. We are going to fight such and such a nation in a few months. I am afraid I will be too late. I want to get into it. They are all niggers. I want to kill some of them." So when you have said that a social order based on war damns individual souls, go on to say that individual souls with such a spirit damn the social order.

Where did the Great War come from? From this or that maladjustment in the public organization of the world, economic, political? Yes, that is crucially true. Yet that alone would be like explaining the Hudson River by the influence of the Palisades upon its channel. Now, the influence of the Palisades upon the Hudson's channel is very important but that is not where the Hudson originally starts. The Hudson starts in multitudinous, individual springs far up among the mountains, obscure, small, insignificant, but in their combined strength the Hudson. So when one traces back our social evils, like war, he finds their springs in the individual souls of men.

How often, having studied in the large some social problem like an equitable economic order, or war, or racial prejudice, have we come suddenly face to face with one man and there, the whole macrocosm of the social problem condensed into his microcosm, the deep damnation of the social order stood plain in the attitude and spirit of an individual soul!

My friends, if we are ever to solve that original and profoundest social problem inside the souls of men, we must have a vital, effective, ethical, personal religion, so that I should suppose that some of you, who have cared about social reform but have thought little of personal religion, might change your tune. You had better help us. We are trying to assist people to get an intelligent, vital, socially

[34]

minded spiritual life. You never will get a better social order without that.

In the second place, when the knightly and chivalrous youth, intent upon a better social order, has now grown up and reached a more sober-eyed maturity, he needs a deep and patient faith. Ah, says the youth as he goes out to save the world, You need only blow on your hands! But after the years have passed almost inevitably one of two things has happened. Either he has thrown over his chivalrous ideals and endeavors in disillusionment and futility or else he has achieved a deep and patient, spiritual faith. How can a man go on year after year at this appalling task of trying to build a humane and coöperative social order in such a world without facing the inevitable question: Is this a world where a more decent social order was ever meant to be or can be?

Sometimes when we preachers talk about theism versus materialism, it must sound dry. It ought not to. It is vital and nowhere more so than in a man's social enthusiasm. What if this universe, with us within it, is only an accident of the dust so that, in consequence, our high-spirited endeavor to build here a better social order is only the hopeless effort to make a silk purse out of a sow's ear? What if that is the case? Many today think it is, so that one of the most pathetic things one sees in America is the disillusioned social reformer who has quit. Once he was aflame for mankind. Now he thinks he knows the truth: "Vanity of vanities, all is vanity."

When in our youth we undertake chivalrous enterprises, we naturally live upon that one word "ought." We ought to stop war. We ought to have a more humane economic order. We ought. But if a man has any thoughtfulness in him he cannot go on many years trying to live on "ought" without running headlong into that other word "is." What if the universe *is* merely a physical machine? What if mankind *is* merely an accident on one of the minor planets? What if the social hope we are giving our life to *is* merely a fantasy by which we fool ourselves? What if the inevitable destiny of man *is* annihilation on a planet that never wanted him, in a cosmos that never cared? One of the most familiar sights today, alas! is the wreckage of a youthful "ought" on that terrific "is."

There is no way out of that situation except a high religion. Religion essentially is a gospel not simply about what ought to be but about what *is*. God *is*. "Now *are* we children of God." So, undiscourageable social hope, like all spiritual life, is grounded in reality. My friend, interested in social reform but not in personal religion, even though your private faith may be burning dimly, do you not wish that wider areas of our population had within their souls a stronger grip on that sustaining "is"?

To be sure, some may be thinking that science can save us socially. Science? Alone? But the typical consequence of our new technological science is to throw men together physically without uniting them spiritually. Society organized on the basis of modern technological science is a good deal like the subway, amazing and in its way very useful, but with this for its crucial human effect: it throws men together in physical proximity without uniting them in spiritual sympathy. Nothing that science can do outwardly can solve that problem. Only spiritual life can solve it, only a better inner quality deep in human souls, only a vital, effective, personal religion.

My young friends, going out with eager enthusiasm to save the world, the launching of a ship is always a gala sight, with flags and bands, bunting and cheering crowds. So you start out on your expedition for a better society. But before that ship comes to its last port it will face long-drawn-out storms, howling northeasters, discouraging delays, and seas that make the heart stand still. Such is the test of a mature man's social hope. You are going to need a deep and patient faith.

Once more, note that nobody is fitted successfully to help society outwardly until he himself inwardly has proved able to rise above society, be superior to it, and carry off an inward victory over it. One of the most outstanding triumphs for a better social ideal in our time has been won by Gandhi in India, at the risk of his life taking his stand against "untouchability." Yet, obviously, Mahatma Gandhi could have done nothing effective about the caste system unless in his inner life he had transcended caste lines and in his own comprehensive sympathies taken in the despised untouchables. No one can help society without until he has won a spiritual victory within. Too few have taken the serious measure of that fact.

Consider, for example, the amazing influence which Jesus has wielded and wields yet over social attitudes. He lived long ago. The peculiar problems of public life that face us he did not face and so he never said a word directly about them. Yet some of us would testify that nobody ever has wielded such powerful influence over our social attitudes as has Jesus. In his own soul he rose so far above the dead levels of common morality that he keeps challenging the things to which socially we consent. He challenges war. I tried, myself, by every devious argument that I could lay my hand on, to harmonize Christ and war until at last I gave up the mad endeavor. Christ *or* war—we can have our choice, but we cannot have both. He challenges our economic inhumanities. Try to be contented with them as we will, there he rises saying, "Inasmuch as ye did it unto one of these my brethren, even these least, ye did it unto me," and seeing him so caring for the lowliest and the least, the things we socially consent to become at last blasphemous and intolerable.

O knightly youth, remember this: anybody who ever yet lifted the world succeeded first in standing above the world himself so that he could lift it.

Every one of us must have discovered this truth in dealing with some individual. Here is our friend in trouble. If it were money that he wanted, we could give it, or if advice, we would offer it, but if life has done to him some terrific thing so that what he needs is faith and inner courage and a victorious soul, we cannot give that unless we possess it. What an empty cupboard we sometimes find when a friend needs vital, spiritual life! No more can we feed society's deep need except out of a full soul or lift the world unless we first of all stand above the world.

When, therefore, one sees some young social reformers proposing to save the world, for all one's instinctive love for their chivalrous hopefulness, one sees the method which they are likely to employ. They will try to improve the play by shifting the scenery. That is not enough. Important? Yes, but it is not enough. The improvement of the play also lies deep inside the minds and spirits of the actors. Call Mrs. Browning mid-Victorian if you will, but she was right about this:

> . . . . It takes a soul,
> To move a body: it takes a high-souled man
> To move the masses even to a cleaner stye.

This, then, is the essence of the matter. Our religion does indeed cry desperately for social reform. I agree with a Christian contemporary who says, "If religion ends with the individual, it ends." So it does, and so long as Jesus has influence in his church there is only one place where the gospel can end—with the kingdom of God on earth, which is a better social order.

Nevertheless, let no one underestimate what spiritually that is going to cost. At the very least it costs transfigured individual lives and sensitized individual consciences. At the very least it costs in social workers a deep and patient faith, proof against cynicism and despair. At the very least it costs superiority of soul that rises high above the world. What, then, are these three things when they are put together? They are vital, personal religion. Church of Christ, if you were only about your business producing that! And you who care for social reform but not for personal religion, would you not do well to look deeper into this? The saving of society does depend on things which only high, personal religion can supply.

Modern Civilization's
Crucial Problem

THE life of each one of us is divided into two factors—the means by which we live and the ends for which we live—and nothing enters much more deeply into determining the quality of a man or an era than the handling of those two factors. This is easily illustrated in terms of the generation as a whole. The fact distinguishing our day from previous times is obviously our mastery over the scientific means of life. One after another the forces of the universe, from steam to the impalpable vibrations of the ether, have been harnessed for our service, until we possess, as no previous age even in its dreams possessed, the means of living. But when we turn our thought from the means by which we live to the ends for which we live, are we so sure that we are on a correspondingly higher level than our fathers?

One remembers the Periclean Age in Greece, when around the Acropolis a people small in numbers but great in mind first created and then preserved from the impinging barbarism a culture that ever since has been an inexhaustible treasury for the Western world. When we think of the means by which they lived, they were crudely primitive, but when we think of the things for which they lived—Praxiteles and Phidias, Æschylus and Sophocles and Plato—Athens moves up into a position in the spiritual history of man that New York and Chicago may never achieve.

Or one remembers a little group of disciples around a Teacher in Galilee. The means by which they lived were crude indeed. A donkey provided the swiftest method of travel that they ever tried. Their houses of one room with two small windows and probably no chimney, where the family slept on an upper platform and the beasts slept on the floor, were roughed out of native stone or sun-dried brick—hovels to live in, poverty-stricken conditions to live under. But when one thinks of the ends for which they lived, ah, my soul!

Everywhere, when we compare ourselves with previous generations with reference to our means for living, we are supreme, but whenever we turn our attention to the ends for which we live, a different picture presents itself. "Improved means to an unimproved end"—how much of our modern life is summarized in that shrewd phrase of Thoreau! We often jestingly recognize this contrast between means and ends as when, for example, we laughed at Voliva of Zion City using the radio to tell the world that the earth is flat. So when the Atlantic cable first was laid, Thoreau, in protest against the popular enthusiasm, said that probably the first use made of it would be to let us know that Princess Adelaide had whooping cough. We do jokingly recognize the contrast between amazing instruments and the trivial uses to which they can be put. How many of us, however, have dropped our plummets deeper into this important matter, improved means to an unimproved end?

The movies, for example, are a marvelous invention and sometimes they are beautifully used. They could be very beautifully used. Yet we all know into what crass, commercialized, conscienceless hands a wide area of movie production has fallen, so that this amazing instrument, teaching boys and girls through their eyes, the swiftest way by which any of us learns anything, is being deliberately used to make vice attractive and dress licentiousness in charm—improved means to an unimproved end.

In our campaign for disarmament, we often remind ourselves how very crude and primitive ancient battles were. The Greeks won Marathon with ten thousand men and lost only one hundred and ninety of them; the charge of the Light Brigade involved only six hundred cavalry; even Napoleon at Austerlitz led seventy thousand French and lost but eight thousand. Now, however, forces are in the hands of military power that in a few hours could depopulate London and Paris of their millions, and the next war, if it comes, will no longer see champion against champion or mere army against army, but whole populations against whole populations—improved means to an unimproved end.

That phrase comes as near as any I know to stating the crucial problem of modern civilization. Ever since James Watt made his steam engine and the era of scientific inventiveness got well under way, we have been absorbing ourselves in the creation, accumulation, elaboration, multiplication of the means of living. But that second matter cannot longer be kept in the background. It crowds up into the front. It is the crux of the situation today. Unless we can reestablish the spiritual ends of living in personal character and social justice, our civilization will ruin itself with the misuse of its own instruments. And just as soon as we begin thinking about the spiritual ends of life we are thinking of religion.

Why is it, indeed, that in this last generation so many people have supposed that they could get on without religion? It is because this last generation has been absorbed in the provision of more means by which to live and that is not religion's realm. When some one says today that the dominant interest of our time is not religion but science, he speaks the truth. That is the fact, and it is the fact because the dominant interest of our time has been the provision of more means by which to live, which is the realm of science. But it is not the function of science to provide the ends for which we live. That is another matter. That is a man's philosophy of life, his spiritual ideals, his religion. What is a generation profited if it gains the whole world of means by which to live and loses its soul, the spiritual ends for which to live?

That is the text we are talking on. That is the voice of religion as it was the voice of Christ. And, mark it! this generation cannot dodge that question. Everywhere we turn, it faces us. Every road we travel on, it meets us. It besets us before and behind and lays its hand upon us. What is a man profited if he gain the whole world and lose the end, the soul?

Before we are through answering that question, we shall

have a revival of spiritual life. It is coming. We may hasten it; we may delay it; but no group of men, and I think no set of ideas, can permanently stop it. We shall have a revival of religion.

Of course, I can imagine objectors who will protest against this statement. Let us consider them.

One person, for example, may say, There is going to be no revival of religion; no likelihood exists that this generation will ask searching questions about the spiritual ends of life, because we are too satisfied with the enjoyment of these new and fascinating means of living. To this I answer, Not so satisfied as on the surface might appear. No city was ever so richly equipped with the scientific means of living as New York. Does it strike you as preëminently happy and satisfied? Upon the contrary!

If you should hear about some individual man that he had a million dollars a year and could buy what he wanted, what is the first question that would rise in your mind? I know the first question that would rise in mine: I wonder if he is happy. Suppose we heard that he had a town house and a country house, a yacht, a fleet of automobiles, and was served by all the ingenuities that science has devised; I still would wonder—Is he happy?

But if you should hear about some man that he had found his work and loved it, that he was creating some beauty, doing something useful, and would rather put himself into that than anything else in the world, you would not wonder. You know that *is* happiness. Happiness is not primarily a matter of the means by which we live; it is a matter of the spiritual end for which we live.

If you should hear even about a humble man that he loved people, that like Peter he had a healing shadow, that like a river he had found his channel, like a garden the fruit that he could grow, like a lantern the dark places of the earth where his light was needed, you would know that he was happy. You do not wonder whether Jesus was happy; you can see he was. You do not wonder whether Sir Wilfred Grenfell has had a happy life; you know he has.

Consider, then, our generation as a whole—long on the means of living, it may be, but short on happiness. For we are not dogs to be satisfied when a few bones are flung to us, though they be automobiles and subways, electric lights and airplanes. There is something else in us that makes the very essence of our humanity; we have to live *for* something. The deepest hell that some of us could ever fall into would be to have everything to live with and nothing to live for.

If this is the law of our being, one by one, do you suppose that the generation is under another law? Statisticians have estimated that a century ago the average man had 72 wants, of which 16 were regarded as necessities, but that today the average man has 484 wants, 94 of which are regarded as necessities, and that, moreover, whereas a century ago 200 articles were urged upon the average man by salesmanship, now 32,000 articles are urged on us. I do not belittle all that. The means by which we live is the underpinning of existence, but it is not the secret of happiness. That is a matter of finding something worth while to live for.

I appeal to your experience. Have you found something worth living for, some beauty to create, some goodness to achieve, some truth to discover, some spiritual aim to give yourself to? If not, you are not happy and not all the accumulation of the means of life can make you happy. What profit, even in happiness, if a man gain this whole modern world of means and lose the soul? The discovery of that fact means a revival of spiritual life.

In the second place, I can imagine a man saying, No, we are not going to have anything like a revival of religion; the materialistic philosophy was never more in the saddle than it is today; what Russia is doing officially against religion millions are doing personally; the atheistic philosophy has swept the intelligentsia along and carried in its wake wide sections of popular opinion. Just so, I answer. That is one reason why we are going to have a revival of religion. For in any generation when a few people merely play with the materialistic philosophy of life, it can remain attractive, but when multitudes go after it, when it is so successful that it begins to reveal, as it does now, all that it thinks, and to show just where it leads, then a reaction is due.

The great triumphs of materialism have been Pyrrhic victories; they defeated themselves. If, therefore, you say that in this last generation the materialistic philosophy has carried off a resounding victory, I answer, That is what is going to ruin it, for when the materialistic philosophy has its swing and goes its limit, it carries us out into a senseless world, full, it may be, of means to live by, but with nothing much in it worth living for.

It carries one out, for example, into an intellectually senseless world. You would not take a billion cards and put a letter on each and throw them up into the northwest wind, expecting them to fall together so as to make sense. You would not expect out of all those billion cards even ten to fall together to make a sentence like "This is a cat." The chance of that happening would be negligible; yet they try to tell us that atoms and electrons, by themselves, fortuitously have fallen together into law-abiding stellar systems, into human personality and social progress. That is believing in sheer magic. As Professor Montague of the Department of Philosophy in Columbia says, the chance of that being true would have to be represented by a fraction with 1 for the numerator and a denominator that would extend from here to one of the fixed stars. Give it enough rope and the materialistic philosophy hangs itself, for it leads out into an intellectually senseless world.

Worse than that, however, it leads out into a spiritually senseless world. Life is not mostly theory; it is mostly something else. For one thing, it is hardship. Not only do troubles come very deep, but love comes also, deeper yet, binding us up into one bundle of life with other people so that what happens to them happens to us, and

> . . . he who lives more lives than one
> More deaths than one must die.

How often a man wishes he had genuine spiritual life,

not so much for his own sake as for the sake of another for whom he cares!

> Old Mother Hubbard,
> Went to the cupboard,
> To get her poor Dog a bone,
> But when she came there,
> The cupboard was bare,
> And so the poor Dog had none.

Queer nursery jingle, but there is depth in it, for even when a man cares about a poor dog, he does want a bone in his cupboard. And when it is not a poor dog but a child, a boy or girl going out to live in this difficult generation, how a man does hate that bare cupboard of his own soul, empty of the spiritual life which comes alone from high things to live for! For what can you give a child worth giving to a child at all if you cannot give something beautiful to live for?

See, then, this cycle that humanity is traveling around, which it has traveled more than once before. A generation starts doubting, doubts the church and the creeds, doubts God and immortality, doubts that there is any purpose in the universe at all or any goal ahead, doubts all the bases of idealistic living, and then, having stripped life of spiritual significance, it begins to doubt its doubts. Like the fabled serpent, disbelief turns and eats itself. The generation cannot even have faith in its own lack of faith. Then the reaction is due. When a materialistic age gets a materialistic philosophy, though it be fabulously rich in the means by which to live, it begins to say, What profit!

Nevertheless, I can imagine one more objector saying, No, nothing like a revival of religion is coming; look at the moral situation—to which I answer, Look at it. A war always brings a long aftermath of moral looseness. We might suppose that war would sober people, and war does sober some. That English mother who had three sons fighting on three fronts and on the same day received from the British War Office three letters telling her that all her sons were dead was probably sobered.

After the war the Prince of Wales went into one of those

hospitals where they keep the utter wrecks—one whole ward filled with men whose faces had been shot away. They begged the Prince not to look at the six worst cases, and when he had seen five of them they fairly insisted that he should not see the last, but he did—nothing left of the man's face except a bit of the forehead—and, white as a sheet, the Prince bowed down and kissed all that remained of the brow. There are sobering things about war.

But the total effect of war is not sobering. Only sentimentalists with no knowledge of the rudiments of psychology suppose it is. People as a whole when they face a terrific situation flee from it psychologically into excitement, wildness, hectic sensuality, drunkenness—anything to make an emotional escape from the pressure of an intolerable situation. Then, when millions of people are making a flight into excitement and wildness, millions of others flock after them and the inevitable next step comes on apace: a philosophy, namely, to rationalize it all—sex-mad psychoanalytic theories, supposedly learned books about the glories of extramarital relationships and the general advisability of moral looseness and the appalling danger of being decent and self-controlled.

Do not suppose that because on Sunday you see a minister in a black gown perched in the carved pulpit of a Gothic church, that he does not know. A working minister can sometimes see more of the seamy side of life in a week than a roué sees in a month, for the roué may see only his own rottenness, but the minister in intimate disclosure will see the deep and varied iniquity of many.

If, therefore, you say, Look at the moral situation! I answer, Look at it. What do you argue from it? If you argue that it is going on and on from bad to worse you have all history against you. Inevitably the pendulum swings. Did you happen to see that recent cartoon—a mother with all the obvious signs of flapperishness from indecent dress up, the very picture of emancipated modernity, and beside her a daughter looking demure, decent, and sensible? The daughter is saying, Mother, do stop trying to be so modern, it is all out of date! Just so!

The dean of one of our foremost colleges recently said that the tide already had turned and in place of the sophistication, the blasé cynicism, the wild experimentation of these recent years, there was coming a renaissance of natural eagerness, earnestness, and idealism. I am not half so anxious about some of this younger generation, in which I think are many of the finest youths this world has ever had, as I am about some of you older ones, the left-overs and relics of the war psychology.

All around us in New York we see families where, if the fathers and mothers would straighten up, aye, if they would sober up, there would be little to worry about among the children.

My friends, this generation is not going to escape the question of our Lord. We may make money and become rich, multiply our means of pleasure, grow wild, tear self-control from the throne and put license there, but up from the gates of the dawn there comes another generation to assess us with discerning eyes. What profit if we lose the soul?

If a genuine revival of spiritual life should really come, what could we not do with this world? When I say a revival of religion, of course I do not mean emotionalism, ecclesiasticism, creedalism—God forbid! I mean a revival of ethical Christianity that will lay its hand on these amazing modern means and dedicate them to human good. There never was such a chance in history. Our ancient forefathers were in comparison poverty-stricken. They always lived under the fear of penury and famine. They never had the means to carry through their dreams, but we have. Our hands are full of scientific means, and see what we are doing with them! We harness Niagara Falls, stupendous achievement! and then use the power to make a brilliant advertisement for a chewing gum—improved means to an unimproved end. That is a parable of too much modern life. With the most amazing means of production in history we have made unemployment. With the most amazing world contacts on record we make world wars. The trouble is not with our means; it is with our ends—and there is no cure for that difficulty except the revival of genuine Christianity with effective intellect to make it work.

For this is the conclusion of the matter. Those who are saying that Jesus is done for, that he is going, not coming, that he is a first-century Palestinian and outgrown, face the surprise of their lives if they live long enough to see it. What has Jesus to do, they say, with an age of subways, airplanes, electric lights, and automobiles? What can he tell us about right and wrong in a machine age that he could not even dream? To this I answer, In so far true! Jesus has no direct contribution to make to the means by which we live, but I should be doing a great piece of business in some consciences here, if I could make them listen to Jesus about the ends of life. That is his realm. What are you living *for*? What profit if a man gain this whole modern world of means and lose the soul?

The Service of Religious Faith
to Mental Health

THESE are days when we need all the resources we can find which will assist in creating and maintaining mental health. We who stand at the human end of this breakdown of economic security are of course impressed by its physical consequences—downright hunger and destitution —but that is not half the story. The mental, moral, emotional consequences are far more terrific. Is there anybody here this morning who one way or another, for himself or for somebody else, does not feel the strain? Listen, then, to this message from the second letter to Timothy: "For God hath not given us the spirit of fear; but of power, and of love, and of a sound mind." Aye! that would be something to get out of one's religion.

This word from the New Testament, so close to our present need, at once suggests that it probably never has been easy to attain a sound mind. We moderns often pity ourselves in this regard. Our new civilization, we say, has so complicated life that the strain is breaking down the mental balance of many; insanity is increasing and nervous breakdowns multiply. To be sure, it is easy to recount those factors in modern civilization which so overstrain many and unbalance some. But let us remember that even though it be true that our modern civilization has in some regards increased the difficulties of healthy-mindedness, in other ways it has decreased them. Think of ancient fears and superstitions that once haunted our fathers which are not in our world at all—mysterious plagues that in a single year took off a large part of England's population, cause unknown, cure impossible; or belief in demons that scared sanity out of generations of common folk; or the paralyzing fear of hell; or the dread of torture for heresy; or in the economic life masses in penury so hopeless that even today it is diffi-

[49]

cult for us to imagine it. No, my friends, it probably never has been much easier than it is today to win that inner victory without which no good life is possible—a sound mind.

When, therefore, an ancient character like Paul talks to us about the contribution which his Christian faith has made to healthy-mindedness, he comes close to our need. For through Paul's burdened lifetime he was a healthy-minded man. He faced the contentious ingratitude of his followers. He faced the limitations of physical ill health, most bitter to an active man. He was brutally maltreated by his public enemies. He endured poverty, always skirting the ragged edge of destitution and ever and again falling over. And at last, after a long-drawn-out imprisonment, he met martyrdom. But through it all he kept a high morale and his last cry came from an unspoiled and unembittered soul: "I have fought the good fight, I have finished the course, I have kept the faith."

I do not see how we can avoid the challenge of a healthy-minded man like that. We had better listen to him when out of so rich an experience he writes, as despite some scholars I hope he did write, in this particular portion of the second letter to Timothy, "God hath not given us the spirit of fear; but of power, and of love, and of a sound mind."

Let us clarify our thought on one matter. "Healthy-mindedness" and "sick-mindedness" are not the common vocabulary of the pulpit. "Righteousness" and "sin" are the preacher's ordinary words. But while "righteousness" and "sin" are good words and have a long future ahead of them, they sometimes confuse the issue. What would you call pride, for example? A sin? Let us rather say that a conceited man has a sick mind. To see the truth of that, turn the matter around and consider the impression made on us by a fine specimen of humility. Mr. Einstein, for example, in his own lifetime by consensus of scientific opinion is ranked along with Newton and Galileo. Already he is among the immortals, and he is told so, so that I suspect a similar thing has seldom, if ever, happened in the history of science. Listen, then, to Mr. Einstein himself: "Many times a day I realize how much my own outer and inner life is built upon the labors of my fellow-men, both living and dead, and how earnestly I must exert myself in order to give in return as much as I have received."

What is your first comment on that? Mine is that that man has a healthy mind.

If some one, now, is fearing that it is dangerous so to translate righteousness into healthy-mindedness and sin into sick-mindedness, I simply ask, What did Jesus call himself? A physician. How did he describe the people he tried to help? "They that are whole have no need of a physician, but they that are sick." Aye, they that are sick!

Indeed, thinking of you young people in particular, I ask you which ideal is the more attractive to you, to be righteous or to be healthy-minded? You know well that some of you here, if I called you sinners, would be moved not at all except, it might be, to hidden mirth, but if I could make you even dimly suspect that you are not healthy-minded, you would be disturbed. Behind all our callous consciences every one of us does want to be healthy—physically, emotionally, mentally healthy.

What tragedies have come from the changed meanings of a word! If in this pulpit today I should cry, "O young men and women, be holy!" what a mistake! Who wants to be holy? Nevertheless, go back to the original meaning of that word "holy"—whole, wholesome, healthy. That is what it means. Well, God hath given us not the spirit of fear; but of power, and of love, and of a sound mind.

In the first place, note that those most competent to interpret the meanings of vital Christian faith unmistakably testify that it does release interior resources of spiritual *power*, and if that is true nobody can afford to neglect it. For, as all the psychiatrists say and as every man must plainly see, one of the commonest sources of mental ill health is the consciousness of deficient resources and of consequent inadequacy for life. Why should we not feel inadequate for life? Look what it does to us! I have just been reading a new biography of George Eliot. When she was a young woman she loved Herbert Spencer. And, what is more, he was very attentive to her, so that their friends supposed of course they were going to marry. But he was coldly philosophical. One day he took a shilling and flipped it: heads he would marry, tails he would not. And it came down tails. Months afterwards, out of her convalescence from heartbreak, the young woman who was afterwards to be George Eliot wrote to a friend: "I am very well and 'plucky' —a word which I propose to substitute for happy, as more truthful." How many of us have had one way or another to learn to substitute "plucky" for "happy" as more truthful!

Multitudes of people today, faced by the cruel things that life sometimes does to them, are pounded quite to pieces, and the consequence is what the New Testament describes as "the spirit of fear"—that is, an appalling sense of inadequacy for life. If there were time, I could unroll a long list of unhealthy tricks which the human mind is guilty of in such a case. For some people, running away from their appalling sense of insufficiency, take to boasting; they talk and act as if they were as conceited as Lucifer, pathetically covering up with a crust of seeming pride their real humiliation and inferiority. Others fall into a persecution complex, blame somebody else for their inadequacy, brood over being hurt and wronged, and end, many of them, in the asylum with paranoia. Others take to day-dreaming, run away from these unhappy situations where they always feel inferior, into a fantastic world of make-believe, where they are always superior and come out on top, and so comfort themselves. Some become downright sick, fall into physical illness, frequently of an hysterical variety, their subconscious minds devising for them this escape, as often happens in shell shock, whereby they may be pitied instead of blamed for their inadequacy.

What consequences a man who works with individuals sees arising from this familiar feeling of inadequacy for life! And all the time, my friends, there is only one healthy way out: power, personal power in life, spiritual resources that can be tapped, in the possession of which a man goes out into life saying like Paul, even though he was in prison when he said it, "I can do all things in him that strengtheneth me."

A religion that does not do something like that for a man is not functioning. Many people suppose that a man has so much power and no more. A man's energies, they think, are in a closed reservoir and when the demands are too much, they are exhausted. So they picture themselves, and the damage done by that familiar but false way of thinking is incalculable. For the seers of the spiritual life agree that the truth is something else altogether. We are channels of power,—not closed reservoirs,—open channels of power, and at the fountainheads of our being it is possible to release power, set it flowing, so that one may not easily put limits around the quantity of power that might conceivably be let loose even through a simple life.

Consider. You are exhausted, limp, done for, and you come into the presence of a radiant personality who touches hidden springs in you and, lo! the channels of your soul fill up and the riverbed of your power overflows. You are not a closed reservoir; you are an open channel through which power can flow. Here is a woman, apparently at the end of her resources, whose child falls ill, and mother-love in her sets free energies and staying power that will see her through long months of tireless watching. This thing we are talking of is not miles up in the air and mystical; it is solidly founded. Now, Christ had a similar effect on men. Simon Peter was not a closed reservoir; he was a channel, limited in size, to be sure, but still a channel, and when Christ released the fountainhead of his passionate loyalty and purposefulness, a power flowed through him that those who knew him in his early days never would have dreamed.

How can we put this, so that some one here who needs it can practically get hold of it? To believe in God, not far off but here; to understand prayer, not as a form of words but as an inner opening of the life to the Divine resources, and so to experience what the prophet said, "They that wait upon the Lord shall renew their strength"; to go out into life, in consequence, not afraid of being overborne, because you know you are not a closed reservoir that can be exhausted but a channel in touch with inexhaustible resources, and that therefore as your day is so shall your strength be— that is vital, personal religion. If you have a little of it, deepen your experience. If you have none of it, for your own soul's health fulfil the conditions of getting it. For some day the sense of inadequacy stands on every threshold.

Recall what John Morley said about Gladstone: "He was one of that high and favoured household who, in Emerson's noble phrase, 'live from a great depth of being.'" Aye, for over fourscore years of amazing vitality! Be sure that a spiritual phenomenon like that is no mere, physical accident. Such healthy-minded souls live from a great depth of being.

In the second place, the New Testament tells us that God has given us not a spirit of fear, but of power, and of *love*. Now, the word "love" in the New Testament has nothing whatever to do with soft sentimentalism. "Love" in the New Testament is one of the strongest words in the vocabulary, representing the kind of undiscourageable goodwill that could carry Christ to the cross or float a soul like Paul's unembittered through many an angry sea. If there is any force on earth, religious or not, that can help a man to keep that undiscourageable goodwill about living, it is worth investigating for, as every one of us can plainly see, one of the most familiar causes of mental ill health is bitterness, plain bitterness about life. It may be some one says:

Why not? Why should one not be bitter? See what life does to us. The idea of pious sentimentalists that this world is just to the individual simply will not hold water; it is not just. Who hung on those three crosses? Christ and two thieves. That is life —the best and the worst nailed up together and no justice anywhere. The poets indeed may sing:

Truth forever on the scaffold, Wrong forever on the throne,—
Yet that scaffold sways the future, and, behind the dim unknown,
Standeth God within the shadow, keeping watch above his own.

Does he? Does he indeed? Well, he waits a long while sometimes before he acts. And in the meantime the merciless heel of the world crushes innocence and guilt alike.

How easy it is to grow bitter about life! And in personal, human relationships, as on an autumn day one walks through a rough country field and comes back covered with nettles, how easy it is to walk through life and accumulate stings! One knows well that some people here this morning are sorely tempted to bitterness and therefore to mental ill health.

For as soon as you see the other thing, an unembittered soul, generous, magnanimous, full of radiant and undiscourageable goodwill, you know that *that* is healthy-mindedness.

Consider a homely illustration of this. A century ago a French citizen left to the French Academy a fund which, increased by others, year after year furnishes prizes for conspicuous exhibitions of virtue discovered in the French population. Here is a typical case: Jeanne Chaix, the eldest of six children—mother insane; father chronically ill; she with no more money than the wages she earns in the pasteboard factory where she works, brings up the family, maintains the entire household, which, says the record, "subsists, morally as well as materially, by the sole force of her valiant will."

With these few facts, what do you know about Jeanne Chaix, standing there to receive her prize from the French Academy? You know this: she had not grown bitter; life had done hard things to her but she had not been embittered; she must have been sustained by an undiscourageable goodwill. She was a healthy-minded girl. Moreover, I suspect that, being French, she was a good Catholic too and that more than once, when the burden did seem unjust and she was tempted to be bitter, she went up to the church and prayed to the Blessed Virgin and came down again sweetened and reinforced. Have we any religion that does anything like that to us?

Bitterness imprisons life; love releases it. Bitterness paralyzes life; love empowers it. Bitterness sours life; love sweetens it. Bitterness sickens life; love heals it. Bitterness blinds life; love anoints its eyes.

In the third place, the New Testament tells us that God has given us not a spirit of fear, but of power, and of love, and of a *sound mind*. The Greek word for "sound mind" is not easy to translate. The Revised Version calls it "discipline." I suspect that the new psychological word "integration" comes close to it. That is to say, Paul's Christian faith pulled his life together, integrated it and so made it sound, saved him from a split, scattered, aimless life, gave it direction and guidance and so unity and discipline, made life seem abundantly worth living, put purpose in it worth living for, and so incalculably contributed to healthy-mindedness.

If Christian faith can do anything like that for anybody, we might well look into it. For we know mentally sick people. What is the matter with many of them? Cynicism, futilism, disillusionment, nothing in life for them, they say, no meaning in the universe to live by, no purpose in the universe to live for—and that is essential irreligion. There are multitudes of people who never will get a healthy mind until they get a vigorous religious faith.

Here in this church, as you know, we are not interested in the minutiæ and peccadilloes of religion. So, I beg of you, do not erect against this truth we are driving at small matters of obsolete church custom, or of belated theology, or of perverted forms of religion that burlesque reality. What we are driving at now is basic.

Listen to this from a contemporary writer: "Is this, then, all that life amounts to? To stumble, almost by mistake, into a universe which was clearly not designed for life, and which, to all appearances, is either totally indifferent or definitely hostile to it, to stay clinging on to a fragment of a grain of sand until we are frozen off, to strut our tiny hour on our tiny stage with the knowledge that our aspirations are all doomed to final frustration, and that our achievements must perish with our race, leaving the universe as though we had never been?" Is this, then, all that life amounts to?

Well, is it? If a man consents to the idea that it is, he has accepted a philosophy which, as a matter of fact, theorize about it as you will, is leading many into cynical contempt for life, an abysmal sense of futility in living life, a disillusioned unwillingness to sacrifice for life. And cynicism, futility, and disillusionment are diseases of the mind.

Look out in imagination on that world we left today and must go back to tomorrow. If ever out of its chaos order comes and a more decent world for our children after us, who will be the builders of that better day? We may be sure of this: it will be the healthy-minded. The cynics and futilists? Never. The disillusioned and discouraged who can find no profound meaning or purpose in life? Never! The healthy-minded must build the better day, and we never will get a robust, vigorous, radiant, hopeful, healthy-mindedness out of the kind of irreligion that reduces man to a hapless victim stumbling by accident into a universe that does not want him, and clinging to the fragment of a grain of sand until he is frozen off.

For myself, I have lived long enough now and have seen enough of the appalling tragedies that fall on man and the broken social hopes that make his progress halting and unsure, to understand how deeply indebted to religion—even though a man may have got only a little of it by indirect contagion—we all are for any healthy-mindedness we may possess.

How strong faith does pull life together, put meaning into it, run purpose through it, put horizons around it! How, when we lose a battle, it reassures us that we may lose a battle and still win the war! In parched years how deep and cool a well it is into which to drop the buckets of our need! And in days like these, when evil seems triumphant and cynicism is easy and courage is hard, how it does unveil upon the surrounding hill tops the horses and chariots of fire!

Inadequacy for life, bitterness of soul, cynicism and futility—these are prevalent diseases today, and because so many are afflicted with them one may be sure that some are here in whom is the last consequence of all these evils, the innermost and final enemy of healthy-mindedness, the sense of guilt. As the psychologists are telling us, behind many nervous breakdowns, emotional maladjustments, insanities, lies the sense of guilt. And we cannot push it out of our souls; it will not go. We cannot argue it out of our souls; it is not amenable to argument. We cannot thrust it down into the pit of our minds and deliberately forget it because always what we try to forget we must remember. There is only one healthy way out from the sense of guilt: penitence, confession, restitution, forgiveness, a new start, and new reserves of strength. How many thus have found, not the spirit of fear, but of a healthy mind!

The Conquest of Fear

WE MAY be sure that every one here, one way or another, faces the problem of fear. If some one says that he does not, a skilled confessor of souls, I think, would take his word for that only temporarily, pending further investigation. Fear runs so far back into the human heritage, takes such diverse forms, works its way out to such disguised results, that nobody, however normal, altogether escapes it. As for the abnormal, one of the leading psychiatrists of the world has said: "If fear were abolished from modern life, the work of the psychotherapist would be nearly gone."

The pulpit has said a great deal about sin but comparatively little about fear. Jesus, however, while he did say, "Go, and sin no more," said again and again, "Fear not," "Be not afraid," "Be not anxious," which shows his clairvoyance into many a broken and hopeless life. Nevertheless, if we should say merely, Be not afraid, if we should think of fear as an utter evil and try to eliminate it altogether from human life, we should be on the wrong track and headed straight for confusion. Fear is the elemental alarm system of the human organism, one of our primary and indispensable instincts. It runs far back into a primitive world where animals and men could never have survived if fear had not made them swift to scent danger, swift to flee, if it had not furnished them, as one scientist puts it, with a "swig of our own internal fight-tonic" from the adrenal glands.

No more can we in the modern world dispense with fear. It keeps us from being run over by automobiles, from being content with unsanitary conditions, from disobeying doctors' orders. The fear of ignorance is one reason why we get an education. The fear of war is one builder of the League of Nations. Fear runs through all of life—wholesome fear not only guarding us from danger but positively driving us to

[59]

constructive enterprises of personal and public protection, so that if by "a fearless man" we mean one who thinks that there is nothing here to dread or from whose constitution the fear instinct has been left out, we are picturing, not a wise man, but a defective mind.

Indeed, this is the difficulty of our problem, that our business is not to get rid of fear but to harness it, curb it, master it. Like fire it is a marvelous servant and a terrific master.

Because fear thus runs the gamut from bad to good, the word "fear" is used, like the word "love," with such confused significance that many people cannot make head or tail out of it. "The fear of the Lord is the beginning of wisdom," said the Psalmist. Surely, being frightened of the Lord is not the beginning of wisdom, but reverent awe in the presence of the Eternal is. A man who can stand before the Eternal Source of this amazing universe without reverent awe, as Einstein says, is blind.

Let no man, then, despise fear or call it wholly evil, for it has many meanings and no good life is possible without its healthful presence. That, however, is not half the story. What ruin cannot fear work in a man's life when it gets loose!

Fear disheartens life. One cannot go on for long with that "old man of the sea" on his back. It drains his energy, depletes his resources, takes the heart out of him. Fear imprisons life. Some one here this morning is looking out on the world now through the bars of an imprisoning fear. Fear distorts life so that though nature be beautiful and music sweet, though friends be faithful and opportunities for lovely living be in our hands, all that is as though it were not, so twisted is our perspective by our obsessing fear. And fear paralyzes life. "Scared stiff," we say. "Scared to death," we say. Both those phrases can be literally true. Can one suppose that in a congregation such as this in days like these there are not some half paralyzed with fear?

Of course the Master talked about this subject. If, as the gospel says, he knew what was in man, how could he help it? Everywhere, all the time, men and women face fear—fear of others, fear of themselves, fear of change, fear of growing old, fear of disease and poverty—and at last many face what the psychiatrists call phobophobia, the fear of fear, being afraid of being afraid. That is why Emerson said, "He has not learned the lesson of life who does not every day surmount a fear."

Well, then, how to do it?

For one thing, there is an area of fear not to be avoided or overcome without a clean and upright moral life. For, my friends, you need expect from me no soft and Pollyanna dealing with this serious matter. I have no pretty embroidered wall mottoes to present to you by whose hypnotic repetition you can banish fear. Jesus never said "Be not afraid" because he thought there was nothing here to be afraid of. Who was it said that if we do not worry we go to the poorhouse and if we do worry we go to the insane asylum? The Eternal has put us in a dangerous world, dangerous to individuals, to nations, to whole civilizations, with actualities and possibilities on every side that all sane men will dread. If, therefore, a man desires a fearless life— that is to say, a life that transcends fear, surmounts it, gains a conquest over it—he must fulfil serious conditions.

One primary condition is a clean and upright life, for if we could be rid of the fears that follow moral wrongdoing we should be a long way out of our problem.

The story of the Garden of Eden goes back to so primitive an age that it pictures God taking an afternoon walk in the cool of the day, pictures a serpent talking and a woman made out of a man's rib. It is a very ancient legend. All the more impressive is it to discover that even then human beings had found out at least one thing that human beings have been finding out ever since. For no sooner has Adam eaten of the forbidden fruit than we hear him saying to God, "I was afraid . . . and I hid myself." As every psychiatrist knows, that is as modern as this morning's newspaper—I was afraid.

One young man I knew plunged gaily into sin. He was no coward, he thought; he was not afraid of anything. So he plunged in and from that time to this he never has known a day free from fear. Has any one of us so entirely escaped that experience that we need to have it described in detail? We sin gaily and then, beyond our power to have foreseen, the sense of guilt knocks at our doors and comes in to live with us. Coleridge described that in "The Ancient Mariner":

> Like one that on a lonesome road
> Doth walk in fear and dread,
> And having once turned round, walks on
> And turns no more his head;
> Because he knows a frightful fiend
> Doth close behind him tread.

Or we sin a little more and, beyond our power to have foreseen, we face a growing habit. At first sin dressed itself in the garments of liberty and said to us, Be free! but now the inexorable laws of habit take charge and that illusory freedom turns out to be the bait to a trap of terrific tyranny. We were free to start. We are not free to stop. Then fear arrives. Yes, a whole troop of fears: fear of the consequence of what we have done upon other people, fear of the gravitation by which a train of evil, once started, goes on and on to disasters we could not guess, and always the dread of being found out. Look at the reputations in the business world which have gone to pieces in the present crisis. Crooked dealing, covered up! Can anybody question what has gone on inside those lives? Fear,—sleepless nights and haggard days peopled by fear of being found out,—until one man kills himself, and another flees the country, and another resigns to save the credit of his institution.

You see what I am trying to say, my friends. At his best a man does desire a fearless life. There is nothing much better that any one could crave. To go out into the world every morning unafraid of the face of mortal clay—what can be worth while without that? One condition of that is imperative—a clean life, no hidden, dirty corners in it, no clandestine Bluebeard's closet whose discovery we dread, an honest, open, upright life. Young man, if you still have

that, keep it! If you have lost it, recover it! For beyond all
the consequences of wrongdoing that moralists commonly
talk about, this, I think, is the darkest consequence of all,
that, one way or another, an evil life is peopled with fear.

This, however, is not the whole story. Another wide area
of fear is caused by trying to face the strain of life with
inadequate interior resources. Did you ever spend a windy
night in a tent when you were not sure how firm the stakes
were and how stout the ropes might be, and when the gales
rose with increasing fury? Nervous business! Multitudes of
people are in that situation. Heavy gales, weak stakes—they
are afraid.

To be sure, some of the fears which people suffer from
they are not responsible for and their phobias cannot be
cured by anything the victims alone can do. Their fears got
a long head-start on them in early childhood from unfor-
tunate accident or unwise parents. A normal baby's fear
instinct has only two expressions, the dread of falling and
the dread of a loud noise. That is all. Every other fear we
possess we have accumulated since, and some children do
accumulate a mass of abnormal fears in unintelligent and ill-
tempered families, so that their subsequent careers are
cursed in consequence and only the skilled service of psychiatry is likely to disentangle them. Fear of the dark, fear
of water, fear of closed places, fear of open places, fear of
altitude, fear of death, fear of hell, fear of cats, fear of
Friday the thirteenth, fear of walking under a ladder—anybody who knows that hinterland and slum district of the
mind knows how tragic it is. We parents have few duties
more sacred than to see to it that our children do not catch
from us unnecessary and abnormal fears.

Much of our fearful living, however, moves in another
realm, where the service of psychiatry is dubious unless the
psychiatrist is a man of religious faith. For the trouble with
us is simply that we are facing the heavy strain of life without adequate spiritual resources. We would call Paul a fearless man, would we not? I think we had better. He was not
afraid of human enemies—faced them down more than

once, even when a mob clamored for his death. He was not intellectually afraid, moving from orthodox to liberal Judaism and then to Christianity, and even then leading the enterprise out from a narrow church for Jewish Christians only into a comprehensive faith that took Gentiles in. He was not afraid of physical danger. It took more than flogging and stoning to stop him, and once in a shipwreck he, most of all, sustained the courage of the company. He was not afraid of prison and even cried victoriously that his bonds had fallen out unto the furtherance of the gospel. In life and death, he was preëminently a gentleman unafraid. And if you take his word for it, his secret runs far down into his religious faith. Listen to him: "I know how to be abased, and I know also how to abound. . . . I can do all things in him that strengtheneth me." You recall how Dr. Moffatt translates that last clause: "In him who strengthens me I am able for anything."

If a man's religious faith does not thus furnish him with adequate spiritual resources for life, there is something the matter with it. Out of the unseen, to one who has experienced the Christian gospel's practical effect, there comes a voice with all the resources of the Eternal Spirit, saying, You can. When fear whimpers, I cannot do what I ought to do, the voice says, You can. When fear complains, I cannot stand what I must endure, the voice says, You can. As Emerson said about youth,

> So nigh is grandeur to our dust,
> So near is God to man,
> When Duty whispers low, *Thou must,*
> The youth replies, *I can.*

In that fine sense, a vital Christian faith keeps a man's soul young. He can.

I should like this morning to do something more than discuss the conquest of fear. I wish that the conquest could be achieved now by some one here who needs it. Fear is a hypnotist. It stares us out of countenance. It says to us again and again, You cannot, you cannot! So fear produces what

[64]

it fears. It is a creative force. Listen to it long enough and its message turns out to be true: you cannot. How often, do you think, in the far country did the Prodigal Son say to himself, I ought to go home? You know that every time he said that something inside of him whispered, You cannot go home; you dare not go home; your father will not welcome you; you have not strength enough to go home; you have got to stay. So, just as a hypnotist can draw an imaginary line around his victim across which the victim cannot step, fear, that Svengali of the soul, imprisons us. It is a terrific experience and the only way out is faith.

"The only known cure for fear is *faith*"—that was said by one of the leading physicians and psychiatrists of America, speaking out of a long scientific experience. For faith also is creative. It produces what it has faith in. Live with it in the deep companionship of your soul, listen to its speaking out of the resources of the Divine world, tap the infinite resources which it can release into your life, and at last you *can*.

This creative nature of faith and fear is illustrated in our present economic situation. President Roosevelt furnished a text for this sermon when in his inaugural address he said that the only thing this nation has to fear is fear. Just so! And there is a dangerous quantity of it—indignant, anxious, fearful loss of public confidence. Let a few more political leaders fail us, let a few more shocking disclosures of dishonesty and chicanery burst upon us, and the loss of public confidence may grow to panic proportions and once more on a large scale fear produce what it fears. We had better balance budgets; we had better finish the question of international debts; we had better overpass our stupid policies of national isolation; and, above all, we had better give the people some assurance that we do honestly intend some deep-seated and far-reaching reforms in our economic system. That is to say, we had better give public faith something to grow on or else we shall inevitably eat the bitter fruit of public fear.

If fear and faith are so creative in the large, they are op-

erative inside us, are they not? I saw a man once, in the grip
of an evil habit, listening to that word out of the Unseen—
You can. I watched him, dubious about it, wanting to believe
it but not daring, wishing that it might be true but seeing
that the whole logic of the situation—his long habit, his
spoiled reputation, his coarsened conscience—argued against
the possibility. Then, catching a note of authority in the
voice, as though spoken by one in whom the power to per-
form is equal to the thing he promises, the voice sank in and
took control and the Divine "You can" was answered by the
human "I will." I saw that man go out to freedom, fear
conquered, faith triumphant, character transformed. That is
salvation!

That might happen here today. You can. You can do what
you ought to do. You can stand what you must endure. As
your day is so shall your strength be. And, however difficult
the circumstances, you can have an inner victory, the conquest of panic and fear.

Even this, however, does not tell the whole story. There
is one more field where fear grows rank and strong and
where the only cure is goodwill, love. So the New Testament
says, "Perfect love casteth out fear." When one stops merely
repeating that text and sits down to think of it, it is a
strange saying. What have love and fear to do with each
other? They have so much to do with each other that one
does not need to go down into the obscure and mystical
depths of the human soul for an illustration. Our international relationships themselves are a perfect picture of the
truth. The last time I was in Geneva I heard Dean Inge
preach the sermon before the League of Nations and his
thesis was that the major cause of war is fear. Of course it
is. There are other causes—economic, political, racial—but
they all spring from and are shot through with fear—France
fearing Germany, Germany fearing the encircling powers,
the Balkan States fearing one another, and the United States
pacific in intention mainly because we are not vividly haunted
by fear of another nation. People commonly talk as though
war came from hate, but the order of events is generally

quite otherwise—first fear, then war, then hate. Fear of another nation's attack, fear of another nation's economic supremacy, fear of lost prestige and lost markets, as in the Far East now—all the causes of war are shot through with fear. Now, the old remedy for fear was great armaments. Armed to the teeth, a nation said, we shall not fear. But how futile is that old remedy in the new world! Great armaments are not now a remedy for fear. They are the major cause of fear.

So, once again, this world, which thought itself so wise, swings round to something the New Testament said long ago. Not battleships and poison gas but only organized good-will can ever give the nations real security and cast out fear.

A fact that works thus in the large is probably operative inside our lives. What are some of us afraid of this morning? We are afraid of the superiority of other people, afraid that somebody is going to get ahead of us or be preferred before us, afraid of other people's disapproval if we do what we know is right. Jealousy, envy, bitterness, vindictiveness, a humiliating sense of inferiority in comparison with others —all such emotions are forms of fear.

Years ago in Free Saint George's Church in Edinburgh, Alexander Whyte ruled the pulpit like a king. Then Hugh Black was called to be his junior colleague. They used to say that in the morning Whyte blackballed the saints and that in the evening Black whitewashed the sinners. As the years passed, Alexander Whyte saw his junior colleague forging to the front. He had a note that caught the ear of the younger generation; he had wider influence, larger con-gregations. Whyte told a friend of his what a bitter struggle with jealous fear that caused him, and the friend, knowing how gracious and lovable Whyte was and absolutely loyal to his colleague, would not believe it. "Ah," said Whyte, "you don't know the black depths of the human heart."

What is the cure, then, of this fear of people, jealous, envious, suspicious, sometimes bitter? We know the cure— God help us to achieve it! Love casteth out fear.

O Master, you were fearless. Men may deny the creeds

[67]

about you but they cannot deny your courage. An upright life that never needed to be ashamed—that was part of it. A great faith that tapped the resources of power—that was part of it. But when one thinks what people did to you, their misuse of power in hurting you, the vindictive humiliations they visited upon you, and how unafraid you were, one sees that only undiscourageable goodwill could have risen to such a height.

Well, add up the sum and see what it comes to. Clean life, great faith, love that takes in enemies—the sum of that addition is a fearless soul.

Handling Life's Second-Bests

WE ARE concerned today about a factual personal problem so nearly universal in its application that we need not be bothered by its exceptions: namely, that very few persons have a chance to live their lives on the basis of their first choice. We all have to live upon the basis of our second and third choices. To one who reads biography this comes to be so much a matter of course that he takes it for granted.

Whistler, the artist, for example, started out to be a soldier and failed at West Point because he could not pass in chemistry. "If silicon had been a gas," he used to say, "I should have been a major-general." Instead, he failed in soldiering, half-heartedly tried engineering, and then tried painting—with such remarkable results as one sees in the portraits of his own mother, Miss Alexander, and Carlyle.

Let us approach this unescapable human problem of handling life's second-bests by way of one of the most impressive exhibitions of it in history. In the sixteenth chapter of the book of The Acts, in the record of Paul's journeys, we read this: "When they were come over against Mysia, they assayed to go into Bithynia; and the Spirit of Jesus suffered them not; and passing by Mysia, they came down to Troas. And a vision appeared to Paul in the night: There was a man of Macedonia standing, beseeching him, and saying, Come over into Macedonia, and help us. And when he had seen the vision, straightway we sought to go forth into Macedonia, concluding that God had called us to preach the gospel unto them."

So simple and succinct is this narrative that one would little suspect that we are dealing with one of the most significant events in human history. Here Christianity passed over from Asia into Europe. It was a momentous day when Columbus set sail from the shores of Spain or Vasco da

Gama discovered the sea route to the Indies, but could even such events be more pregnant with consequence than the day when Paul carried Christianity out of Asia, in a few centuries to be overrun by Mohammedanism, through Troas into Macedonia and so to Europe, where Christianity was going to have its chance? But Paul had not planned to go to Europe. That was a second choice. Paul had planned to go to Bithynia. "They assayed," it reads, "to go into Bithynia." And no wonder, for Bithynia was one of the richest provinces of Asia Minor, and to have carried Christianity there would have been a triumph indeed.

Moreover, we may be sure that if Paul wanted to go into Bithynia he wanted to go very much and tried to go very hard, for Paul was never a half-way man. And he could not go; the way was blocked; his plan was broken. We read, "The Spirit of Jesus suffered them not," but that is only another way of saying that some circumstance blocked their course. It must have seemed to Paul lamentable at first. I picture him arriving on the shores of the Ægean, saying, I wanted to go to Bithynia and here I am in Troas! And lo! through Troas a way opened to the preëminent ministry of his career. Paul rendered his most significant service with the left-overs of a broken plan.

Wanting Bithynia and getting Troas, how familiar an experience that is! But to take Troas, the second-best, the broken plan, the left-over of a disappointed expectation, and make of it the greatest opportunity we ever had, how much less familiar that is! Yet, as one reads the story of human life, one sees that powerful living has always involved such a victory as Paul won in Troas over his own soul and his situation.

When a career has at last been finished and the halo of well-deserved reputation now hangs over it so that one cannot think the name without thinking of some high enterprise with which the name is indissolubly associated, then in the glamour of that retrospect we are tempted to forget that almost always the turning point of the career is the experience that Paul had—getting Troas when he wanted Bithynia.

When, for example, we think of Phillips Brooks, we think of spiritual ministry, a great personality pouring his soul out with abundant power upon the people. Of all the letters that Phillips Brooks received, it is said that he cherished most this one from a small tailor shop near Copley Square in Boston: "Dear Mr. Brooks: I am a tailor in a little shop near your Church. Whenever I have the opportunity I always go to hear you preach. Each time I hear you preach I seem to forget all about you, for you make me think of God." Nevertheless, remember that Phillips Brooks did not plan to be a preacher. He planned to be a teacher. That was his Bithynia. As soon as he graduated from college he plunged into his chosen profession of teaching and he failed. He failed completely. Listen to young Brooks writing about his scholars as he is failing: "They are the most disagreeable set of creatures without exception that I have ever met with. . . . I really am ashamed of it but I am tired, cross and almost dead, so good night." Listen to Phillips Brooks after he had failed and been dropped from his position: "I don't know what will become of me and I don't care much"; "I shall not study a profession"; "I wish I were fifteen years old again. I believe I might make a stunning man: but somehow or other I don't seem in the way to come to much now." Listen to Phillips Brooks' father, concerned about his son, so humiliated that he will not talk even with his friends: "Phillips will not see anyone now, but after he is over the feeling of mortification, he will come and see you."

There is a sense in which Brooks never recovered from the disappointment. At the flower of his career he came down once from the office of President Eliot of Harvard white as a sheet and fairly trembling because he had declined what he knew to be his last opportunity to become a teacher. He wanted Bithynia and he got Troas but through Troas he found the door into a service that if he had lived a hundred lives he might never have found again.

Or consider Sir Walter Scott. We think of him as the novel-writer whose stories charmed our youth so that for many years some of us would have voted Ivanhoe the best

tale ever told. Sir Walter, however, did not want to be a
novelist; he planned to be a poet, but Byron's sun rose and
dimmed his lesser light. "Byron hits the mark," he said,
"where I don't even pretend to fledge my arrow." Then he
turned to writing novels, so ashamed that, as you know, he
published the first of them anonymously. He did not want
any one to know that he was writing novels. He wanted
Bithynia; he got Troas and through Troas an open door to
the best work he ever did.

Is there anybody here who has not wanted Bithynia and
gotten Troas? We older people watch the youths come up,
as we did, with their ambitions and plans for Bithynia and
we wonder what they will do when they face the unescapable
experience. When they are shut out from some Bithynia and
land in Troas, will they know how to handle that? Will they
have the spirit and attitude and the technique to make of it
their finest chance? And since it is so unescapable a problem,
we well may ask what it was in Paul that enabled him to
turn his defeat into victory.

For one thing, his religion entered in. Whatever else was
shaken when he got to Troas, his conviction still was there
that God had a purpose for his life, that if God had led him
to Troas there must be something in Troas worth discovering, that God's purposes included Troas just as much as
Bithynia, that God never leads any man into any place where
all the doors are shut. Paul's religion entered in.

It is in just such situations as this that one can tell how
much real religion a man has. We hear a man reciting a
familiar creed: "I believe in God the Father Almighty,
Maker of heaven and earth," but no matter how serious he
may seem about it you cannot tell from that alone how real
it is to him. You hear a man singing,

> He leadeth me: O blessed thought!
> O words with heavenly comfort fraught!
> Whate'er I do, where'er I be,
> Still 'tis God's hand that leadeth me.

But however much in earnest he may seem you cannot tell

from that alone how deep it goes with him. When, however, you see a man who, wanting Bithynia, gets Troas and, still certain that there is a purpose for his life, takes a positive attitude toward Troas as if to say, If God has led me here there is something worth while here to do, you know that that man's religion is practically operative. If, therefore, Paul had merely said what he did say, "To them that love God all things work together for good," we might have cocked suspicious eyebrows at him, thinking that that proposition is extraordinarily difficult to prove. What is impressive about Paul is that whenever he did land in a disappointing Troas, and he landed in a good many of them, he did so effectually love God that he *made* all things work together for good. Paul's religion meant to him a positive faith about life and a positive attitude toward life so effective that watching his career is again and again like watching the Battle of Marengo—in the morning an obvious defeat, in the afternoon a resounding victory.

Consider a modern counterpart of Paul, Adoniram Judson. When Judson was a young man he gave himself to missionary service and his ambition centered on India. That was his Bithynia. When at last he reached India they would not let him in. The East India Company would not allow him to stay and the governor told him to take the first ship back to America. For a year he labored to open the doors of India and they were bolted shut. So he turned to Burma. That was his Troas, unknown, untouched Burma. Can one suppose that through all that humiliation and disappointment Judson could always see the leadership of God? Of course he could not; he was human. Can one suppose during those months that he lay in the prison of the Emperor at Ava and Oung-Pen-La he could always see evidences of the divine purpose? Of course he could not; he was human. But he did so handle the affair in Burma that the doors began to open until no well-instructed man today can think of Burma without thinking of Adoniram Judson, or think of Adoniram Judson without thinking of Burma; and when the consequence began to appear he could look upon his life in retrospect as though it had been planned of God. To live your life through—not argue it through; that never is sufficient—to *live* your life through into the conviction that there is an eternal Purpose with which a man can ally himself is one of the finest achievements of the human spirit.

Altogether the most thrilling story in the Old Testament is on this theme. One day in Palestine we stopped our automobile by the roadside and ate our lunch at Dotham where long ago Joseph had been sold by his brethren. Still the camel trail goes up from across Jordan, and then runs down to the coast cities and so to Egypt. Now Joseph, stolen from his home, betrayed by his brethren, dropped into a pit, sold to Midianite slave-dealers, made a man-servant in a household in Egypt, lied about by his master's wife and put in prison—can one suppose that during all that humiliation and disgrace he could see where God was taking him? Of course not. But he so kept his faith and handled his life that the doors opened into the biggest business of his career, and when at last those penitent and frightened brethren stood before him, you remember what he said: "I am Joseph your brother, whom ye sold into Egypt. And now be not grieved, nor angry with yourselves, that ye sold me hither: for God did send me before you to preserve life. . . . So now it was not you that sent me hither, but God."

Such was Paul's feeling as he looked back on the day he missed Bithynia and found Troas, and such will be ours if in Troas we will let our religion enter in.

In the second place it was not simply Paul's religion that enabled him to win this victory but the fine fruit of his religion, his care about people.

The trouble with so many of us when we land in Troas is that we begin to pity ourselves. Paul could have done that. He could have started the process we indulge in—"ifing."

If I had not missed Bithynia; if my plans had not been broken, if, if! I have given up everything for Jesus Christ. I could today be one of the great rabbis of Jerusalem saluted in the market place. I have given it all up for Christ. I spent a long time in Arabia thinking through the gospel. I have been fourteen years in a trying, difficult, unrecognized ministry in Cilicia, at odds even with my Christian brethren because once I persecuted them. And now, when I am beginning to get on a good footing with my fellow Christians, with Barnabas and a few others trusting me, I have come up through Asia Minor on a preaching mission. See what they have done to me. They stoned me and left me for dead in Lystra. Even after that, all I asked was that I might have a chance to get into Bithynia and do some good work, and now I cannot; I am foiled; my plan is broken.

How easy it would have been for Paul in Troas to feel sorry for himself!

Upon the contrary, he at once began thinking about other people. He wondered if there was not some one who might be better off because he had landed in Troas. He had not been there a night before he saw a man from Macedonia saying, Come over and help us. It was Paul's unselfishness, his generosity, his magnanimity that opened the doors for him in Troas.

Once there was a man named William Duncan who gave himself to the missionary cause and in time was sent by his board to a little Indian island off Alaska called Metlakatla. It was an unlikely Troas for a young man to land in who had doubtless dreamed of some Bithynia, for those Indians were a poor, ignorant, miserable tribe, and their morals were vile beyond description. Dean Brown of Yale, however, who visited Metlakatla after William Duncan had been there about forty years, makes this report, that you will find every Indian family in a separate house with all the decent appointments of home life, that you will find a bank, a coöperative store, a saw-mill, a box factory, and a salmon cannery run by Indians in profitable industry, that you will find a school where Indian boys and girls learn to read and write and think and live, and a church where an Indian minister preaches the gospel of eternal life and an Indian musician, who once was a medicine man playing a tom-tom, now plays a pipe organ, and a congregation of Indians sing the great hymns of the church to the praise of Almighty God—and all because a man named William Duncan, landing in Troas, cared enough about people to find there the chance of his life!

My friends, there is nothing in that spirit or consequence that cannot be transferred to our lives. We are all in Troas. Just as at Sebastopol each heart thought a different name while they all sang Annie Laurie, so when today we say "Troas" each one of us thinks of some situation we would not have planned to be in. There is only one way—love. Was it not George Macdonald who said: "Nothing makes a man strong like a cry for help"? You walk down the street utterly fatigued, so tired that you would like to lie down on the curb and go to sleep, and suddenly there is a cry; there has been an accident; a child is hurt; and you never will remember how tired you are until it is all over. Nothing makes a man so strong as a call for help.

A mother is completely fatigued. She has been telling her friends for weeks that there is nothing left of her, and then a child falls ill and needs her. Week after week, by night and day, she stands by and never thinks of being tired. Nothing makes a man strong like a call for help.

It would be strange indeed if there were not some young men and women here not altogether dull to the dangers of our civilization, not altogether blind to the possibility of losing it, thinking that perhaps there is something in them that might help build a more decent world for human children to be born in. That is their strength. Nothing makes a man so strong as a call for help. And the trouble is that when we get into Troas we pity ourselves; we miss that man from Macedonia, saying, Come over and help us.

Indeed, so true is this principle of life that it holds good of even small excursions into Troas. When annoyances and irritations come, when one is lied about and hated and denounced, there is only one way out—goodwill. You remember Edwin Markham's lines:

> He drew a circle that shut me out—
> Heretic, rebel, a thing to flout.
> But Love and I had the wit to win:
> We drew a circle that took him in!

If in the midst of life's harassments and irritations one has grace enough to do that, he sometimes will find in that very difficulty his choicest opportunity for usefulness.

This, then, is the conclusion of the matter: that because Paul had these two elements in his life, as soon as he landed in Troas his imagination was filled, not with defeat but with victory. Coué was right that it is the imagination which makes or unmakes us. If you put a thirty-foot plank as high as a cathedral tower hardly anybody can walk it, and it is not because the physical difficulties are greater than they would be on the ground but because one's imagination keeps picturing him falling off. So when we get into Troas we think we are defeated. I wanted Bithynia, we say; I have got Troas. So we think defeat, we say defeat, we imagine defeat, and we are defeated. But as soon as Paul landed in Troas he saw an open door, a beckoning man, a new chance, and a successful issue.

What helped him most, I suspect, was that his thought went back, as it so habitually did, to the cross of his Master. That was a Troas to land on! What a Bithynia it would have been if his people had accepted Jesus as Messiah! And now, shut out from that Bithynia, he came to his Troas, his Calvary, and he so clothed it with the purpose of God and the love of man that

> All the light of sacred story
> Gathers round its head sublime.

He took a very hard thing and he made of it a triumph.

Keeping One's Footing in
a Slippery Time

ONE of the most familiar ideas in modern preaching is that the Christian life is an adventure. So it is. Faith in the Christian God is a daring interpretation of this mysterious universe. Christian morals are a venturesome pushing out of goodwill as far as we can make it go into human relationships. Christian prayer is an adventure of the soul in fellowship with the Unseen. As for a redeemed society, the kingdom of God on earth, that will take adventurous thinking and doing before it is achieved. Important as this element in Christian living is, however, it does not cover the case. How constantly in days like these we find ourselves faced with another problem altogether, not exciting, forward-looking adventure, but the more prosaic task of maintaining our own interior stability, keeping on our own feet, standing our ground, holding on! Moreover, this is certain: a man who cannot maintain his own footing cannot be venturesome; a man who cannot hold on cannot carry on.

All this caught fire in my imagination when, reading Dr. Moffatt's translation of the book of Job, I came, in the fourth verse of the fourth chapter, to this sentence: "Your words have kept men on their feet." To be sure, that was said to Job by Eliphaz, one of his friends. Now, these friends of Job were a poor lot and much of what they said turned out to be false, but no one can talk so continuously as they did without saying some true things. As another has put it about this very passage, even a clock that has stopped is correct about the time twice in twenty-four hours. So Eliphaz, remembering the years when Job was in his prime, a helper and encourager of his people, said to him, "Your words have kept men on their feet."

We need words that will do that if any generation ever

did. Many intimate, personal things about a congregation like this it is impossible to know, but we may be certain that many of us are not well fitted to be adventurous for enterprising undertakings because we have a prior problem—we are having difficulty not to be swept off our own feet; we cannot go on unless we can hold on. What if there are words that can keep men on their feet!

When history writes of us a century from now, it will say that this was one of the most chaotic periods through which mankind ever passed, when from every side torrential currents poured together in confusion. If some stout soul says, Just so, and in consequence we all ought to fall to and help harness these unruly streams so that, like Niagara, they may drive the turbines of a new and better civilization, I agree. But some of us are in no position to help harness torrential streams. We are having difficulty maintaining our own footing. We ourselves are slipping. In a generation full of change, with external circumstances kaleidoscopic and new ideas shifting like clouds in our mental skies, we are even tempted to lose, almost without knowing when we do it, the old spiritual convictions that once did keep us on our feet.

In an Illinois village recently a woman, housecleaning, in the enthusiasm of her spring renovation sold for ten cents to a traveling ragman old books which she did not want. Then, hours afterward, she remembered that she had hidden four thousand dollars in one of those books. Too late! At last accounts she has had to make up her mind that she sold something very valuable very cheap.

That kind of loss is being suffered spiritually by multitudes of people. Spring housecleaning is mild compared with the upheavals and renovations of this generation's interior life, and in recent years many have morally and religiously parted with old things which they thought obsolete and useless, only to wake up too late to discover that they have sold something very valuable very cheap. Challenge them now to be adventurous for great causes and you will discover that that is not their problem. They have lost something which keeps a man's footing secure. They have forgotten the words which keep men on their feet.

With a subject such as this, one is not likely to say anything new. This sermon must frankly be an excursion in remembrance, an endeavor to recall some of the old words which century after century, through stormy days, have kept men on their feet.

One such word is that *life is an entrustment*. That sounds simple but it runs deep. Indeed, when we stop discussing the theoretical contrast between religious and irreligious theory and get down to the thing we really are talking about in terms of daily life, much of the difference between irreligion and religion can be swiftly summed up.

It may be that life is an accident. It may be that once long ago, when the planet was cooling, the heat was just right so that from a fortuitous collocation of matter which we do not understand and have not as yet been able to reproduce, life emerged, and being here has gone mechanically on into intelligence, creative purposefulness, and love. It is strange, of course, that such things should casually have emerged as fortuitous by-products of a physical system, but so to explain them is one way of looking at the matter. That is sheer irreligion. Concerning man's presence on this earth, it ultimately says merely that we're here because we're here, because we're here, because we're here.

It may be, however, that life is not an accident. It may be an entrustment. So Jesus said, "The Father hath sent me." To him, at any rate, life was an entrustment, not to be thrown away, not to be misused, too sacred to be profaned, too significant to be wasted, too purposeful to be frightened —something that he had been trusted with.

In a university community like this are many people who say that religion is an elective in life, that it does not matter much, that if you must have it, all right, but that intelligent people could probably get on better without it. Now, there is plenty so-called religion which an intelligent man might better get on without but, as for the essence of the matter, we should at least face this obvious fact: irreligion ultimately says to us, You are an accident, a fortuitous by-product of a physical process. I challenge you: make that your daily meat and drink. In the morning do not pray, as we Christians do, to a Father who seeth in secret and by whose will and purpose we are here. Say to yourselves instead, I am an accident, a fortuitous by-product of the dust. Salute yourselves at night with what the honest, thoroughgoing irreligionists are plainly saying and printing—this, for example: I am "a parasite infesting the epidermis of a midge among the planets." Do you really think that such words help to keep men on their feet?

There is another attitude toward life that some of us can remember as far back as we can remember anything in our childhood's homes. We breathed it in the very air. We caught it in the unconscious accents of our parents' conversation—that life is something we are trusted with. To be sure, a man does not go about continuously saying that to himself. He does not constantly make of it a solemn pronouncement. So in Geneva, Switzerland, one does not all the time see Mont Blanc. It is often shrouded in mist. But once in a while one sees it. Sometimes its mighty summit, glorious and dominant, shines out. One knows it is always there. So some lives here have been dominated by a towering idea which rises out of the very nature of religion, that life is something sacred with which we have been trusted. What a powerful motive to keep men on their feet!

To be sure, there may be treachery against trust. Judas betrayed Jesus, but afterwards he hung himself in remorse for doing it. He waked up to face a thought with which he could not go on living—that he had been trusted and had been false. As for the noblest living which the world has seen, I venture that always, one way or another, you find underneath it this basic idea that life is a trust.

Even Mr. Walter Lippmann, one of the finest of the nontheists, in his *Preface to Morals* says characteristically that a wise man can regard life as "comedy, or high tragedy, or plain farce," and still enjoy it. Well, maybe! But as one considers the spiritual heroes of the race, they seem to be thinking about life as something more than comedy or tragedy or farce.

When Lincoln, against the advice of his friends, decided to make the speech which defeated him for the Senate in 1858, saying, "If it is decreed that I should go down because of this speech, then let me go down linked to the truth," was he dealing with life as comedy or tragedy or farce? He was dealing with life as a trust. Or when Dr. Trudeau, smitten with tuberculosis, took to the mountains and for forty years poured out such service as never before had been rendered to his fellow-sufferers, was he thinking of life as comedy or tragedy or farce? Upon the contrary, I wish that some of us might say to ourselves this morning what he must have said to himself many a time: Life is a trust; I will not desert it or surrender it or betray it; the Eternal has entrusted me with it. Life is hard. To be sure, it is! Life is often unjust to individuals. Of course it is! But underneath, life is something else, a trust which a man must carry finely until without stain he can lay it down. How that word has kept men on their feet!

Here is another word that might help, that *the supreme successes of the world have been defeats.* I am sure that is a neglected emphasis in American preaching. We ministers, wanting to be hearty and optimistic like all the rest of the Americans, have been tempted to say, Of course you can win; blow on your hands; have faith and courage and nothing is impossible. That message does not go deep enough, does it? Sometimes we cannot win outwardly. Sometimes we have to face defeat externally. In these days especially, alas for those religious quacks in the pulpit who, like the advertisers in the newspapers promising perfect health or amazing eloquence after six lessons, say to the people that nothing is impossible! But there is another kind of message which ministers of the Christ, who was himself crucified on Calvary, might bring to the people,—that even in defeat a man can win the kind of victory which has meant most to the world. In Story's words:

[82]

Speak, History! who are Life's victors? Unroll thy long annals,
    and say,
Are they those whom the world called the victors—who won the
    success of a day?
The martyrs, or Nero? The Spartans, who fell at Thermopylæ's
    tryst,
Or the Persians and Xerxes? His judges or Socrates? Pilate or
    Christ?

The amazing successes of defeat!

Of course, it may be that some of us here do not need to
fail even outwardly. When the Wright brothers were ex-
perimenting with airplanes in Dayton, Ohio, one citizen of
that state is said to have exclaimed: "Nobody's ever going to
fly; and if anybody ever did fly it wouldn't be anybody from
Dayton." That is typical of the cynical words that knock
men off their feet. One can hear them on every side: We
cannot, they say, we cannot stop war or build a decent economic order, or educate the world to better racial attitudes.
We cannot overcome sin or surmount trouble. Nobody is
ever going to fly, least of all anybody from Dayton.

How indispensable faith is! Religion or no religion, how
indispensable it is! Not the faith of credulity—Heaven forbid—but the faith of creative confidence! Nothing is ever
done in any realm without it and this morning if some soul
here should rise from doubt and fear to faith he might go
out on his feet again to win even outwardly.

Nevertheless, life is full of another kind of story altogether. Helen Keller as a little child was struck blind. Everything they could do they desperately tried in the battle for
her sight. No use! She faced defeat and then out of the limitations of defeat she rose up to win one of the shining
successes of human history. That is a most indispensable
kind of victory. Mankind could muddle along without flying
at Dayton but mankind cannot muddle on without this inner
victory, triumph on a cross, success in defeat.

Let us say it to ourselves this morning. It might put some
of us on our feet: I myself do not need to be a failure. No
matter what happens on the outside, I myself need not be a

failure. Outwardly I am defeated. Well, then, there are plenty of people left on earth who can succeed outwardly, but the spiritual enrichment of mankind has come chiefly not from the men who succeeded outwardly but from men and women who, defeated, won an inner victory. Some of us have heard Walter Hampden in "Cyrano de Bergerac" more than once, and we would go back to hear him again if only to listen to the gallant Cyrano at the end, defeated but saying,

> . . . . One thing without stain,
> Unspotted from the world, in spite of doom
> Mine own !—
> And that is . . .
> My white plume.

So Socrates, defeated, fell on sleep, his white plume unstained. So Jesus, defeated, gave up the ghost on Calvary, his white plume unstained. So some whom we have loved, to whom life was not kind, within the limitations of defeat won a success that has been the major inspiration of our lives, their white plumes unstained. The supreme successes of history have been defeats.

One more word might help, that *there is ample power available to see a man through.* As you know, that conviction lay at the heart of old-fashioned Christianity. When we have said our worst about the obsolete elements in old-fashioned religion, there was in historic Christianity at its best, for those who understood it, an experience which kept men on their feet. They were inwardly strengthened with spiritual power ample to see them through. Many modern Christians have lost that. Christianity to them has become a set of ethical principles to live by or a series of social causes to live for. But ethical principles to live by and social causes to live for require power but do not of themselves furnish it. So many modern Christians find themselves with moral ideals and a new social order to struggle toward but with no deep consciousness of interior, personal, spiritual power to do the struggling with. Their religion demands something of them without supplying anything to them. So in a turbulent time like this, when men are called to give themselves to difficult enterprises, they discover themselves preoccupied with a prior problem—they cannot keep their own footing. True, is it not? Many modern Christians have sold something very valuable very cheap.

The disintegrating forces all around us are obvious. Can you imagine anything much more likely to knock a man off his spiritual feet than a steady diet of novels, movies, and dramas compounded fifty-fifty of sex and cynicism? I will not advertise them by name. I imagine you know them.

As for much of the current thinking which passes for philosophy, I read the other day in a book that all we men and women on this planet with our aspirations, our age-long sacrifices, our progress hardly won, our dreams of nobler days for our humanity, are like so many spiders in the basement of the universe, spinning dusty webs that soon will be brushed down and quite forgotten. A grand idea *that* to keep men on their feet!

A moment ago I quoted Mr. Walter Lippmann critically. Now let me quote him with profound gratitude. Recently speaking at the University of California, among many highminded things he said this: "Underlying the disorder in the outer world, there is disorder in the spirit of man. . . . Where there is no vision, the people perish. . . . Only the consciousness of a purpose that is mightier than any man and worthy of all men can fortify and inspirit and compose the souls of men." Just so! And what does Mr. Lippmann think we Christians mean by God or are trying our best to persuade our generation of except this, that at the heart of the universe there really is a purpose mightier than any man, worthy of all men, that alone can fortify and inspirit and compose the souls of men? That is a word which might keep men on their feet.

To be sure, there are many steadying influences closer at hand and homelier than this. Human friendship, for example. Were some one to come to me, his morale slipping and his footing insecure, perhaps the first thing I would say to him would be, You still have friends? You still have some who love and trust you? Then you must not cave in. Robert Louis Stevenson, in his long fight with tuberculosis, was not thinking of a theory but of a poignant experience when he said to us what he doubtless had said to himself many a time, "So long as we are loved by others, I would almost say that we are indispensable; and no man is useless while he has a friend."

Tremendously important as such friendship is, however, and little as any one of us ever would keep on our feet without it, how can a man live through days like these without feeling the deep and lonely need of power from the wells of the Eternal? A man need not have a complete philosophy or an adequate answer to all the questions he would like to have answered about God before he can avail himself of that spiritual power. All around us we use power concerning which we theoretically know little. Men breathed for ages before Lavoisier discovered what breathing really is in terms of chemistry, and even yet on spring days amid the fresh green of the countryside one does not need to know anything about respiration chemically in order to breathe life. So in the spirit, if you have, as Jesus said, faith as a grain of mustard seed that there is a realm above you, a spiritual life superior to you, a purpose mightier than any man and worthy of all men, or, as I would say it, a Personal Life which puts mind and meaning into the universe, then pray, lift up your spirit to The Spirit, sink deep the shafts of your need into the resources of the Eternal. Such words have kept men on their feet.

A few years ago, a man, they say, was lost in the fog on the Welsh mountains. For two nights and a day he wandered lost. So, sitting fatigued and discouraged, suddenly out of the unseen he heard a voice say, "I wonder if by any chance he could have come this way." Who can measure such salvation? He was being searched for out of the unseen. May some such word come to some one here who thinks himself lost in the fog! May he hear a word out of the invisible that will put him on his feet!

Is Our Christianity Appealing to Our Softness or Our Strength?

WE FACE today a question which, before we are through, ought to come home to our consciences— Is our Christianity appealing to our softness or our strength? For Christianity as it actually operates in experience appeals to and brings out all sorts of qualities in the people whom it touches. It brings out one man's intolerance and sectarianism so that, holding that one special church or one special set of theological opinions alone is true, he who in other realms of life is benign and amiable becomes in his Christianity dogmatic and bitter. It brings out another man's credulity so that he who in other fields exhibits intelligence and hard-headedness counts it a virtue in his Christianity to throw down the safeguards of evidence and believe almost any incredible thing which the Christian tradition happens to have picked up.

You see, Christianity, as it is variously interpreted, can appeal to diverse qualities in its devotees. It can lay its hands on a Quaker's love of peace and lift it up to powerful testimony. It can lay its hands on a crusader's belligerence and send it forth on dastardly exploits, saying, "Deus vult"— God wills it. It can bring out St. Francis of Assisi's tenderness and Torquemada's cruelty. In this regard religion is a fearful thing. It accentuates anything it touches. It brings out into powerful exercise whatever qualities it gets its hands upon.

Most of us are Christians. We have been under Christian influence for years. To what, then, is our Christianity appealing? In particular, is it appealing to our softness or our strength? You remember Paul's admonition to his young friend Timothy, "Endure hardness, as a good soldier of Jesus Christ." The military metaphor need not trouble us. Paul was no militarist. Just as he took a simile from the

[87]

prize fight, although he would have made a poor prize
fighter, so he, who would not have made a soldier, took a
metaphor from the battlefield: "Endure hardness, as a good
soldier of Jesus Christ." That is to say, beware of the kind
of Christianity that appeals to, brings out, and accentuates
your softness.

A great deal of our contemporary Christianity fails at this
point. We can interpret faith in God so that it becomes a
pillow to lie down upon. It does not so much challenge us and
call out our strength and courage to serve high aims as it
mollifies us, soothes and lulls us, becomes, as the communists say, an opiate to the people, and makes us soft.

We can interpret the personality of Jesus until only his
sweetness and gentleness fill up the picture. Recall Renan's
idea of Jesus. "Tenderness of heart," he wrote, "was in him
transformed into infinite sweetness, vague poetry, universal
charm." In that soft portraiture where do we find the linea-
ments of him who endured his cross on Calvary?

We can interpret prayer so that that deep resource, from
which men like Paul drew their courage to face the wrath
of devils and the scorn of men, becomes merely a spiritual
lotus land, a place of soft, esthetic retreat.

We can even interpret forgiveness of sin so that in the
end it makes God seem merely merciful, pardon very easy,
punishment quite unreal, the law-abiding nature of the moral
world exceedingly vague, and the whole, deep difference
between right and wrong as soft as mush.

Christianity thus can be set forth so that it appeals to
and brings out our softness. There are doubtless members
of this congregation who wish that I would preach more
consoling and comfortable sermons. Well, years ago I did
preach a sweet, consoling sermon. The text was "Lord, thou
hast been our dwelling-place in all generations." The sermon
was about God's being our home and about the lovely and
comfortable ministries characteristic of a home that spiritually come to us from God, until we all go back to him as our
eternal home. It was a sweet sermon. I remember one man
who specially liked it. He liked it so much that he had to

[88]

have a copy of it so that he might read it over and over again. Yet inside a year it was discovered that all the time he had been gambling in speculative stocks, stealing his business firm's money to make up the losses, and falsifying his accounts. Since then I have been afraid of sermons which are too sweet and of people who like sweet sermons too much. Indeed, after many years in the Christian ministry, I offer this generalization: whenever you find anybody clamoring for a type of Christianity which is merely sweet and consoling, you are dealing with somebody in process of moral deterioration.

Certainly, when we stop talking about Christianity in the abstract and begin thinking about the historic Jesus, there is no question—is there?—about the qualities in us to which he would appeal. On what powers in those first disciples did he get his fingers that they so went out to turn the world upside down, though like Peter they were crucified head downward or like Paul decapitated on the Ostian Way? He did not bring out men's softness, only their strength.

If, now, some one says, He did comfort people too, I answer, Indeed he did. He poured out friendliness without stint. He could be as tender as a mother. He could say, "Come unto me, all ye that labor and are heavy laden, and I will give you rest"; in Tennyson's fine phrase, he had

. . . that gentleness
Which, when it weds with manhood, makes a man.

But, when you consider the nature of the comfort which he gave to those first disciples, there is no mistaking its quality. "The rain descended, and the floods came, and the winds blew, and beat upon that house; and it fell not: for it was founded upon the rock"—that is comfort. Security, peace, stability, adequacy for life,—that is great comfort,—"How firm a foundation, ye saints of the Lord!" But it is not soft.

To what qualities of strength in us, then, let us ask ourselves, would Jesus appeal, if he had a chance?

For one thing, he would appeal to an unconsenting conscience. He had it himself and he brought it out in anybody he seriously influenced. Why did he preach that first sermon in Nazareth against racial prejudice until the synagogue's service broke up in turmoil and they tried to kill him? He had an unconsenting conscience. Why did he run into such headlong collision with the popular religion of his day or try single-handed to cleanse the temple of its commercialism? He had an unconsenting conscience. Why the cross? Oh, my soul! his unconsenting conscience. He had it himself, he always challenged it in other people, and, when one sees it anywhere, it reminds one of Christ.

I am thinking this morning about my friend Yukio Ozaki, seventy-three-year-old liberal Japanese statesman. He is on a ship now going back to Tokyo, expecting to be assassinated. He does not call himself a Christian but one of the most interesting evenings I remember was spent in his home in Japan discussing what attitude Christ would take toward war. Since 1890 he has been a member of the Japanese Diet, a fearless, anti-militaristic liberal. Three times already assassins have tried to kill him but he never has modified his courageous testimony against the militaristic policies of his own people. The Japanese cherry trees that bloom along Potomac Driveway in Washington were his gift to this nation. The last time I saw him he came to see this church and left his benediction upon its liberal attitude. I had a note from him this last week. He has just buried his wife in England and now is going back home again, where fanatical militarists have taken their solemn vow that this time he shall surely die. He is expecting death. "Any one," he has written, "who claims to be a first-class public man must be prepared to meet a tragic death." He does not call himself a Christian but when I think of the multitudes of us soft Christians who years ago forgot that there was any such thing in Christianity as a real cross, I know where the Master sees his likeness.

Despite the fact that loyalty on our part to the real Christ would cost us infinitely less than a tragic death, we can answer Christ's appeal for an unconsenting conscience. We had better answer it. Against the militarism of our Western

world, where war costs mount to dizzy heights, we need an
unconsenting conscience. Against the debasing of our government and the inhumanity of an economic order that,
breaking down the security of millions of American families, shakes the foundations of the nation, we need an unconsenting conscience. Yes, against this loose, prevalent idea
that just because prohibition now has gone to pieces our
problem is solved, the whole nation is going to enjoy its
liquor and make as much money in taxes as can be made by
selling as much liquor to the people to drink as possible, so
that every time we turn on the radio some one will be as-
suring our sons that the more beer they absorb the better
men they will be and every time we open our magazines we
shall see advertisements advising our daughters to keep
kissable by drinking somebody's gin,—this insane idea that,
just because prohibition has broken down, our troubles are
over and we have escaped the age-long horror of the liquor
traffic,—we need an unconsenting conscience. And how some
of us need it in private character only God and our own
souls know.

You see what we are trying to say. Christianity can be
interpreted so as to call out softness, but Christ never did
that. Far back in the life of every one of us there are, as
Dr. Jacks has said, a hero and a coward. When we are tired,
timid, and afraid, how we like to have that coward sympa-
thized with and coddled! Yet how much more stimulating it
is when something or somebody reaches farther back and
wakes the hero in us so that with his strength released we
go out to face our duties and our difficulties! That is comfort. That is real comfort. Christ did that for every man
he ever seriously touched.

Again, Christ would surely try to lay his hand upon another element of strength in us. I mean the capacity to be
possessed by something worth serving. Bishop Brent of the
Episcopal Church, whom many of us knew and loved, said
once of the cause of Christian unity, which absorbed him,
"It is not so much that I possess it as that it possesses me."
This quality, which had been so brought into play that the

good bishop found himself laid hold on by something which used his personality as its vehicle, is one of the most powerful elements in human character.

Indeed, in every realm greatness involves that. All great souls have been great because they were laid hold on by something worth being mastered by. Michelangelo as a little boy was possessed by the love of painting. His father was enraged; he was willing that peasants should be artists, but not the sons of his house. When he was a small lad his father and uncles used to take turns beating him to make him give up his desire to be an artist, but Michelangelo was possessed so that, as a boy of thirteen, despite the opposition, he stepped out into the studio of Ghirlandaio.

To be sure, I understand what some of you are saying. That lets me out, you think; I am no Michelangelo or Paul; I am a plain man in the common ways of life. Yes, my friend, but plain people in plain ways also have this strong capacity in them. This last week I saw it exhibited within the borders of this congregation until my soul bowed humbly down before it.

A few years ago off the coast of New England a liner was wrecked on a reef. The Coast Guard went to the rescue under the captaincy of an old seaman but with some young men on the crew. One of the young men, seeing the situation presented to them, turned a white face to the captain. "Sir," he said, "the wind is offshore and the tide is running out. Of course we can go out, but what good will it do? Against the wind and the tide we cannot come back." And all the captain said was, "Launch the boat. We have to go out. We don't have to come back." That seaman, possessed by his duty, was a plain man.

We do not suppose—do we?—that we can get through life without being possessed by something. It is psychologically impossible. One man is driven by sensuality, ridden like a jaded horse flogged by a brutal rider. Another is possessed by the love of money so that no member of a chain gang is a more helpless prisoner. Another is possessed by love of ease, until softness rots his very soul away. And another is possessed by high aims, great faiths, serviceable causes, becoming their disciplined and able servant.

We are certain to be taken hold of by something or other before we are through with life. Be sure of that. The question is, Have we let Christianity take hold on this capacity in us? When I honestly face my own life, I am not very much afraid of what is ordinarily called sin. The probabilities are that at this late date I shall not go all to pieces in sin. But softness? To live in a generation like this that calls for strength, for courage to see straight and then to speak and act straight, to be a Christian minister, preaching amid all this loveliness, and growing soft—that might happen. O Christ of God, say it all over again so that we will know Thou dost mean us: "If any man would come after me, let him deny himself, and take up his cross, and follow me."

If he did say that, I am sure he would be trying to lay his hand upon another element of strength in us, the love of adventure. He had it himself. He aroused it in others. He sent those first disciples to turn the world upside down with it.

Indeed, while as a Christian minister I feel free to criticize Christianity because it often is interpreted so that it brings out softness, there are times when, hearing that criticism from another source, it awakens my ire. Here is a youth with a sweet face and a fair cheek, upon whose innocent chin the dew of his first beard is not yet evident and who has probably never done anything much more daring than play tennis, who says, Christianity appeals to softness; the weak need it; strong men do not. To which I answer, Since when has Christianity appealed to softness? Was Paul soft? Were Augustine and Martin Luther and Hugh Latimer soft? Were the great pioneers and missionaries of the faith, from David Livingstone to Wilfred Grenfell, or social reformers like Shaftesbury, soft? Say what else you will about Christianity, yet when you know its history, the sacrifices that it has inspired, the far-flung battle line it holds today across the world, the men whom Christ has really mastered and made his martyrs and pioneers, the thing you cannot say is that it

[93]

appeals to softness. At its best it has appealed, as it did at first, to the spirit of adventure.

That is true, but the question is, Is it doing that in us? You see, in any highly developed religion there always are two tendencies in conflict, the spirit of conservatism and the spirit of adventure. On the one side, Christianity, making sacred to its followers the personal habits and social customs around which it has been entwined, tends to encourage conservatism toward the status quo; on the other side, Christianity, presenting the ideal of a new social order where God's will shall be done on earth, where personality shall not be trampled as it is around us now, where fraternity shall make beautiful the relationships of men and nations, also presents a standard of revolt against the status quo and calls for social adventure. The spirit of conservatism and the spirit of adventure always are present in a highly developed religion, and what I fear most in modern Christianity is that there should be too much of the first and not enough of the second.

We hear continually that there is a conflict between science and religion, and it is almost always stated in intellectual terms. But is it not more true to say that the real conflict between science and religion is in another realm altogether? Science appeals to the adventurous spirit in youth. New things to be learned, new achievements to be wrought out, a new kind of world to be built—so youth hears science speaking. But religion often sounds to youth as if it were singing a soothing lullaby. Yet there never was more need of a Christianity on fire with the passion of that first church for a better world.

I am troubled by the way some people are contented to talk about communism. Of course, I could not endure communism, and as for trying it in the United States, I think it would be utterly ruinous. Nevertheless, this other thing is true: those Russian communists are on fire with a sacrificial and determined zeal at all costs, even at the cost of ruthless persecution, to build what seems to them a just society, and the only way in which we ultimately can compete with them is to care, at least as much as they do, about social justice. What if in the end it should turn out that those atheists in Russia really care more about social justice than we Christians in America? This is the moral crux of our competition with them. How much is there left among our churches of that old spirit of adventure to which Christ long ago appealed?

Doubtless, in spite of oneself, a sermon like this sounds dour and demanding, and yet, while we have been talking against softness and have been trying to reconstruct in our imagination the splendor of that early church enduring hardness as good soldiers of Christ, we really have been appealing for our own happiness. The courage of an unconsenting conscience, the glory of a life possessed by things worth serving, the spirit of adventure for a better day— that is the highroad to the most durable satisfactions in human life. God speed us on it! God bring us to the end of it with joy, saying, "I have fought the good fight, I have finished the course, I have kept the faith."

The Peril of Worshiping
Jesus

THE world has tried in two ways to get rid of Jesus: first, by crucifying him, and second, by worshiping him. The first did not succeed. It required more than a cross to stop the influence of that transcendent character. Like an airman taking off against the wind and using the very force of the opposing air to rise by, so Jesus took off on his amazing flight. The cross did not crush—it lifted him.

The world, therefore, foiled in its first attempt to be rid of Jesus by crucifying him, turned to the second, far more subtle and fatal way of disposing of great spiritual leadership—it worshiped him. Throughout history it has been true that when a spiritual leader has been too powerful to be crushed by opposition there has been still another way to escape his moral insights and his ethical demands, and that is to worship him. To dress him up in elaborate, metaphysical creeds, hide his too-piercing eyes in the smoke of sacramental adoration, build beautiful sanctuaries where his challenging social ideals may fade out in vague mysticism, get him off somewhere on a high altar, pray to him, sing to him, do anything for him rather than let him get back again where he started, walking the common ways of men and talking about how to live—that always has been the most successful way of getting rid of Jesus.

If at first this seems a dangerous thing to say, remember that Jesus himself said it. He did not fear being opposed. He knew that the blood of the martyrs is the seed of the church, and concerning his own cross John reports his saying: "I, if I be lifted up from the earth, will draw all men unto myself." He did not fear being opposed; he feared being worshiped.

For one thing, he saw his own contemporaries by this method getting rid of their prophets. First, their fathers had hated the prophets, opposed them, stoned them, sawn them asunder. Then, when the prophets proved too powerful in personality and influential in message to be disposed of in that way, the ever-available, second method had been tried. Listen to Jesus, himself, as he describes it—"Woe unto you, scribes and Pharisees, hypocrites! for ye build the sepulchres of the prophets, and garnish the tombs of the righteous, and say, If we had been in the days of our fathers, we should not have been partakers with them in the blood of the prophets. Wherefore ye witness to yourselves, that ye are sons of them that slew the prophets."

Jesus saw that stoning the prophets on one side and garnishing their sepulchers on the other, different as the two things appear, come practically to the same end: they are two ways of getting rid of the prophets, escaping what the prophets really stood for, dodging their moral message. The fathers who killed the prophets and the children who garnish their sepulchers belong to the same race, says Jesus, and are up to the same thing—they are evading the spirit of the prophets.

Even in his lifetime, Jesus feared this way of being evaded. How else will you explain his stern rebuke to the sentimental woman who cried, "Blessed is the womb that bare thee, and the breasts which thou didst suck"? Jesus came back at her like thunder, saying, "Yea rather, blessed are they that hear the word of God, and keep it." It is as though you could hear him saying to himself, See, they are beginning to worship me; they are evading what I am driving at by adoring emotions about me; they will get rid of me yet, as they have gotten rid of the prophets, by idolizing me. Or how else will you explain his swift retort to the man who came bowing to him, saying, "Good Teacher"? Said Jesus, "Why callest thou me good? none is good save one, even God." One can fairly read his thoughts as though he said to the man, Beware of worshipful deference to me—I fear it; come, stop this bowing and this "Good Master"; what about your attitude to the kind of living I am standing for, whose springs are in God? And once, as though to leave no doubt that this fear of being worshiped was ever before him, he cried, "Not every one that saith unto me, Lord, Lord, shall enter into the kingdom of heaven; but he that doeth the will of my Father who is in heaven." O, wise Master, with what prophetic eye you saw the way men would successfully evade you! For all these centuries since, cherishing evils that your spirit would have spurned, all Christendom has been saying from countless temples, "Lord, Lord!"

It is an amazing thing that the historic church has so unanimously worshiped Jesus and has so seldom stopped to ask what Jesus himself would think of it. Is it not true that most Christians have taken it for granted that Jesus would enjoy it—enjoy being prayed to, sung to, talked about in exalted, theological terms, and enshrined on the high altars of the church? Do not many Christians still suspect that he would feel grieved, hurt, rejected, and jealous if he were not thus adored? All this, however, obviously is the reflection of our own littleness. Little people like extravagant praise, adoration, flattery. Little people push their egos to the front, claiming attention and wanting to be idolized; but great personalities are never like that. When a capacious soul comes, standing for something that he cares so much about he will die for it on Calvary, you cannot flatter him. He has identified himself with something greater than himself, of which he regards himself as the incarnation and instrument. He thinks of himself as the vehicle and agent of an eternal matter. He does not want his ego idolized; he wants his cause supported.

Take the truth into a realm quite different from religion and consider Abraham Lincoln, who, if you use the word "worship" as we are using it this morning, in its general and human sense, comes as near being worshiped as any American. That began when he died. While he lived men tried to crush him by opposition, but he was too strong to be overcome. When he died, however, they began using the other method to dispose of him. They adored him. They garnished his sepulcher. Nothing too marvelous could be said of him. But in the ten years after he died Congress put into effect a policy towards the South that denied everything Lincoln had stood for and wanted. They praised his name and they scuttled his policies. They flattered his memory and denied his magnanimity. They alike adored Lincoln and refused to follow him, so that they made the reconstruction era in the South one of the horrors of our history.

What would Lincoln have said? We know. Stop this evading of my spirit by praising me! What do I care about the idolizing of my ego? I want my cause supported. Of course Lincoln would have said that because he was a large soul, not a little one.

Can one doubt, then, what Jesus' attitude would be? We all sing, for example, that great hymn,

> In the cross of Christ I glory,
> Towering o'er the wrecks of time.

Who wrote that? Sir John Bowring. Who was he? He was the British Governor at Hong Kong at a time when the British Empire was forcing the opium traffic on China, and he was the agent of the imperial policies. Everybody acknowledges, our British brethren first of all, that the forcing of opium on China was one of the most outrageous things in Western history. Well, the man who was Governor of Hong Kong while that policy was in force had written, years before, "In the cross of Christ I glory."

You will recall the man who said that he could take care of his enemies himself, but prayed to be delivered from his friends. Jesus Christ might have said that. The most disastrous events in the history of his movement have not come from his opposers, but from his worshipers who said, "Lord, Lord!"

When today I plead against the peril of worshiping Jesus, you see it is not because I, myself, do not exalt him. You know I do exalt him. He is supremely great. That constitutes the seriousness of the situation. He is really great—not to be flattered, not to be pleased by creedal praise or sacramental worship, wanting just one thing so much that he died for it—the Divine Will done in personal lives and social relationships. And the tragedy is that it has proved too deceptively easy to join in forcing opium on China while at the same time singing "In the cross of Christ I glory." I am not specially blaming Sir John Bowring; we cannot do that. He was like the rest of us. He was not consciously hypocritical, but a sincere, honest, and in many ways eminently admirable man. He simply fell victim, as many of us have fallen, to this most popular of all ways of getting rid of Christ. We would not crucify him, not one of us, but, alas, we worship him—we dispose of him that way. We say, "Lord, Lord!"

Consider, for one thing, how easy it is to get rid of Christ by worshiping him, because thereby we can substitute emotions for morals. There are two sets of faculties in us, the esthetic and the ethical—the sense of beauty and the sense of duty—and Christ appeals to both. Especially as the tradition of history has woven its alluring spell about him, setting him in stories that begin with singing angels over Bethlehem and end with worshiping women in a garden, he is beautiful. He has been set to music, glorified in poetry, enshrined in architecture, until the approach to Christ is clothed in beauty. But when we approach Christ esthetically, through beauty, it may end in emotional adoration only, saying, "Lord, Lord!"

So you, a youth here in New York City, may adore your mother. How do you adore her, emotionally or morally? That is, do you simply love her with tender sentiment, or are you living the kind of life which does honor to her and developing the sort of character which, if she knew about it, would make her glad? The difference is deep. Mothers at their finest are beautiful and most men adore them; but it is one thing to have the emotional sentiments of the heart go out to a mother and it is another thing to be morally true to her. It would be strange, indeed, if some youth here did not at this moment acutely feel the difference. Well, Christ must acutely feel the difference in his disciples. Indeed, he never said, "Worship me!" He said, "Follow me!"

To put the matter in a figure that combines both beauty

and morals, Christ played his life like music meant to be played over again. When Beethoven wrote a symphony, he did not write it merely to be admired but to be reproduced. When once a Beethoven has created harmony, one does not have to be a Beethoven to reproduce it. It can be played again and again. So Christ, in his unselfishness, his faith in God, his reverence for personality, his practice of brotherhood, his devotion to a nobler social order, was not creating a piece of music for the world to stand before and cry, "How lovely!" He wanted it reproduced—played again and again by boys and girls, men and women, on all the human instruments that God had given them, until the whole earth should be full of his music.

He wanted that, but he has not seen that—only here and there has that come to pass. What he has seen is something different—countless millions of people worshiping him emotionally but not morally. Emperors like Constantine, drenched in blood, who murdered his own wife, his son, and other more remote and less significant relatives, worshiped Christ. Ecclesiastics who sold their influence for private gain and stained the garments of the church with fornication and simony have worshiped Christ. Men who believed that little babies were damned to eternal hell have worshiped Christ. Men who persecuted their fellows for conscience' sake and made the torture chambers of Christendom the horror of the world have worshiped Christ. Churches that have shut off their fellow Christians from the kingdom of God because of diversities in theology that Jesus never heard of and would have scorned as mint, anise, and cummin, have worshiped Christ.

John Newton ran a slave-ship between Africa and the slave-markets of his time in the days when the horrors between decks were enough to make even the reading of them turn one white. He wrote in his diary that he had never known sweeter or more frequent hours of divine communion than on some of his slave journeys, and every Sunday he read the church liturgy twice with his crew. How incredible, in retrospect, such a combination of worshiping

Christ with ruthless inhumanity appears! Yet how many have been and are guilty of it and how few, like John Newton, see new light, repent of their blindness, and change, as he did, both opinion and life!

You see what we have done with Christ—we have kept his name on the label, but we have changed the contents of the bottle. That is a summary of much of Christendom's history—the name kept on the label, "Christ," but the contents not of his moral quality.

We cannot suppose—can we?—that that suddenly has stopped in our time. Upon the contrary, the churches of this country are full of people who worship Christ, who have no more idea what Christ means about war, race relationships, the color line, about the money standards of the day, the profit motive in industry, than Constantine had about Christ's attitude toward his bloody imperialism, or the Duke of Alva about Christ's care for the victims of his persecution. This seems to me the very nub of the Christian problem today. The crucial matter is not theological controversy. Real problems are involved there, but they are not the crux. The crux is moral. A Christianity that worships Christ emotionally but does not follow him morally is a conventional sham, and too much of our ecclesiastical Christianity today is precisely that. Let us say it to ourselves in our beautiful churches, amid the loveliness of our architecture, lest we should ever be tempted to substitute esthetics for ethics or formal worship for downright righteousness. Jesus would care more about our attitude towards the color line or war than he would care about all our processionals, however stately, and all our architecture, however fine. For obviously, Jesus, above all else, intended to be taken in earnest morally.

We cannot, then, leave our text in history. It comes down the centuries, accumulating significance with every year, and walks up to our own doors and knocks. "Not every one that saith unto me, Lord, Lord."

Consider how easy it is to dispose of Christ by worshiping him, because we can thereby substitute theological opinion for spiritual experience. In this regard much of Christianity has gotten rid of Christ just as Buddhism has gotten rid of Buddha. Think what you will about the basic presuppositions of Buddha's philosophy—and I heartily disagree with them—he, nevertheless, was a tremendous character, and his noble eightfold path of moral living *is* noble. At first men fought against him, but that did not succeed; he was too great to be overthrown by opposition. Now, however, conventional Buddhism has gotten rid of him by worshiping him. It is one of the strangest ironies in the history of religion. For Buddha himself did not believe in a personal God at all, and now Buddhism has made a personal God out of him. That disposes of him! Now they can build up rituals, construct theologies, worship him in sacramental regularities, and his noble eightfold path of moral living can be obscured in the smoke of incense. The Christians, however, are no better than the Buddhists in that regard. That is what we have done with Jesus.

I can imagine some one saying, But, then, do you not believe in the divinity of Jesus? To which I answer that I believe in the divinity of Jesus with all my faculties if we can come to an understanding about what we mean by *divinity*. Are you willing to start with John's idea of *divinity* in the New Testament: "God is love"? That is divinity—love. Divinity is not something supernatural that ever and again invades the natural order in a crashing miracle. Divinity is not in some remote heaven, seated on a throne. Divinity is love. Here and now it shines through the highest spiritual experiences we know. Wherever goodness, beauty, truth, love are—there is the Divine. And the divinity of Jesus is the divinity of his spiritual life.

If some one says, Well, we all have some of that divine spark in us; we all have some goodness, truth, love, and therefore on that basis the divinity of Jesus differs from ours in degree, indeed, but not in kind, I answer, Are you afraid of that conclusion? Of course the divinity of Jesus differs from ours in degree but not in kind. You cannot imagine there being one God and two kinds of godlikeness. Paul prayed that his disciples might be filled unto all the fulness of God. John said, "He that abideth in love abideth in God, and God abideth in him." Was the God that Paul and John prayed might be in them a different kind of God than was in Jesus? To be sure not. There is only one God. To say therefore that God was in Christ seems to me no theological puzzle at all. I think God was in my mother, the source of the loveliness that blessed us there! And I rise up from that with a profound sense of the reality of what I am doing when I profess my faith that God was in Christ.

If, now, some one says, Very well, but that reduces Jesus to our level, I answer, How do you make that out? I feel in relationship to Christ like a land-locked pool beside the sea. The water in the land-locked pool is the same kind of water that is in the sea. You cannot have one sea and two kinds of sea-water. But look at the land-locked pool, little, imprisoned, soiled it may be in quality, and then look at the sea, with deeps and distances and tides and relationships with the world's life the pool can never know. So is my life beside his. So is my soul beside his soul. The same God, to be sure, but what a contrast the difference in capacity can make!

If, then, we mean by Jesus' divinity the quality of his spiritual life, of course I believe in it and glory in it. But the historic church too often has meant something else, has pushed him far off to a supra-mundane world, throned him in a distant heaven, garbed him beyond all recognition in heavily brocaded garments of theology, until the real Jesus has been gotten rid of altogether. Listen to this about Jesus of Nazareth: "The second person in the Trinity, being very and eternal God, of one substance, and equal with the Father, did . . . take upon him man's nature," so that "two whole, perfect, and distinct natures, the Godhead and the manhood, were inseparably joined together in one person, without conversion, composition, or confusion." They have done that to the divine teacher of Galilee, and they have gloried in it when all the time they were getting rid of him,—at last successfully crucifying him,—laying him in a theological tomb and rolling a great stone before the door.

I read recently a passage from a sermon that seemed to me to cry out for an answer—the preacher was glorying in the fact that Jesus had conquered Europe. Very conceivable, said the preacher, that Jesus might appeal to Asia, but what a marvel that he should appeal to Europe, to hard-headed, practical, militant Europe! How glorious a thing that Jesus should conquer Europe! What does the preacher mean—Jesus conquering Europe? What Jesus conquered Europe? A conventionalized Jesus as unlike the real one as the floral patterns on wall paper are unlike the flowers of the field. A Jesus who was called by the most resplendent, metaphysical titles in history, but who supported bloody imperialism, blessed bloody persecutions, gave his benediction to economic exploitation, put his cross on the banners of the most sanguinary crusades in history, insisted on the damnation of infants to hell, and said that slavery was ordained of God. That caricature of Jesus has, as a matter of plain history, too largely conquered the Western world. But the Jesus of the Good Samaritan, the Prodigal Son, the Beatitudes, the Jesus who used a little child as his symbol of the kingdom's spirit, the Jesus who said, "Ye cannot serve God and mammon," and "A man's life consisteth not in the abundance of the things which he possesseth," the Jesus who reverenced every human personality and died that there might come a kingdom of God and human brotherhood on earth—that Jesus has not yet conquered either Europe or America.

To be sure, I know that this is not all there is to religion. Christianity is more than ethical effort. If you take the word "worship" in its original meaning, "worthship"—the recognition of worth—then there are few things more important that we ever do. And especially we moderns need ever to grow quiet, like pools at evening, in the presence of the highest that we know in Christ, that his beauty may be reflected in us. If that is what one means by "worship" then we should worship him with all our hearts. We need, however, to imagine what would happen if somehow he could be released from all the brocaded velvets and golden crowns of our too-conventional and formal adoration and could speak to us in his own voice. How little he would care for anything that did not involve personal character and social righteousness! How little he would care whether a man idolized his ego, if only he possessed his spirit! What a company he would claim as his own—men and women of all races, colors, creeds, religions, some who had worshiped him and some who had not, in whom he found his spirit! For he supremely would care that what he stood for should permeate the world. Not every one, not *any one*, who merely says, "Lord, Lord!" but he that doeth the Father's will!

Facing the Challenge
of Change

WE OFTEN sing,

> The changes that are sure to come
> I do not fear to see.

That, I suspect, is one of the falsehoods in which hymn singing commonly involves us, for what most of us fear more than anything else in the world is precisely the changes that are sure to come. Somehow or other we must deal with change. It is inevitable. The mere process of growing up through childhood, adolescence, youth, early married life, mature married life, old age, with their constant demand for practical and emotional readjustment, makes plain the fact that we need some philosophy and technique with which to handle change. As for the external world, evolutionary and full of vicissitude, where the one thing certain is that tomorrow will be different from today, that not only faces us with change but plunges us into it and often whirls us along with it.

The importance of this matter is clear when one considers what this changefulness does to people. Many souls go to pieces before life's continual demand for readjustment. They are upset emotionally, suffering from a kind of spiritual vertigo. They are upset morally in a world so kaleidoscopic that there seems nothing steady to be loyal to. They are upset philosophically, seeing on every side process but nowhere purpose, until at last they surrender to bewilderment and cry, "Whirl is king." This familiar experience makes it evident that unless we manage well in handling change, change will manage ill in handling us.

Nevertheless, we would not live in a changeless world. Suppose ourselves now possessed with power to freeze our life into static immobility, or in some much fairer state of human society to create unalterable changelessness; we would not dare to use the power. Change is our dear enemy. It often bewilders us. Sometimes like an earthquake it fairly ruins us. It commonly destroys our peace of mind. But we would not and we could not live without it.

While there are modern factors in this experience of change, it always has been a problem for mankind to face, so that this morning our thought turns naturally back twenty-five centuries to a classic word of wisdom concerning it from Jeremiah. He faced change. Those of you who have followed his career, from that day beside the almond tree in Anathoth when he was called to prophethood, through reform and counter-reform, battle, siege and two captures of Jerusalem, until at last by frightened fugitives he was dragged off to die in Egypt, understand he did not need any modern to explain to him "Change and decay in all around I see." Yet while doubtless he often was confused, as we are, at the changefulness of his life, he did have a philosophy about it. There across Jordan, thirty miles away, was Moab, lying outside the track of world empires. It was static, undisturbed, stagnant. Yet, between changeless Moab on the one side, and on the other confused Judah, forced by shifting circumstance to rethink its positions and readjust its life, the hope of the world lay not with Moab but with Judah. "Moab," cried Jeremiah, "hath been at ease from his youth, and he hath settled on his lees, and hath not been emptied from vessel to vessel." Well, not to be poured from vessel to vessel is about the most hopeless situation possible for any personal or social life. Disturbing as change may be, it is an invaluable discipline of life, if we have faith, character, philosophy, and technique with which to handle it.

How, then, can a man live in a changeable world like this, making change his friend and not his enemy?

In the first place, of course, change wakes us up, discourages sluggishness and stagnation, encourages alertness and vigilance. That is precisely what many of us do not want, so that the constant demand for it seems to some people one of the cruelest aspects of life. We want to settle down, get into a situation we can count upon, rest back on security. We are tired. We have readjusted ourselves to life so often that it seems cruel to have to begin again. When life begins to pour us once more from vessel to vessel, we cry out in vexation of soul: Leave us alone; is that too much to ask, the simple peace of being left alone? But the alarm bells of change ring without mercy. They wake us up. We are tumbled out of bed.

What happens to us as individuals happens to us as societies. We move from one social order to another, not because we want to but because change forces readjustment. We start, for example, with a laissez-faire, individualistic, industrial order not badly fitted to the days of hand labor, and with a theory to match it, as in Adam Smith's *Wealth of Nations*. We are thus comfortably well off with a theory and practice which are harmonious and seem secure. Then the machine comes, grows mighty, cries "Change!" and upsets the world. Processes transferred from hand labor to machine labor become ruinous. Adam Smith's ideas become ridiculous. We do not want to change but we must. We have been tumbled out of bed. In consequence, alert and vigilant minds are trying today to think their way through into the new, planned economy which must come.

In the religious realm the same effect of enforced change appears. No one wants, for example, to begin rethinking missions. Rethinking anything is painful. But the alarm bells of change ring out. I do not see how any one can go to the Far East without hearing them. The old theologies will not work in the awakening East. The old attitudes toward other religions are not based on fact and are destructive of the finest missionary endeavor. The spread of educational and medical work into governmental control faces the missions with new aims and new techniques. And as for the personnel, a Japanese Christian in Tokyo said to me, "Take back ten of your $1,000 missionaries and send us one $10,000 missionary." I believe in the missionary enterprise and I plead for its support with all my heart, but its theories and its methods need rethinking. Yet look on many of our churches and you will find human nature running true to form; they do not want to rethink. They resent being poured from vessel to vessel.

This reluctance to come to terms with inevitable change is one of the most ruinous factors in human life. This is a pity because, when one does face change with intelligence and courage, it presents one of the finest opportunities that mankind has. Jeremiah was right about the Jews. One of the deepest secrets of the strength of that amazing people is their capacity to make opportunity out of change. They have been poured from vessel to vessel—poured from the desert into Egypt and back again, poured from the wilderness into Palestine, emptied from Palestine to Babylonia and back again, and through centuries of such vicissitude as no other race has ever faced they have enlarged their influence beyond the wildest dream of any ancient prophet. From Jeremiah to Spinoza and Einstein, the great Jews have faced change, risen above it, grappled with it, and gone on everlastingly rethinking.

Some one here may be saying, Yes, but change is dangerous. Of course it is. Change is one of the most perilous things in the world. There is only one thing I can think of more dangerous—not to change: to go out into a new era of international relationships and still cling to old nationalistic ideas, to go out into a new industrial order implemented with machinery and still cling to the laissez-faire individualism of the eighteenth century. One of the deadliest delusions of the human mind is the idea that to stay still is to be safe. But to stay still is to be safe only when the world is staying still and to stay still when the world is moving is ruinous. That fact is behind the tragedy of the Great War. That fact is behind the tragedy of this depression. We tried too long to stay still in an individualistic, militaristic, nationalistic system when the circumstances of the world were moving.

My friends, whether we like it or not, the Eternal has put us in a world where stagnation is a deadly sin. To be sure, I know the people who change superficially with shallow readiness, the weather vanes that swing with every breeze, the cheap souls who call themselves modern because they know the latest wisecracks, can enjoy jazz and the blues, and, having forsaken the ancient sanctities of moral life, plunge into the still more ancient license of promiscuous sensuality. How contemptible they are, not only in character but in intellect, when they call themselves modern! There is a burlesque for everything but what I am pleading for this morning is genuine and deep. It is seen in a man—how we do admire him when we meet him!—who, facing the changes of the passing years and the growing world, hears ever the call for thinking more deeply and living more effectively. Such a man never grows old. Such a man never surrenders to sluggishness or stagnation. He does not stop rethinking. Each new era brings out in him new ideas, wider outlooks, deeper character, stronger faith. Poured from vessel to vessel, he makes change his friend.

In the second place, without some such attitude as this, one cannot be genuinely Christian. This is not simply a matter of being modern, up to date, progressive. This concerns the essential nature of Christianity, if by Christianity we mean sharing the spirit of Jesus.

To be sure, by some people Jesus himself is interpreted in terms of restfulness and peace. Living tired, stagnant lives, some please themselves by saying that the Master so has spoken peace to their souls. Now, peace when it is genuine is a profound matter and Jesus did say, "Peace I leave with you; my peace I give unto you." But we surely shall misunderstand that unless we understand the situation out of which it came—that upper room, with Gethsemane and the cross ahead, toward which his venturesome message was inevitably driving him, and around him those disciples going out to incredible vicissitudes, as the New Testament says, to turn the world upside down. The peace which Jesus promised to his disciples in the upper room was not the restfulness of an unchanging life. It was the spiritual stability that carries a man through change. It was the inner gyroscope that makes steadiness possible in stormy days of change. More than that, it was the firm standing ground from which a man can produce change. Let all Christians be careful, therefore, when they talk about peace. What Jesus said was, "Think not that I came to send peace on the earth: I came not to send peace, but a sword." The context makes plain that he did not mean a literal sword. He was a pacifist. When he talked about literal swords he said, "All they that take the sword shall perish with the sword." But he did mean to say, I came not to send peace upon the earth but division, strife, change; deliberately to plunge man into a contest for a better world.

Professor Seeley Bixler, of Harvard University, has lately made some shrewd comments on our new psychological talk about the well-adjusted life. At its finest, the well-adjusted life is so beautiful an achievement that we might even identify it with salvation itself. But in much of our popular rendition the well-adjusted life settles down into contentment with the status quo, fitting into things as they are, shading life off into the personal and social color scheme of popular custom until we are not disturbed any more. Against that we need to lift up the Christian ideal of the maladjusted life. The sacredest obligation of the Christian is to be maladjusted—to the war system, to the inequities of an acquisitive economic order, to the wrongs of race prejudice, to the vulgarities of popular morals, to the crude sectarianisms of the churches, to the belated ideas there which represent in new forms those very things against which the Master himself fought in the ancient synagogue. The deepest obligation of a Christian, I should suppose, is to be maladjusted to the status quo. Christ in this generation is saying, I came not to send peace, but change.

In view of this what would you say is the commonest sin of Christians? I should say, Respectability. In such a congregation as this, your ministers, sometimes in you and sometimes in themselves, discover nearly all the kinds of sin there are, but if you should ask me what the commonest sin is, I should say, Respectability.

Christians never were meant to be respectable. The Master

was not. They crucified him between thieves. He was mal-adjusted to the status quo. But we who bear his name are so unlike him that we do not remind anybody of him, and at no point is the dissimilarity more marked than in our conventional, easy-going respectability. One thinks at times that we get that way in part because we substitute one word for another. We talk about saving the world. That is not disturbing. That even sounds beautiful. We can put that into poetry and sing it. I can preach about it so that you will go out to say, How pleasing it is to think about the world's being saved! My friends, alter the phrase. We cannot save this world without changing it. That has another sound. We cannot save our banking system without changing it. We cannot save our international relationships without changing them. We cannot save our economic system without changing it. We cannot save ourselves without being changed, radically changed, transformed by the renewing of our minds. Sometimes I think we would do well to declare a moratorium on that word "save." It is too much like its kindred word "safe." In our usage it has grown smooth, easy-going, respectable. But *change* is what the New Testament means by it—changed lives, changed human relationships, a changed society, a changed world.

We Christians are supposed not simply to endure change, not simply to profit by it; we are supposed to produce it. The deadliest enemy of Christianity today is not theoretical atheism; it is the stealing of the churches' thunder by non-Christians so that some of the most devoted and sacrificial efforts now afoot on earth to change the world toward humaneness and brotherhood are going on outside the church, while within the church too many Christians settle down into well-adjusted conformity. The deadliest thing that ever can happen to Christianity is that non-Christians should beat Christians at what the Master intended to be their own game, pouring mankind from vessel to vessel.

In the third place, all this would be incomplete if we did not add another and, at first sight, strange matter, that no

[113]

one can adequately deal with change until he gets his eye on the unchanging. There is deep insight in that swift shift of the familiar hymn:

> Change and decay in all around I see;
> O thou who changest not, abide with me!

Hardly a realm exists, for example, where change has taken place more revolutionary than in man's interpretation of the planets and the stars. To the primitive eye they were like a swarm of flies, without sequence or law. Then to the Chaldeans they were like an army maneuvering with mysterious strategy. So astrology arose and out of it astronomy. From one astronomical theory to another, our minds have been poured from vessel to vessel, until with our new telescopes we are expectantly looking forward to new data and new theories. Yet when one inquires what has given meaning to all this change, the answer is clear: *the steady stars themselves*. You recall Walt Whitman's listening to an astronomer lecture and writing about it afterward:

> . . . I became tired and sick,
> Till rising and gliding out I wander'd off by myself,
> In the mystical moist night-air, and from time to time,
> Look'd up in perfect silence at the stars.

Unless one can have some such perception of the unchanging amid the changing, I do not see how he adequately can handle change.

Look about you and see. You must know souls who are so obsessed by change that it is all the universe to them—not only is life entirely vicissitude but the cosmos itself is merely flux. They see on every side constant process but nowhere integrating purpose. They have lost out of their world-view unity, continuity, and meaning—that is, the idea of God, which alone has ever given to the world as a whole unity, continuity, and meaning—so that at last, in this whirlpool of fortuitous electrons, life seems to them, as Shakespeare said, like

. . . a tale
Told by an idiot, full of sound and fury,
Signifying nothing.

So we get our modern cynics and futilitarians, to whom life is only whirl and flux and endless alteration, without sense or significance.

I confess I do not know which I pity the more: the people who will not change—the standpatters, the Moabites, the Beckmessers, the stick-in-the-muds who want a frozen world—or the people who see in all the universe nothing but change, to whom the things that are seen are temporal but to whom the unseen is not eternal.

Whether we are dealing with large matters or small, I suspect that there is no getting wisdom until one's eye rests on the changeless amid change. Consider our American family—that is changing. The modern world is forcing on the American home critical vicissitudes of outward circumstance, inward theory, and personal relationship. Alas for parents who refuse to change! But alas for parents also who are swamped by change, who think the family done for, with nothing solid left to build on, so that in the end in the dictionary "home" will be marked "obsolete." If some of you are thinking that this morning, will you say three words to yourself: Father, Mother, Child? There are permanent elements in those relationships,—are there not?—biologically, psychologically, economically, racially permanent. The creative unit of the race is not the individual, as these new, sexual anarchists are saying to us. The creative unit of the race is a human trinity, father, mother, child. Without that there never would be any individual—no, nor any race. If by "home" you mean father, mother, child, and all the ineffable possibilities in those relationships, that is solid ground. New domestic structures to be raised on it, to be sure, but an abiding basis!

Carry out this attitude, which brings thus the changing and the changeless into one world-view, and see what a deep Christian faith means to some of us. It helps to make us fearless about life. To be sure! This is God's world and, as David Livingstone said, we will "go anywhere—*provided it be* FORWARD." It puts upon us the obligation to produce change. To be sure! "Thy kingdom come. Thy will be done." But it also puts upon our lips this other word: "O thou who changest not." Some of us here this morning crucially need that. This last year has forced on us changes that have shaken us to the depths. Who can tell what changes will face some of us tomorrow? The difference between people does not lie primarily in the fact of change. The difference between people lies in what they have inside themselves to meet it with. Some go out through stormy vicissitudes to end at last, like Paul in prison, still crying, "I have kept the faith"; others go out through stormy days to end in prison like Napoleon on St. Helena, concerning whom one commentator said, "No great principle stood by him." What a way to face a changing world:—no great principle stood by him! Yet for you and me it will be so,—or else, "O thou who changest not"!

Making the Best of a
Bad Mess

LET us get at our subject through a letter which Paul once wrote to a young disciple of his named Titus. I shall take it for granted that Paul wrote this letter, although some scholars think that he did not. Paul, so the record runs, had left Titus upon the great island of Crete in the eastern Mediterranean, and the island of Crete was not at all a desirable place for a Christian to be left. The situation is summarized in one blistering verse of this letter: "One of themselves," says Paul, "a prophet of their own, said, Cretans are always liars, evil beasts, idle gluttons. This testimony is true." Such is Paul's summary of the situation in Crete and of the character of its inhabitants. But listen to him as he writes to Titus: "For this cause left I thee in Crete, that thou shouldest set in order the things that were wanting."

That is a queer reason for leaving a man in Crete, that the Cretans are always liars, evil beasts, and idle gluttons. It sounds like a good reason for getting out of Crete. But Paul was a man of stern fiber. He himself never shrank, and he never wanted his followers to shrink, from the challenge of a difficult situation. He felt the stimulus of a hostile environment. There is something profoundly characteristic of the man himself and of Christianity at its best in that attitude. Crete—a hard place; the Cretans—a bad lot: "For this cause left I thee in Crete."

Put yourself in Titus' place as he received this letter. I surmise that it must have been a letter that Paul wrote to Titus in answer to one which he had received from him, and it ought not to be difficult to reconstruct the spirit in which Titus wrote. "Dear Paul," I suspect he had said, "this is an awful place. The inhabitants are hopeless, and the poor, struggling Christian movement is only rags and tatters. I am remaining here until you say 'Go' but I can't get away fast enough. For pity's sake, don't make me stay here all winter. There isn't a decent chance. Obediently but unhappily yours, Titus." And then he got this letter. "Titus," said Paul in effect, "you are right about the Cretans. They are liars, evil beasts, idle gluttons. There isn't anything too bad that you can say about them. Crete is in deep need. For this cause left I thee in Crete."

Let us put ourselves in Titus' place. It ought not to be difficult. One way or another we are always getting into Crete. There are many differences that separate us here this morning, but any preacher could be sure of one thing which unites us: we all have been in Crete, we are all going to be in Crete, probably most of us are in Crete now. Moreover, we are human and complaining, and we want to get out of Crete. I wonder what Titus said to himself when he faced this ringing message, "For this cause left I thee in Crete."

In the first place, he must have reminded himself of some simple but profound common sense about life which he ought never to have forgotten. I think he said to himself, "Paul is right. After all, happiness is not something that you find. It is something that you create. And if you start with that attitude you might just as well create happiness in Crete as anywhere else."

When a man lands in Crete, you see, as probably Titus did, hoping to find it a pleasant place, he is foredoomed to disappointment. He walks up and down Crete looking for happiness, but it isn't to be found. The Cretans are a bad lot. Then he gets this message that changes his inner attitude. He walks up and down Crete now, not looking for ready-made happiness, but looking for an opportunity. He has been left in Crete to use it as so much raw material out of which to make something. He is saying to himself over and over again, "Life is not something that you find; life is something that you create." And, lo! approached in that way, Crete becomes an El Dorado. That is not poetry; that is history. Crete did turn out to be one of the greatest opportunities that Christianity had in that ancient world. Today in Crete they are excavating the foundations of stately churches from which, in those early days when the gospel went out in the crusade against the paganism of the Roman Empire, came teachers, preachers, and missionaries of the cross. Whose name is on those churches? Titus'! Whose shrines were built there? Titus'! Saint Titus'! Think of it! In the very place from which once he could not soon enough get away! Paul was right. "For this cause left I thee in Crete, that thou shouldest set in order the things that were wanting."

Surely, this principle runs through all of life. Life is not what you find; it is what you create. Many people wander into the world and pick up everything they can get their hands upon looking for life. They never get it. What they get is existence. Existence is what you *find*; life is what you *create*.

Biography is a running commentary on that. Who, for example, is this Scotch boy who landed in Boston a half century and more ago? He came over in the steerage when the steerage was a beastly place. His old Scotch father had told him that his abilities were below the average. He began his life in America as a foundryman and he roomed over a liquor saloon in the north end of Boston. Such was his existence to start with. What he made of it, however, was a great life. For he was George A. Gordon, one of the best scholars Harvard ever graduated, who in Old South Church, Boston, a few years ago celebrated the fortieth anniversary of his pastorate—one of the most notable for intellectual quality and spiritual influence in the annals of American churches—and who now has fallen on sleep, full of years and honor. His existence was what he found; his life was what he created.

One wonders if this ability to tackle life as Titus tackled Crete, without which America would lose nine-tenths of her glory, is going to be distinctive of the new generation. Many of our children are going to schools where, as Dean Hawkes of Columbia says, they are asked in the morning what, if anything, they wish to study that day. We are surrounding them in our families with luxuries that we never knew, that our fathers never dreamed. They are told on every side that personality is a creature of environment and that the great thing is for everybody to be surrounded by commodious and comfortable circumstances. I do not think that that is going to make them morally wild, but I am sure that it is deceiving many of them as to the real secret of living. They are expecting to find life, pick it up, get it out of circumstances, and that is a fallacy. You never find life; you create it. Often the best friend a man ever has is not comfort but the stimulus and challenge of antagonistic environment to awaken the resistance of his slumbering soul.

This principle, that all life has to be tackled as Titus tackled Crete, applies not simply to an elemental matter like character, but also to some of our dearest relationships. What is the matter with our sadly shaken married life in the United States? Many people say that the laws are wrong. The laws about divorce are very chaotic and should be greatly improved, but all the tinkering that we do with the laws will not solve the problem of our family life. The deeper trouble is that young people approaching marriage think of it merely as a road to happiness. They expect magically to alight on happiness in marriage. They expect some day to fall in love and float into bliss. The fact is, there is little about marriage in itself to make happiness, while there are plenty of things about marriage to make perdition. Two personalities wanting to be happy come into a relationship the most intimate that earth knows, where all the peculiarities of one are thrust at the sensitiveness of the other. That situation by itself is much more likely to make agony than bliss.

There is, however, one glorious thing about marriage. It is an opportunity, the most beautiful opportunity that life knows. It is an opportunity to create a friendship stronger than death. It is an opportunity for children, the loveliness of their companionship, and the social service rendered to the world by their fine upbringing. It is an opportunity to build a school for character which shall make it easier for all who see it to believe in the fatherhood of God and the brotherhood of man. Take marriage as a spiritual opportunity, the raw material, with many hostile and difficult elements in it, out of which strong souls can build a great result, and you will have a real home. But you never will find one. Real homes are never found; they are spiritually created.

All life must be tackled as Titus tackled Crete. What existence hands us is raw material out of which something must be spiritually made. A man who faces life like that needs a soul undergirded by great faiths, overarched by high convictions, and blessed with inward power. As a man thinks of life in this way, he hears the echo of an old word, "What shall a man give in exchange for his soul?"

A second thing Titus must have said when he received Paul's letter. "Paul is right," I think he said. "This principle which he recommends is not only common sense; it is good Christianity." There is no use pretending to be a disciple of Jesus if we are unwilling to stay in Crete because it is difficult. Jesus belongs in Crete. Jesus particularly belongs in Crete. He belongs in Crete, not in spite of the fact that the Cretans are liars, beasts, gluttons, but because they are. "This man receiveth sinners, and eateth with them," said his enemies. He was always trying to discover Crete. "The publicans and sinners were drawing near unto him to hear him." He always attracted Crete to himself. There is no use pretending to be his disciples if we are dodging Crete!

Imagine the Master, if you can, in some discouraged hour when things were going badly with his ministry, saying, "O God, human beings are a cruel lot. They are selfish, sensual, hateful, brutish. Already I can see that what their fathers did to the prophets they are going to do to me. A crooked and perverse generation!" What voice would he have heard out of the unseen? "For this cause sent I thee into the world." You cannot imagine the Master going into any situation without making it his first business to look up Crete. "They that are whole have no need of a physician, but they that are sick . . . I came not to call the righteous, but sinners."

Ah, we respectable Christians! We have gone on building churches, elaborating complicated creeds, worshiping through splendid rituals, but how often the real spirit of Jesus has been somewhere else! Wherever in this modern world there is a Crete, where the situation is difficult and people needy, where for love's sake some soul puts itself alongside the need and lifts, there is the real spirit of Jesus, who "though he was rich, yet for your sakes he became poor, that ye through his poverty might become rich."

One cannot speak of this without thinking of some of our modern Tituses, whom one knows personally, who have really gone to Crete. I baptized one years ago. She has graduated from college since. She has had all that American culture and education can give her. She has married a young physician. This morning they are up the Congo in Central Africa. I suppose still the Cretans are liars, beasts, gluttons, but in that spot, where under the magic of unselfish service a better day is dawning, there is a challenge in the very degradation: For this cause sent I thee to Crete.

When a man does live in this spirit of Jesus, it is more satisfying than anything beside. Consider: the deepest joy in life is creativeness. To find an undeveloped situation, to see the possibilities, to brood over it, pray about it, think concerning it, work for it, to get something done there that would not have been done except for your creative soul—that is a satisfaction in comparison with which superficial joys are trivial.

This is true even when creativeness is turned toward things physical, like the conquest of the air. Some time ago one of our aviators, who carried mail from New York to Cleveland, fell in the mountains of Pennsylvania and was killed. They found upon his body a letter addressed "To My Beloved Brother Pilots and Pals" and marked "To be opened only after my death." Listen to what he said: "I go west, but with a cheerful heart. I hope what small sacrifice I have made may be of use to the cause. When we fly we are fools, they say. . . . But every one in this wonderful aviation service is doing the world far more good than the public can appreciate. We risk our necks, we give our lives, we perfect a service for the benefit of the world at large. . . . But stick to it, boys. I'm still very much with you all. See you all again."

You pity that boy? I don't. He had more fun in his short life than all the satiated pleasure-seekers who habitually try to feed their souls on superficial foam. For the elemental joy is creativeness and when that spirit of creativeness is turned to spiritual ends and helps to transform personalities and societies it is so satisfying that I do not know whether it is selfish or unselfish. After Titus got started in Crete you could not have dragged him away.

The joy of every true preacher is not that he preaches to this number of people or that, but that once in a while he comes within reach of an individual soul upon whom he can exercise a creative influence. I am thinking today of a Christian home, one of the most promising Christian homes I know. Who is the wife? She was a chorus girl on Broadway. The current was too strong for her. She went under. She touched the bottom of the pit in this perilous city. You never would guess it now. Christ did in her a thing so beautiful that not only have the wounds been healed, but I do not know how you ever would find the scars. Columbus must have gotten deep satisfaction out of discovering America, but no more thrilling, I think, than to discover a soul in Crete and lead the way up. Don't dodge Crete. If in this city we have not found our Crete,—the area of human need that belongs to us,—then we are not quite Christians until we find it.

One other thing I think Titus said when Paul's letter came. I suspect he thought to himself: "Paul is right. The ultimate test of a man's faith in God is its power to see him through a hard place." Perhaps we have not been sympathetic enough with Titus. Crete was a hard place, so hard and the people so unlovely that I suspect moral indignation had a good deal to do with Titus' first attitude. It would have been such a relief to his sense of what was fitting to tell them what he thought of them—liars, beasts, gluttons—and then leave them so. How natural! Many of us here, I suspect, are tempted to deal with some situations which we face by that cheap and easy method of moral indignation. It is much easier to denounce than to build.

Consider the church, for example. Nothing is easier than to berate the church. Sectarian, obscurantist, belated, out of touch with the major movements of thought and life in our time—the churches do face the most perilous situation they have faced since the Protestant Reformation. Here is a chance for irresponsible critics to revel in denunciation, and they are taking full advantage of the opportunity. But they get us nowhere. The situation calls for another attitude altogether—for Tituses who will stay in Crete, not content with Crete, not complaisant about Crete, but building the better Crete that is to be. As Paul said, to "set in order the things that were wanting."

When one is in Crete how much easier it is to be indignant than to be constructive!

Most of us, however, face this problem in much more intimate relationships. You know your Crete; I know mine. And we know that our serious inward problem is somehow to keep Crete from becoming our spiritual enemy and to make it our spiritual friend.

An eminent expert on child psychology was called in some time ago to help a young boy who every night dreamed of a frightful tiger. Night after night that dreadful vision came, and the repetition of the fear was shattering the lad's nervous system. So one evening the psychologist gathered the lad into his lap and said to him, "See here, my boy, I understand that every night you meet a tiger. Now, really, he is a nice, friendly tiger and he wants you to like him, so the next time you meet him just put out your hand and say, 'Hello, old chap,' and you will see." So the boy crawled into bed and fell into his restless, apprehensive, tossing sleep. But presently he stirred and thrust a small hand out from under the bedclothes and said softly, "Hello, old chap."

Then his frightened breathing quieted into the restfulness of natural sleep. Away at the center of his life he had made friends with his tiger.

That is about the hardest thing some of us have to do: to take a situation that we hate, and say: I am not going to let you be my spiritual enemy; you shall not scare me nor intimidate me nor embitter me nor crush me; like the dragons in old myths, which, boldly faced, turned out to be princesses in disguise, you yet shall be my friend. Happy is the man who so transforms his Crete! Happy is the man who so makes friends with his tiger!

Six Ways to Tell Right
from Wrong

OUR thought starts with the plain fact that it is not always easy to tell the difference between right and wrong. Any pulpit, therefore, which keeps up the traditional exhortation, Do right! Do right! as though, with a consensus of popular opinion as to what right is, all that the world needs is to be urged to do it, is indulging in a futile kind of preaching. Behind a great deal of our modern immoralism is not so much downright badness as sincere confusion as to what is right. In many a dubious situation how we wish that some one would tell us that!

The factors that enter into this condition must be obvious to anybody.

For one thing, change of circumstances. Old customs and old codes of behavior in family life or in the relationships between men and women, let us say, undertake to tell us how to act, but the circumstances in which those codes and customs are supposed here to function are radically different from the circumstances in which they first emerged, so that although their basic principles may be valid their applications are endlessly perplexing. In consequence, old patterns of behavior smash up and old prescriptions for right and wrong do not seem pertinent, and every day human beings, who always like to have their roadways plainly marked, go astray, not because they deliberately want to but because they are honestly confused about which the right road is.

Again, our cosmopolitanism, pouring all the cultures of the earth into one melting pot, has, among other consequences, resulted in ethical confusion. Our Pilgrim forefathers, with a wilderness on one side and a sea on the other, in their comparatively isolated community and with their comparatively homogeneous population, could reach a popular consensus of moral judgment or even a dogmatic certainty as to how men ought to act. But in a city like this most of the ways of behaving known on earth are poured together, so that the issue is not a single clear right against a single clear wrong, but such diverse and competing ideas of right as to befuddle the minds even of the elect.

The upshot of all this is that conscience is not enough. Of course, conscience never has been enough. Many of the most terrific deeds in history, from the crucifixion of our Lord down, were conscientiously done. Listen even to Paul in his first letter to Timothy: "I was before a blasphemer, and a persecutor, and injurious: howbeit I obtained mercy, because I did it ignorantly in unbelief." Paul throughout his life had been conscientious. Toward the end of it he could say to his Jewish brethren, "I have lived before God in all good conscience until this day." That did not mean, however, that as he looked back over his life all the things he had conscientiously done seemed to him to have been right. Upon the contrary, he confessed: a blasphemer, a persecutor, an injurious person, such was I, conscientiously but ignorantly.

Today I propose talking about this matter with homely practicality to my own soul and to yours. We may take it for granted that we would not be here in a Christian church if in general we did not desire to do right. We may even take it for granted that if, as in Shakespeare's "As You Like It," some one should ask us Touchstone's question, "Hast any philosophy in thee, shepherd?" we would say, Yes indeed, we have; we believe the basic ideas of Christianity about life's meaning—that is our philosophy. But we had better take it for granted also that this general desire to do right and this general acceptance of the Christian philosophy of life do not solve our problem. So as automobilists our problem is not solved when we desire to take the right road or when we hold a true cosmology about the solar relationships of the earth on which the right road runs. Oh, for a homely sign-post now and then, some practical, directive help amid the confusion of competing ways to tell us where to turn! So this morning I invite you to no airplane trip into the lofty blue but to a practical land journey as we set up six homely guide-posts to the good life.

In the first place, if a man is sincerely perplexed about a question of right and wrong, he might well submit it to the test of common sense. Suppose that some one should challenge you to a duel. What would you say? I would advise you to say, Don't be silly! As a matter of historic fact, dueling, which was once a serious point of conscientious honor, was not so much argued out of existence as laughed out. The common sense of mankind rose up against it, saying, Don't be silly! So Cervantes in *Don Quixote* finished off the ridiculous left-overs of the old knighthood, saying, Don't be silly! So Jesus, in his parable of the rich man who accumulated outward things but cared nothing for the inward wealth of the spiritual life, did not say, Sinner! but Fool!—"Thou fool, this night thy soul shall be required of thee: then whose shall those things be, which thou hast provided?"

So, too, more intimately, here is a youth whom you may know, whose behavior burdens with anxiety his family, his teachers, and his friends. They argue with him; they exhort him; they penalize him to no effect. But some day a fine girl for whom he cares says to him, it may be no more than three words, Don't be silly! and lo, something happens in that boy that home and school and church together could not achieve.

What we are saying now is that this is a healthy thing for a man to say to his own soul before somebody else has to say it to him. One wonders how many here would be affected by it. You do not really care anything about drink, and left to yourself you would not drink at all, but it is so commonly offered to one nowadays and is so generally taken as a matter of course, that you are drinking too much. Don't be silly! Or you may have in your hands today a choice between promiscuous sexual liaisons and a real home where two people love each other so much that they do not care to love anybody else in the same way at all; where romance deepens into friendship and overflows into children; where, as the sun grows westerly, the family life becomes every year more beautiful. And with that choice in your hands you are playing with promiscuity. Don't be silly!

Or it may be that you have a good set of brains and real ability so that if you wanted to you could prepare yourself for some worth-while work in the world, and just because you are financially able you are trying to be aimlessly happy, not going anywhere,—just meandering,—endeavoring to pick up all the sensations that you can accumulate. I should not think it worth while to call you first of all bad, but I am sure it would be true to call you silly.

That is the first test and, alas! twenty years from now somebody here this morning, listening to this and paying no heed to it, will be looking back on life and saying that bitter thing, "God be merciful to me, a fool!"

In the second place, if a man is sincerely perplexed about a question of right and wrong, he may well submit it to the test of sportsmanship. Now, the essence of sportsmanship is that in a game we do not take for ourselves special favors which we deny to other players but, making the rules equal for all, abide by them. In daily life that means that a man should always question concerning his conduct whether, if everybody acted on the same principle, it would be well for all. There is no doubt, then, why it is wrong to crowd in ahead of your turn in a line at a ticket office. Play the game! There is no doubt why it is wrong to cheat the government with petty smuggling or to join whispering campaigns about people when you do not know the facts, or to treat contemptuously a person of another race or color. Play the game! In all such cases we know well that we would not wish to be treated ourselves as we are treating others and that if everybody acted on that principle it would not be well for all. Sometimes one thinks that half the evil in the world is simply cheating. People do not play the game.

Do not, I beg of you, restrict the application of this test within the limits of individual behavior. There are ways of making money in our economic system, not simply illegal but legal, speculative gambling with the securities of the people, using public utilities as a football to be kicked all over the financial field in hope of making a goal of private profit with it, or betting day after day on stocks that represent genuine values which honest business once created but which now can be used merely for a gambler's chance without creating anything. If everybody acted like that there would be no values even to gamble with and no welfare for any one. Be sure of this, that this rising tide of public indignation against the economic wrongs has this much justification: we have a right at least to ordinary sportsmanship and in wide areas we have not been getting it. The Golden Rule, my friends, is a grand test. Husband and wife, parents and children, employers and employees, black and white, prosperous and poor, Occident and Orient—what if we did not cheat! what if we did as we would be done by! what if we played the game!

In the third place, if a man is sincerely perplexed about a question of right and wrong, he may well submit it to the test of his best self. Notice, I do not say to his conscience, for the conscience merely urges us to do right without telling us what the right is, but deeper than conscience and more comprehensive is this other matter, a man's best self. For, of course, no one of us is a single self. How much simpler life would be if we only were! There is a passionate self, reaching out hungrily for importunate sensations, good, bad, and indifferent. There is the careless self taking anything that comes along, excellent and vulgar, fine and cheap. There is the greedy self in whose eyes an egoistic want blots out all the wide horizons of humanity beside. But deeper than all these is that inner self where dwells the light that, as the Fourth Gospel says, lighteth every man coming into the world.

Let us illustrate it from biography. You know the story of Pasteur, great scientist, devout Christian, builder of modern medicine. In 1870, when the Germans invaded France, he already had had a paralytic stroke and was a cripple. He could not help repel the invaders. His friends urged him out of Paris that he might not be "a useless mouth" to be fed through the siege. His biographer tells us that sometimes when he was sitting quietly with his wife and daughter, in the little village of Arbois, the crier's trumpet would sound, and forgetting all else, he would go out of doors, mix with the groups standing on the bridge, listen to the latest news of disaster, and creep like a dumb, hurt animal back to his room. What could he do? What ought he to do? "Unhappy France," he wrote to a friend, "dear country, if I could only assist in raising thee from thy disasters!" Then something happened inside Pasteur that has changed the world. He, half paralyzed, a man already warned of his end, determined that he would raise France again to glory by a work of pure beneficence, that he would erect a monument to his country's honor that would make the military monuments of the conquerors seem puerile. In his biography you can read it all, how by years of inspired and sacrificial labor he at last fulfilled his purpose. So Pasteur, wondering what he ought to do, what he could do in a perplexing situation, carried the decision up to that finest self.

Sometimes when I preach here I wonder if there may not be in this congregation a youth who, so choosing his vocation, so testing his ambition, so dedicating his intelligence, will not help to raise America again. She needs it, unhappy country!

Be sure of this, that if, in large ways or small, any one of us does help to ennoble our society and build a better nation for our children and their children to be born into, it will be because we have taken our secret ambitions up to the tribunal of our finest self. There *is* something in us like a musician's taste, which discriminates harmony from discord. There *is* something in us like a bank teller's fingers, which distinguish true money from counterfeit:

> . . . . To thine own self be true,
> And it must follow, as the night the day,
> Thou canst not then be false to any man.

In the fourth place, if a man is sincerely perplexed over a matter of right and wrong he may well submit the question to the test of publicity. What if everybody knew what we are proposing to do? Strip it of secrecy and furtiveness. Carry it out into the open air, this conduct we are unsure about. Suppose our family and friends knew about it. Imagine it publicly talked of whenever our name is mentioned. Picture it written in the story of our life for our children afterwards to read. Submit it to the test of publicity. Anybody who knows human life with its clandestine behavior understands what a searching and healthy test this is.

How often in politics, in church life, in business, in personal character we see things that remind us of a claque at the theater hired to applaud a play! They can get away with it as long as the public does not know it is a claque. It depends on secrecy for its success. What a test publicity is!

Granted that ex-Mayor Walker may not have done anything illegal. Yet all those clandestine funds, those furtive sources of supply, would not stand the test of publicity. Granted that the Insulls may have succeeded in keeping within the margins of the law. Yet all this clandestine juggling with public utilities, this making millions out of the people by speculative greed, which acts as a parasite upon those real values that creative business produces but which produces no value itself, those secret lists of preferred and powerful men who received hundreds of thousands of dollars for reasons not disclosed—all this will not stand the test of publicity.

Do you remember how Phillips Brooks put it?

To keep clear of concealment, to keep clear of the need of concealment, to do nothing which he might not do out on the middle of Boston Common at noonday,—I cannot say how more and more that seems to me to be the glory of a young man's life. It is an awful hour when the first necessity of hiding anything comes. The whole life is different thenceforth. When there are questions to be feared and eyes to be avoided and subjects which must not be touched, then the bloom of life is gone. Put off that day as long as possible. Put it off forever if you can.

I know one business firm in this city which in a few weeks will crash into a receivership under the tremendous blow of a righteous court decision. Ten years ago that firm did a secret thing which would not stand the test of open knowledge. For ten years those men have lived in deadly fear that it might be known. And now the light has fallen.

Yes, and just the other day in personal conference I talked with an individual on the ragged edge of nervous prostration because in the secret furtiveness of private life something was afoot which it would be disastrous to have known.

Things that cannot stand sunlight are not healthful. There is a test for a perplexed conscience. How many here do you suppose would be affected by it? Imagine your behavior public.

In the fifth place, if a man is perplexed about a question of right and wrong he may well submit it to the test of his most admired personality. Carry it up into the light of the life which you esteem most and test it there. Why is it that some of us do not like cheap jazz? It is because we have known and loved another kind of music. Why is it that some of us do not think that Coney Island is a beautiful place? It is because on autumn days when the artistry of heaven has been poured out in lavish loveliness upon the trees we have walked in the spacious woods alone with our own souls and God. Why is it that some of us regard with a deep distaste all this promiscuous sexuality? It is because we have lived in homes where love was deep and lasting and dependable.

My friends, it is the beauties and the personalities that we positively have loved that set for us the tests and standards of our lives. Why is it, then, that conduct which seems to some people right seems to some of us cheap and vulgar, selfish and wrong? It is because for years we have known and adored the Christ. There is a test for a perplexed conscience. Carry your behavior up into the presence of the Galilean and judge it there.

If some one protests that he does not propose to subjugate his independence of moral judgment to any authority, not even Christ's, I answer, What do you mean by authority? There are all kinds of authorities—ecclesiastical, creedal, external, artificial—against the imposition of whose control on mind and conscience I would as vigorously fight as you. But there is one kind of authority for which I hunger, the insight of the seers. In science, in philosophy, in literature, in art, in music, not simply in morals and religion, I would, if I might, enrich my soul with the insights of the seers. A modern essayist says of Wordsworth, the poet, that he "saw things that other people do not see, and that he saw with quite unique clearness and frequency things which they see at most rarely and dimly." Aye! More than once some of us have carried our perplexed consciences up into the presence of the Christ and have made a saving use of his eyes.

In the sixth place, if a man is perplexed about a question of right and wrong, he may well submit it to the test of foresight. Where is this course of behavior coming out? All good life, my friends, depends upon the disciplining of clamorous and importunate desires in the light of a long look. We Christians who are trying to be intelligent long since gave up our belief in hell, but one suspects that many of us, throwing over the incredible and picturesque impossibilities of that belief, have dropped also a basic truth which our forefathers carried along in it. Every man who picks up one end of a stick picks up the other. Aye! Every man who chooses one end of a road is choosing the other. Aye! Every course of behavior has not only a place where it begins but a place where it comes out.

Life is like a game of chess. Some youth is here this morning with all his pieces on the board and freedom to commence. They tell me, however, that when a man has once played his opening, he is not so free thereafter. His moves must conform to the plan he has adopted. He has to follow the lead with which he has begun. The consequence of his opening closes in on him until at last, when checkmate is called, See! says the expert, when you chose those first moves you decided the end. Well, with what gambit are we opening our game?

We really do not need to be so perplexed about right and wrong as we sometimes are. To be sure, there is nothing infallible about all this. Goodness is an adventure and "Time makes ancient good uncouth." Nevertheless, the test of common sense, of sportsmanship, of the best self, the test of publicity, of our most admired personality, of foresight,— these are sensible, practical, high-minded ways to tell right from wrong. I call you to witness that in all this I have not been imposing on you a code of conduct; I have been appealing to your own best moral judgment. Alas for a man who neglects that! For though, as in Paul's case, one may come out at last to a good life, it is a bitter thing to have to look back and say, A blasphemer, and a persecutor, and injurious —such was I—ignorantly.

Superficial Optimists, the Peril
of a Serious Time

ONE of the most dangerous evils in the world is the highly prized habit of always looking on the bright side of things. To be sure, I should desperately dislike having to live with anybody who habitually looked on the dark side; nevertheless it still remains true that one of the most dangerous ideas in the world is the supposition that of course everything is coming out all right, that at any rate it is a shining virtue to keep on saying that it is, that nice people always see the silver lining to every cloud, and that in general God's in his heaven and all's right with the world. That attitude is sheer sentimentality and there is no health in it.

During recent years we have had an illustration of this attitude in the slogan that prosperity is just around the corner. People who ought to have known better told us *that* at the start and, ever since, people who wanted a substitute for facing hard facts, like disarmament, tariffs, technological unemployment, international debts, and a planned economy, have been busy saying the same thing. A recent writer on medical subjects tells us that there are millions of people in this country who still believe that smallpox can be cured by repeating incantations. In view of what millions more of us have been doing with the economic situation, that seems highly probable.

Do not suppose that such an attitude as this is alien to the deep interests of religion. Indeed, the classic utterance about this matter was made centuries ago by a prophet of religion. Jeremiah also lived in a distracted time that cried aloud for great statesmanship among national leaders and moral reform among the people, and he too heard on every side promises of prosperity around the corner. It was in a situation like our own, then, that he said, "They have healed the hurt of

the daughter of my people slightly, saying, Peace, peace;
when there is no peace." What a genial, amiable, easy-going
fault that attitude is which the prophet criticizes and yet
how ruinous!

We Americans in particular are susceptible to this genial
fault. For two major reasons, I suspect, we have become,
as all the world knows, notoriously optimistic. In the first
place, until about 1895, when some of us were graduating
from high school, we still had in this country the open frontier. Always there was more beyond. To be sure, in those
days also we had disastrous economic depressions, but still
people, too hard pinched, could trek west and pioneer new
lands. There in the west was an open spillway for the adventurous and the hard-bestead; there was a safety valve for
social pressures too severe. Moreover, beyond the practical
effects of the open frontier were its psychological and spiritual consequences. There were no closed doors around our
hopes. We had been given the richest, self-contained continent on the planet to exploit and we had not covered it yet
with even the first layer of our pioneers. Kipling caught the
essential spirit of our hope:

. . . A voice, as bad as Conscience, rang interminable changes
  On one everlasting Whisper day and night repeated—so:
"Something hidden. Go and find it. Go and look behind the
    Ranges—
  "Something lost behind the Ranges. Lost and waiting for
    you. Go!"

If, now, some one says that this spirit of undiscourageable hope, this vision of possibilities not yet fulfilled, which
has entered into the very texture of the American temperament, is a great heritage, I say, Indeed it is, a priceless and
magnificent gift, which if rightly used may lead us out to the
most happy days that any society on earth has known—if,
if we do not let it degenerate into incantations about everything coming out all right, if we do not let it lead us into the
fatuous policy of drifting, sending "our heavy technical machinery," as the President's Research Committee just has

said, "over crumbling roads and shaking bridges," if we do not fall into the burlesque of optimism, saying, Peace, peace; when there is no peace.

Alongside the fact of the open frontier, a second element in the easy-going optimism of the American temperament is the fact that, by and large, we are religious. Christianity has entered too deeply into the traditions of our people for our temperament altogether to escape the consequence, and as we always like to enjoy the genial, amiable, comfortable aspects of any experience, so we have absorbed hopefulness from Christianity. For Christianity is hopeful. It has a hopeful idea of God, a hopeful estimate of man, a hopeful ideal of the kingdom of righteousness on earth, a hopeful outlook on eternity. The consequence is that multitudes of Americans have just enough Christianity to brighten up their general optimistic outlook and to add religious tone to their conviction that everything will come out right in the end. That is what faith in God means to many people—that probably everything will come out right. They no longer believe in the old creeds, the stern, hard-bitten creeds which men like Calvin and John Knox bet their strenuous lives upon. But they have a creed which represents about all the Christianity that has succeeded in percolating into them, and it might run like this: I believe that every cloud has a silver lining, that we ought to brighten the corner where we are, and that in general everything is coming out all right.

Well, I am a modernist but I have a much deeper intellectual and moral respect for the great historic creeds and for the kind of character which came out of them than I have for that.

What do we mean—everything coming out all right? My friends, Calvary is only six miles from Bethlehem. That is all. Climb in imagination the hill of Neby Samwil outside Jerusalem and you will see them both together: six miles down the Judæan ridge the white houses of the little town of Bethlehem hallowed by the reminiscences that fill Christmas day with song, and at our feet Calvary, where once three crosses stood. Ah, Mary, mother of the Lord, how few the miles are between the place you bore him and the place you saw him die!

What, then, does one mean—everything, of course, coming out all right? If one means that in the long run Bethlehem and Calvary together will yet win their way against the stubbornness and cruelty of man,

> . . . life of long life
> Distilled to a mere drop, falling like a tear
> Upon the world's cold cheek to make it burn
> Forever,

I believe that! If one means that there is an eternal purpose which God purposed in Christ and that around the smaller horizon of Bethlehem with its beauty and Calvary with its tragedy there is a larger horizon wherein he yet shall see of the travail of his soul and be satisfied, I believe that. But this soft and sentimental kind of optimism which tries to leave Calvary out altogether, which leads us to drift in critical times with no intellectual and moral seriousness, saying Peace, peace, when there is no peace, is a thoroughly degenerate religion. God does not guarantee that everything will come out all right. What God guarantees is that this is a law-abiding universe, where whatsoever a man or a nation soweth, that shall he also reap. What God guarantees is that there is no salvation, personal or social, without sacrifice.

One might suppose that in a serious time people would be serious. That shows how little we understand psychology. In a very serious time everybody is tempted to run away from seriousness and forget it. Some run into frivolity and dissipation; some run into easy-going, sentimental, optimistic clichés; some run away to feather their own nests and cuddle down in such private luxury as they can afford. As the old chronicler Salvianus said about the Roman people when their empire was crashing down about their ears, *"Moritur, et ridet"*—they die and laugh. Every one here feels that pressure. We all are tempted to say, Peace, peace; when there is no peace.

I beg of you, therefore, join with me as on this matter I search my own soul.

For one thing, our American democracy is not going to escape from its present disreputable estate by any policy of optimistic drift. We cannot say, Peace, peace, about a city like New York. There is no peace and there will be none until we can have a revival of serious, sacrificial citizenship.

I hardly dare tell you how I feel about this city. There is something so disgraceful about the spectacle of this great community held in the grip of a confessedly corrupt machine, which generation after generation has robbed us and today, in ways so well known that they can be set down in specific detail has worked out the most ingenious devices of political thievery in the history of municipal government—there is, I say, something so intolerably shameful about our helplessness and our supineness in the presence of this disgrace that I should suppose that the hour would strike before long when we would stand it no more.

Do you remember what Ralph Waldo Emerson wrote in his diary when the news reached Boston that the national Congress had passed the Fugitive Slave Law forcing northern states and citizens to return runaway slaves? "This filthy enactment," wrote Emerson, "was made in the nineteenth century, by people who could read and write. I will not obey it, by God," "the infamy that has fallen on Massachusetts, that clouds the daylight and takes away the comfort out of every hour. We shall never feel well again until that detestable law is nullified in Massachusetts."

Does some one say, That is growing rather serious about it? But, my friends, this nation was founded in the first place by people who cared seriously like that and it will be preserved only by people who still care. If this city ever comes back to decency so that a self-respecting man can hold up his head in it, it will be because a great body of the people have said that they never will feel well again until this detestable régime of inefficiency and corruption is ended.

I am not saying, Give up hope! The most hopeful days in American life are ahead if we will have it so, but not if we drift, not if we repeat self-complacent incantations, not if we idly trust God to bring everything out all right.

Again, our personal moral life, with its far-reaching social consequence, will never be redeemed from its present estate by any policy of sentimental drift. We have said Peace, peace, too long already in the moral realm. We have been tolerant and broad-minded and easy-going and genial about many current practices which we know well are personally and socially rotten. I plead with you today to stop all that. Let us get our ethical backs up. Let us come straight out for moral aristocracy. Only that is likely to lift us out of this vulgar mess that has made the last ten years what one of our citizens called it, "the dirty decade."

To be sure, I believe in democracy after a fashion. It is the most efficient rough-and-ready way of reaching public decisions that we are likely to discover, and in a town like this if we could get proportional representation so that an intelligent minority might secure at least a share in the government, it might work out well. But to believe in political democracy as a rough-and-ready governmental device is another thing altogether from subjecting one's conscience to a moral democracy. Let a man stand clear of that. The mob is a vulgar beast. Its tastes are vile; its habits are disgusting. We are swamped by vulgarity. In our personal habits, our standards of judgment, our social customs, we are suffering another invasion of the barbarians. I plead for moral aristocracy.

Do not misunderstand me. I am not making a distinction now between Third Avenue and Park Avenue—not by a great deal. I am not making a distinction now between the sons and daughters of privilege on college campuses and those outside—not by a long way! Much of the wholesomest, soundest moral life of this country is among the poor and underprivileged. The healthiest roots of our nation's character are still there. I am not talking about rich and poor, about educated and uneducated. I am pleading for genuine moral aristocracy: good taste, sound character, personal integrity, simple living, faithful family life, unselfish public

service. My soul! how the nation does need that! "Ye are
the light of the world," said Jesus; "Ye are the salt of the
earth." "Come ye out from among them, and be ye separate,"
said Paul, "and touch not the unclean thing." You see, this
is not the first generation when this appeal was needed, but it
is needed now.

Again, we are not coming out of our present economic
debacle on any policy of superficial, optimistic drift. Indeed,
I suspect that these years ahead will see some very deep-
seated and far-reaching economic changes and that we had
better give our serious thought to them. Some of you here
this morning are socialists and you do not need that I should
talk to you about eagerness for social change. You are eager
already; you have the blue-prints with you for the changes
which you desire, and I honor you for that. But most of us
here, I suspect, are not socialists and, being thus unpersuaded
of the adequacy of the new collectivist blue-prints, we are
thrown back on a general hope that somehow a reformed
capitalism may prove equal to the task.

Any man who finds himself occupying that position would
better talk to himself seriously about the matter. For, you see,
our danger is that since our present economic system is
called capitalism and since we are hoping that somehow capitalism will meet the new problems, we are tempted to an
easy-going expectation that we may drift back again into the
old ways. Peace, peace, we are tempted to say; we will ride
out the storm and then the old ship will poke along much as
it did before.

My friends, that is about the most dangerous attitude in
America today. The only hope I see of capitalism's being able
to meet the new emergency lies in the fact that capitalism
itself is capable of revolutionary changes, that it never yet
has been the same in two successive generations, so that if
we call the economic system of the middle nineteenth century capitalism, we need another word altogether for what
we have now because it is not the same thing at all. The hope
of capitalism's meeting the new problems is not in drifting
back to the old ways—there is no hope there. It lies in the

elasticity of capitalism itself, in the radical changes which it already has accepted and absorbed and in the apparently endless capacity for change still inherent in it.

If the laissez-faire capitalists of the mid-Victorian era should see what we call capitalism now they would roll over in their graves! What with social legislation and workmen's compensation, and laboring men's organization, and public education, what with old-age pensions and unemployment insurance just ahead, to say nothing of great Federal organizations of assistance and control, which on every side interfere with individual initiative, the old capitalists would not recognize what we have now as capitalism at all. Indeed, one of our economists has gone so far as to say that if we take three points of comparison—capitalism as it was in 1848, shortly after Karl Marx wrote *The Communist Manifesto*, and capitalism as we have it now, and Russian communism— capitalism as we have it now is nearer communism than it is to the capitalism of 1848.

Phrase it as you will, what I am driving at is clear—just because a man is not a communist or a socialist is no excuse for his falling back on the policy of drift. Capitalism is not a static system. It never has been a static system. It always has been changing. Today and tomorrow it faces more radical changes than ever before. We must not drift. Drifting leads not to peace but to revolution. We need the massed intelligence and conscience of this nation eagerly to seek for changes and wisely to guide them.

In particular, we Christians, who ought most poignantly to feel the human consequences of our economic distress—not only unemployment itself but thousands of children under sixteen in Pennsylvania, according to the Federal Council, working for two dollars a week, women in factories in New Jersey working for from two to five dollars a week, girls in sweatshops of Connecticut working between eighty-one and eighty-five hours a week—we Christians ought to see that towering figure of our Lord, saying, "Inasmuch as ye did it unto one of these my brethren, even these least, ye did it unto me." Woe unto us if in a day like this we try to heal the hurt of the daughter of our people slightly, saying, Peace, peace; when there is no peace.

I should be distressed if anybody thought that this sermon sounded hopeless. Upon the contrary, the greatest advances in history have uniformly come out of just such upset, disturbed, and chaotic generations. In retrospect how magnificent a time to live when, for example, Magellan lived. Within his generation Columbus discovered America, Dias rounded the Cape of Good Hope, Vasco da Gama found the sea route to India, Balboa stood on a hill in Darien and saw the Pacific, one of Magellan's ships circumnavigated the earth. It was one of the most upset, chaotic, distracted times in history but how magnificent the consequence! So, I suspect, our children's children may yet look back on us. For with our scientific mastery over the latent resources of the universe we have achieved a power to do what we will which makes the achievements of our ancestors childlike, *if* we can muster intelligence and character enough to handle it, *if* in this country now we can have a genuine revival of spiritual life that will cleanse the souls of our people and dedicate their abilities to the common weal.

That is the gist of the matter. We have said we need better city governments, a higher ethical tone, a more serious recognition of the need of social change. Indeed we do, but back of all that and penetrating that we need a profound revival of spiritual life among our people. You never can cleanse the water of a well by painting the pump. You must have renewal in the deeps. You cannot change the bareness of a winter wood into the glory of a springtime forest by hanging leaves on the trees. You must have a revival of life at the roots. You never can redeem American society by external adjustments only. The deepest trouble is inside of us.

> Create in me a clean heart, O God;
> And renew a right spirit within me.

Unless one by one we are praying *that*, we are trying to heal the hurt of the daughter of our people slightly, saying, Peace, peace; when there is no peace.

[144]

The Sermon on the Mount

LET us raise with ourselves the question whether we Christians are disciples of Jesus or even seriously propose to be, or whether in our religious life we have largely substituted something else altogether. To be sure, we may call this substituted article Christianity but, for all that, it can be very different from the serious endeavor to put into practice the principles of the Sermon on the Mount. We may be Christians in the sense that we believe a theological creed accepted as Christian, or belong to a church that is called Christian, or practice rituals that have been associated with Christianity. But to be Christian in the sense of being disciples of Jesus, seriously endeavoring to live his way of life, is another matter altogether.

Let us, then, question ourselves about our inward attitude toward the Sermon on the Mount. What adjectives would you naturally choose to describe its admonitions, all the way from considering the birds of the air and the flowers of the field and being correspondingly without anxiety, to turning the other cheek when you are smitten on one, or loving your enemies and doing them good? Would not some here say at once that these injunctions are ideal, not to say saintly? Would not others go further and say they are visionary and impractical? And perhaps some would go further and say they are wrong and that it would disrupt human society really to practice them. One independent preacher even said that the Sermon on the Mount ought to be called the Sarcasm on the Mount.

Turn, then, to the adjective which Jesus uses about his own injunctions. Dr. Moffatt has given us a suggestive rendering of that first verse of the final paragraph, in which the Master brings his great discourse to its conclusion: "Everyone who listens to these words of mine and acts upon them will be like a sensible man who built his house on rock." Of all adjectives that would occur to most of us to apply to the Sermon on the Mount, surely the last is "sensible."

We may well at the beginning put ourselves in the place of those who find difficulty with the Sermon on the Mount and agree with them on one point: we cannot always take Jesus literally. Jesus does not always take his own words literally. He said, "Judge not, that ye be not judged," but you have only to read the twenty-third chapter of Matthew's Gospel: "Woe unto you, scribes and Pharisees, hypocrites!" to see how severely he could judge. He said, "Be not anxious," but on the threshold of his tragedy he cried, "Now is my soul troubled; and what shall I say?" and in the agony in the Garden he prayed that this cup might if possible pass from him. He said, "Whosoever smiteth thee on thy right cheek, turn to him the other also," but when at last he was smitten, though in patient silence he bore the contumely and brutality of the Roman soldiers, there is nothing to indicate that he literally turned the other cheek.

The Master did not always take his own words literally because, for one thing, a true Oriental takes no one literally. A native Syrian, born a little way north of where Jesus lived, says that when he goes to visit an old friend, his host, expansive with genial hospitality, addresses him as follows: "This house is yours; you can burn it if you wish. My children also are at your disposal; I would sacrifice them all for your pleasure." Does he mean it literally? Of course not. But he does mean it seriously.

Miss Maude Royden has rightly pointed out that there is a great difference between those two ideas—taking Jesus literally and taking him seriously. Too many people, seeing the obvious fact that you cannot always take him literally, are trying to escape the deep obligation to take him seriously.

He said that it is harder for a rich man to get into the kingdom of heaven than it is for a camel to go through a needle's eye. Take that figure literally and it is absurd. But it is to be taken seriously. Every man with money would better take it seriously. All man's social history is a commentary on the truth of it. "It is hard to carry a full cup."

He said, "Whosoever smiteth thee on thy right cheek, turn to him the other also." Do that literally and see how foolish you will look. But it is to be taken seriously. Generally that passage is interpreted to indicate the way a man should act when he is in a fight. But when we fight do we slap each other on the cheek? Smiting on the cheek is not easily made a symbol for a fight; it is a symbol for an insult. It corresponds to thrusting out the tongue or thumbing the nose. Whosoever insults thee in one way, let him insult thee in another—as a man grows older and experiences a little what it means to be insulted, the more he is impressed with the fact that one who acts upon that principle is a sensible man.

We said that the Master did not always take his own words literally but, surely, he took them seriously. He said, "Love your enemies," and he meant it. To be sure, it was not a literal law that made him soft and prevented severe denunciations of men's woes and wrongs when occasion demanded it, but one has only to climb Calvary and hear from the victim of that central cross prayer for the men who put him there to see that Jesus, an Oriental, often speaking in hyperbole and not taking his own words literally, meant what he said seriously.

With this understanding of the Sermon on the Mount, let us turn to look at it and consider certain propositions which indicate that Jesus' adjective "sensible" is justified.

For one thing, the most sensible thing that the church of Christ could do today would be to rediscover Jesus and his way of life. Look at this strange salmagundi that we call Christianity, that, expressed in innumerable rituals and creeds, one runs across as he traverses the Western world from New York to Jerusalem. In what sharp contrast with that elaborate, sophisticated development does Jesus' way of living stand! For while the principles of the Sermon on the Mount run deep they can be swiftly summarized:

In dealing with ourselves, absolute genuineness within, so

that not only will we not murder but we will not hate, not only will we not commit adultery but we will reverence too much the sanctities of personality to propose it, that we will not require an oath, for our word is as good as our bond, and if ever on the branches of our lives hangs apparent fruit it will not be like the tinsel on Christmas trees, tied on for show, but a spontaneous expression of good life within. In dealing with ourselves, absolute genuineness.

In dealing with others, absolute goodwill, goodwill so un-qualified that no one's ill treatment will ever spoil its quality or reduce it to retaliation, so that, like the God of nature, sending his rain and sun on just and unjust, we will show goodwill to grateful and ungrateful, to the friendly and the hostile, and never allow any one's ill will to reduce us to the level of hating back. In dealing with others, absolute goodwill.

In dealing with God, absolute trust, so that our religion will not mean praying on street corners or thinking that we can be heard for our much speaking, but the serene experience of an inward fellowship with the Unseen Friend so that, giving ourselves primarily to seeking his will upon the earth, we shall be tranquil about lesser matters—

Round our restlessness, His rest.

In dealing with ourselves inner genuineness, with our fellows utter goodwill, with God perfect confidence—that, in brief, is discipleship to Jesus.

We have gone a long way from that in Christianity. Look about you and see what goes under the name of Christian. The history of a spiritual revelation, springing up fresh in some lofty soul, is like that of a mountain stream. The pure water flows down among the haunts of men; societies grow up along its course; they use it to drive their mills, they pour their refuse into it, they turn it from its natural chan-nels; it becomes unlovely, undrinkable, unclean, and at last empties polluted into the sea. Why must it always happen so?

St. Francis of Assisi was a soul through whom God burst in a revelation of light and life upon the souls of men. Says the historian, "Not since Christ has any one else inflamed the human heart and fired the imagination to so great a degree as St. Francis. And yet," wrote the historian, "within a century after the founding of the Franciscan order it became a disgrace." That is the tragedy, that if St. Francis had come back, even within a century, he would have had to insist that, as for him, he was not a Franciscan.

So has it happened to Jesus and his movement. His message, gathering alien elements even from the minds of the first disciples, went out into that ancient world. Greek philosophy took hold upon it, erected enormous intellectual superstructures on the basis of it, made a colossal orthodoxy out of it. The Greek mystery religions took hold upon it. Long before, they had practiced magical sacraments of baptism and sacred meals to imbue their devotees with immortality. They took the simple rituals that spontaneously had sprung up in Palestine and made magical sacraments out of them. The Roman Empire took hold upon it, became the mold for the church's organization, until within the falling institutions of the imperial state the church stood forth absolute, infallible, tremendous.

Will you say now that Protestantism redeemed the Christian movement? Does it look that way? Let us cease our foolish idealization of Protestantism! Magnificent were some of those great souls who joined in that fight for freedom, but, after all, the Protestant Reformation was a half-way affair. It left dogmatism almost more accentuated than it was before. It took the old world order, that at least had had the ideal of unity, and broke it up into separate nations, each with its own state church, and so helped to lay the foundations of that spectacle of disrupted Christianity and triumphant nationalism that is the major problem of the modern world. It took the old church, that at least had the ideal of unity, and broke it up into multitudinous little sects so bitter-spirited that many a deeply religious man has turned his back at last on Christianity because of it. "A little squeaking idiot," wrote Ruskin with impatience, "was preaching to an audience of seventeen old women and three louts, that they were the only children of God in Turin; and that all the people in Turin outside the chapel, and that all the people in the world out of sight of Monte Viso, would be damned."

Is it not the plain truth that if Jesus had come back any time after he left, with his way of living, seeking disciples who would actually try his principles out, one of the chief obstacles that he would have faced would have been Christians? "What are we doing?" asks E. Stanley Jones. "As someone has suggested, we are inoculating the world with a mild form of Christianity, so that it is now practically immune against the real thing." Aye, nearly fifty million folks in the United States calling themselves Christians, inoculated with a mild form of Christianity so that, as one can plainly see from the estate of private character and social life, multitudes are immune from the real thing.

The Sermon on the Mount not sensible? There isn't anything half so sensible the church could do as to go back and rediscover Jesus and his basic principles of life. He is the one great asset that Christianity possesses. The Christian movement has been bad enough but not altogether bad. Once in a while it has been glorious, so glorious that the best hopes of the world yet are to be found in Christianity, and wherever it has been glorious this one thing has happened: somebody has rediscovered Jesus. Wherever in the history of Christendom there has been a vital reformation that even for a little time has lifted the church to be a cleansing and transforming agency in human society, there at the heart of it somebody has rediscovered Jesus.

In Roman Catholicism it may have been St. Francis in humility serving the lowliest and the lost and leaving his radiant spot of beauty at the heart of the thirteenth century. One could not have walked with him a day without seeing what had happened there. A man had refound Jesus and his way of life.

In Protestantism it may have been John Wesley turning his back upon the dry-as-dust formalism of the English Christianity of his time, going out from the sedate edifices of the church to preach to numberless hungry souls upon the open hillsides, but one could not have watched him starting that reformation, the consequences of which are not over yet, without seeing that what had happened there was a rediscovery of Jesus.

And when, just behind us, men like Rauschenbusch raised their call for a social reformation, showing us that six days in the week we were doing things that denied what we said on Sunday, there at the center of their movement, the source of its power and the secret of its passion, was the rediscovery of Christ.

Is anything like that, according to our power and measure, to happen among us? There is no use trying to present to this new generation that vast amalgam of diverse elements that history has lumped together and called Christianity. They will not have it and they are right. But to present Christ himself and his way of life—that is another matter. There is no use trying to present to the non-Christian world our Western sectarianism and our Western theologies, that have associated themselves with the historic development of the Christian movement. They will not have them and they are right. But to present to them Christ himself and his way of life—that is another matter. If it comes hard from a Christian, will you take it from a Hindu? "Though today," says a great Hindu, "Christianity but feebly reflects the spirit of its Master, the personality of the Master himself stands before the world in compelling grandeur. Never before have so many earnest minds of all races and creeds turned to him for light and guidance in perplexities." If any church will listen to the words of Christ and act upon them, it will be a sensible church built upon rock.

Let us push our thought a stage further. The most sensible thing that Western civilization could do today would be to rediscover Jesus and his way of life. So often, when folk think of the conflict between Christianity and anti-Christianity, they think of it in theological terms: God versus no-God. In that and similar propositions moving in the intellectual realm, they think the crucial conflict lies between Christ and Antichrist. Such problems are important. But I am sure the deepest conflict between Christianity and anti-Christianity does not lie there. The deepest conflict is between two ways of living.

Nietzsche, I should suppose, is the most outspoken and impressive representative of the anti-Christian life, but while we use his name let us remember that the principles for which he stood are age-long and that from the days of ancient Greece what we might call Nietzscheanism has had its exponents. This, in brief, is what Nietzsche would say: This world belongs to the strong; not only does might make right, but might is right; Christianity with its ideal of care for the weak is a delusion concocted by the weak to prevent the strong from the rightful use of their own strength for themselves. It is an inversion of all true values, says Nietzsche, that the strong should care for the weak; let the weak serve the strong; let them be fertilizer, even, to make rich the soil out of which the superman may grow; humility is vice, pride is virtue; let the mighty man glory in his might and use it as he will. And as for Christianity, said Nietzsche, it is "the one great curse, the one enormous and innermost perversion, . . . the one immortal blemish of mankind."

There you have the very opposite of the Sermon on the Mount. There you have the crucial conflict between Christ and Antichrist. On the one side, this doctrine: we that are strong ought to squeeze the weak into our cups and drink their blood like wine to make us stronger still. And on the other this doctrine: we that are strong ought to bear the burdens of the weak and not to please ourselves. Take a look at the world. Who wins? Nietzsche or Christ?

Note that in our Western world we have given Nietzscheanism a long, fair chance. In our business, in our industrial expansion, in our imperialism, in our national policies, in our Nordic myth calling ourselves the superior race, we have given Nietzscheanism a long, fair chance. And in these recent years we have seen one climactic outburst and exhibition of it. Do you like it? Do you think that it is sensible?

The last war ruined more reputations than any other

catastrophe in history. Who got out of the war with an undamaged reputation? Did Mars, the god of war? We used to say fine things about him when I was young, that Mars ran a school of manly virtue, that he must come occasionally to tone up the spirit of the nation, that like a thunderstorm he healthily cleared the air. Mars came out of this last war with damaged repute. He left the world half devastated, not only materially, but morally, and many a year we will be reaping the miserable harvest of his lamentable sowing. Who again in his senses will trust Mars for service?

Did science come out with an undamaged reputation? We used to say fine things about science and the way it was going to save the world. In 1912 an eminent American professor said this: "To-day we have no fear of war, famine, pestilence, or failing resources. The advance of knowledge has safeguarded men from all those evils." He said that in 1912. I wonder what he thinks now. Marvelous have been the gifts of science to the hands of men, but that creates the problem; it does not solve it. Under the Nietzschean philosophy every gift of science will be used to destroy, not build. As another has put it, science is mounting man upon a bigger horse than he knows how to ride. So far as being a savior of the world is concerned, science came out with a damaged name.

Did progress come out with an undamaged reputation? How we used to trust this automatic escalator of evolutionary betterment that was to lift us ever and ever to higher things! In every intelligent mind this last catastrophe destroyed that fairy tale of inevitable progress. Some of us have walked over the graves of ancient empires—Egypt, Tyre, Babylon, Greece, and Rome—which practiced the Nietzschean philosophy. Their ghosts rise up to haunt our Western world. Progress came out with a badly damaged reputation.

Who did come out from this catastrophe with an unsullied name? Not Mars, not science, not progress. Did nationalism? It is a new doctrine, in the modern form in which we know it today, this idea that each nation is a separate, isolated, absolute unit and that it must play its selfish game against all the other separate, isolated, absolute units. Before a man calls that sensible let him take full and just account of the outcome to which it is bringing us in this generation where, long ago, all the major interests of humankind became international.

Has even Christianity come out of this last war with undamaged repute? Upon the contrary, with a name badly smirched. Over 564,000,000 people claiming to be Christians —see what we did to one another! Conventional Christianity and real Nietzscheanism—that is the spectacle we presented to the world.

What has kept an undamaged reputation? Not Mars, not science, not progress, not nationalism, not Christianity. Nothing, however, has happened to discredit Jesus' way of life. Everything has happened to make it shine more than ever before, like a beacon across stormy seas. On how many people, even hard-minded folk, must it have dawned from time to time that perhaps, after all, he is right?

Recall what George Bernard Shaw said. You do not go to George Bernard Shaw for sentimental opinions. "I am ready to admit," he wrote, "that after contemplating the world and human nature for nearly sixty years, I see no way out of the world's misery but the way which would have been found by Christ's will if he had undertaken the work of a modern practical statesman." "Though we crucified Christ on a stick, he somehow managed to get hold of the right end of it, and . . . if we were better men we might try his plan."

This is the conclusion of the matter. It would not be merely ideal, it would not be merely saintly, it would be sensible for the church and civilization to rediscover him and his way of life. Would it not be sensible for you and me then? How many of us have been inoculated with a mild form of Christianity so that we are immune to the real thing? A minister in New York tells me that lately, while talking with one of his prominent parishioners, the man broke out in an impassioned confession: "I have been a member of the church for all the twenty-five years since I was baptized.

Why hasn't anything vital ever happened to me?" How many in any church would say that: Church members twenty-five years—why hasn't anything vital happened to us? And nothing vital will happen until back behind formal, conventional Christianity we go to Christ at the heart of it. Christ is Christianity—all of Christianity that matters much. To know him, to be his disciples, to take him seriously, to practice his way of life, is the hope of the church and of civilization and of us who would be members of that band of transfigured men whom the world cannot tame!

Christianity's Supreme
Rival

OTHERS are considering, because others must consider, the vital interests that are involved for them in the problem of nationalism and internationalism. That politics, for example, is concerned is clear. To be sure, our two great parties back and fill because they are afraid that the issues involved in internationalism may spoil some local and temporary success, but, as with slavery so with this problem, politicians, hem and haw as they will, must some day face it and find it the rock of their standing or their falling.

That business has a tremendous stake in this matter is plain. To be sure, some businesses have customarily made large profits out of war, but this does not represent the general consequence of war on the economic situation. War is commercially disruptive. Indeed, one of the most hopeful signs of peace is the growing consciousness that not simply our ideals but our economic interests are against conflict.

While, however, books, newspapers, and magazines continually discuss the stakes which business and politics have in this matter, our concern is with Christianity. So entangled are Christianity and internationalism in their interests that if we in our churches try to content ourselves with the intimate and comfortable aspects of personal religion we are living in a fool's paradise, as though one fitted out a little room and made it very lovely in a large, unstable building that at any moment might come crashing down, room and all, about our ears.

This concern of the Christian gospel with nationalism is not new. If you would see an ancient exhibition of it, turn to the sixteenth chapter of the book of The Acts. Paul has been preaching in Macedonia. He has just crossed over from Asia Minor into Europe—one of the great events in the world's history because then, for the first time, Christianity invaded the Western world. And there, at the beginning, the gospel was met, as it has been met ever since, by the challenge of nationalism. "These men," said Paul's enemies in Philippi, "being Jews, do exceedingly trouble our city, and set forth customs which it is not lawful for us to receive, or to observe, being Romans." Quite so—being Romans! This attack on Christianity, you see, was not launched from the citadel of an opposing religion but from the citadel of an opposing nationalism. These ancient patriots instinctively felt that, if they were to be Romans in the accepted meaning of that term, they would have to withstand Christianity.

Let us take it for granted that at one point we do not need at length to guard ourselves against misunderstanding. In one sense we are all loyal nationalists, as we are all loyal members of our families. It may be that God can look with absolutely equal eyes on all our homes and nations alike, but we cannot, and it would be disastrous if we tried. Each man primarily belongs to his own family; there are the centers of his affection and there the tendrils of his devotion are entwined. Moreover, this unique allegiance to one's own family, when it is rightly used, is beautiful in its results. Because I have loved my own mother supremely I understand better the meaning of everybody else's mother and know, as I could not otherwise have known, the significance of motherhood around the world. Because I am devoted to my own children as I never could be devoted to anybody else's children, I feel, as otherwise I never could have felt, the meaning of parenthood and childhood everywhere. That is what a home is for. It is a hothouse where in a certain isolation of sheltered loyalties beautiful things are grown—affections, sympathies, insights, devotions—which afterwards can be transplanted and applied to the common good of humankind.

Such is the deep meaning of a fine nationalism. No other nation can mean to us what our nation means. Here are the roots of our heritage, and here our central loyalties belong. But, just because we feel so deeply about our own land, we understand how other people feel about their lands, and, using our patriotism to interpret theirs, we grow, not in bitterness but in understanding and sympathy. So all fine internationalism must be rooted back in the noble significances of nationalism.

Let us take it for granted, then, that nationalism has two meanings, one good and one evil, and that we are not forgetting the fine uses of it when we employ the word in an untoward sense. For, whatever words we use, we must somehow get at the modern counterparts of those patriots of Philippi who could not stand Christianity, being Romans.

The gist of the matter lies in the fact that the dogma of nationalism, as it has developed in the last two centuries, has become a competing religion. I think it the most dangerous rival of Christian principles on earth. The crucial conflict today is not primarily Christianity versus Buddhism or Christianity versus Mohammedanism, but Christianity versus nationalism, and until one has clearly envisaged that fact one does not understand the crux of our situation.

Here are the three major items in the nationalistic creed:

First, that each nation is a sovereign unit acknowledging no control save its own independent will. If its interests demand war it may make war, for it is free of all governance beyond itself, being by nature a sovereign unit competing with and, when necessary, fighting with other sovereign units for supremacy.

Second, that within its own borders each sovereign unit may exercise an almost absolute authority over the lives of its citizens. We must be ready on call to sacrifice to the nation our lives, our fortunes, our sons and daughters, even our consciences. Especially in war time the nation can conscript a man's food, a man's business, a man's money, a man's life, a man's family, and a man's opinion. If a pacifist find his conscience in conflict with his nationalism, he may be compelled to give up his conscience or else go to prison.

Third, that each nation, in some point congenial with its pride, is supreme. This doctrine, highly colored with emotion, is necessary to support the tremendous claim of the modern dogma of nationalism over the lives and consciences

[158]

of its citizens. Cecil Rhodes said that he thought the British "the greatest people the world has ever seen." Voltaire prophesied: "Some day, to be approved of others, it shall suffice for one to say: This was the taste of the French; it is thus that this illustrious nation thought." Wrote Professor Lasson of Berlin: "We are morally and intellectually superior to all, without peers. It is the same with our organizations and with our institutions." Said a great American diplomat, my personal friend: "God has yet made nothing or nobody equal to the American people; and I don't think He ever will or can." That is nationalism: each nation a sovereign unit, each unit claiming almost absolute power over the lives and consciences of its citizens, and each nation on some point congenial to its pride thinking that it is the best.

Were there time, one might trace the history of this dogma, unravel the strands that, woven together, have produced it. In its present form it is a modern phenomenon developing from the eighteenth century on, but that it is now dominant in the world is clear. Our children's children, looking back upon our time, will know it as the era of nationalism, as we look back and call another age the era of feudalism, and they will see, whether we see it or not, that Christianity's most crucial fight was with the sinister significances of this dogma.

Consider, then, the sharp conflict between the principles of Jesus and this perverted dogma of nationalism.

In the first place, it makes any genuine monotheism impossible. Some people still think that monotheism is primarily an intellectual *tour de force* and they marvel at the flight of imagination and thought which enabled the great Isaiah, centuries before Christ, to think of this vast and varied universe as created by one Power and controlled by one Purpose. The fact is that the doctrine of monotheism developed not so much in spite of an opposing theology as of an opposing nationalism. Those primitive peoples believed in tribal gods because they wanted to, because they hated their enemies and did not wish them to have the same god, because they craved freedom to slaughter their foes untroubled by any haunting and to them blasphemous idea that their god cared for their enemies. One of the first great internationalist utterances in the world's history is in the nineteenth chapter of Isaiah, where the prophet hears God saying, "Blessed be Egypt my people, and Assyria the work of my hands, and Israel mine inheritance." It is as if, during the Great War, some one had imagined God saying, "Blessed be Germany my people, and Austria the work of my hands, and America mine inheritance." Thus the great prophets of Israel, amid international hatreds that exalted many gods, wrought out the high doctrine of monotheism to displace tribal deities.

One does not need at length to say to you who lived through the last conflict that, when nationalism works its inevitable consequence in war, we suffer even today a theological reversion to the primitive type. For war still rips God into tribal gods and sets us praying, each before his own deity, for the blood of his enemies.

Mark Twain was a humorist who often, in his humor, said more serious things than the most solemn preacher says. Once he wrote a prayer for war time:

O Lord our God, help us to tear their soldiers to bloody shreds with our shells; help us to cover their smiling fields with the pale forms of their patriot dead; help us to drown the thunder of the guns with the wounded, writhing in pain; help us to lay waste their humble homes with a hurricane of fire; help us to wring the hearts of their unoffending widows with unavailing grief; help us to turn them out roofless with their little children to wander unfriended through wastes of their desolated land . . . —for our sakes, who adore Thee, Lord, blast their hopes, blight their lives, protract their bitter pilgrimage, make heavy their steps, water their way with their tears, stain the white snow with the blood of their wounded feet! We ask of one who is the Spirit of love and who is the ever faithful refuge and friend of all that are sore beset, and seek His aid with humble and contrite hearts. Grant our prayer, O Lord, and Thine shall be the praise and honor and glory now and ever, Amen.

You see, humorists have a special license to tell the truth—like old court jesters who could take liberties with their lords that no one else dared—and Mark Twain does tell the truth. When as nationalists we pray in war time, beneath our pious phrases that is what we are praying for. And as Mark Twain saw rightly, that is not monotheism but a return to tribal gods.

I am not speaking about this matter as though I were an economist—I am not an economist; or as though I were a politician—I am no politician; but as a man of religion. For religion is involved in war. I believe in God the Father Almighty, Maker of heaven and earth—we cannot really believe that and believe in the tribal gods of war time.

In the second place, this dogma of nationalism not only spoils monotheism but enslaves the Christian conscience. The son of a friend of mine said to his father, "Dad, what is conscience?" and my friend answered, "Son, I don't know, but when that telephone bell rings, you take down the receiver!" If it means anything serious at all to be a Christian, it means *that*. What God and our consciences say to us we must do. There is the supreme allegiance of a religious man. As of old, we must obey God rather than men.

But this runs into direct collision with the new dogma of nationalism. Listen to this announcement of an early nationalist: "The state, it seems to me, is not at all made for religion, but religion is made for the state. . . . The state has supremacy in everything. . . . When the state has pronounced, the church has nothing further to say." That is, all our religious loyalties are to be subservient to the nation and in a pinch we Christians must think what the nation thinks, do what the nation says, believe what the nation believes. No infallible church in all history ever tried to impose upon its devotees a more absolute obedience than this dogma of nationalism would impose upon the citizens. In the United States more popular sentiment than one likes to think is represented in the oft-quoted slogan: "Our country! In her intercourse with foreign nations may she always be in the right; but our country, right or wrong." Right and wrong, God and conscience are to be bent to nationalism. "The king can do no wrong," said the monarchists, and we transfer that idea to the republic.

It is strange how history repeats itself. Why did the Romans persecute the early Christians? Was it because of intolerance toward their religion? Not in the least! The Roman Empire had no interest in persecuting anybody on account of his religion, and the United States today is hardly more free for all sorts of religious faiths and practices than the Roman Empire was then. There is one central reason why the Roman Empire persecuted Christians. They would not worship Cæsar. They would not acknowledge the supreme authority of the state. They put Christ first and, because they would not even scatter incense on the burning altar before Cæsar's statue as an outward symbol acknowledging his supremacy, they went to the lions.

Our American forefathers in the early days of democracy would have agreed with those first Christians. They had just broken the shackles of absolute monarchy and they had not the slightest intention of putting in its place any kind of absolutist state whatsoever. They would have fought this developing dogma of nationalism as they would have fought Satan himself. Even in time of war they held to the primacy of their individual consciences. Abraham Lincoln in the House of Representatives lifted his voice against the Mexican War and on the floor of the same house Joshua R. Giddings called it "a war against an unoffending people, without adequate or just cause, for the purpose of conquest," and said, "I will lend it no aid, no support whatever. I will not bathe my hands in the blood of the people of Mexico, nor will I participate in the guilt of those murders which have been and will hereafter be committed by our army there." In Massachusetts, James Russell Lowell in the *Biglow Papers* poured out his withering scorn against the wickedness and folly of the nation, and in his Boston pulpit Theodore Parker thundered his denunciation against the nation's leaders.

Today, however, were we to exercise such liberty in war time we should be locked up. For the absolute religion of nationalism grows apace and while the old religions have gradu-

ally sloughed off external penalties for heresy, it is nationalism that now has its spies, its Judge Jeffreys on the bench,
its prison cells. A federal judge in this country, with much
unnecessary insult and objurgation, has even refused citizenship to a woman because in her opinions she is a Quaker
about war.

So stealthily has this new conflict between freedom of
conscience and the absolutism of the nationalistic dogma
come upon us that many of us do not recognize its presence.
But it is here. According to this dogma the individual conscience of the religious man is not to be supreme but is to
be harnessed. The bit and the bridle are to be put into its
mouth and it is to be driven by the state. In 1897, in an
audience with the German ambassador in Constantinople,
Sultan Abd-ul Hamid, though a Mohammedan, said that he
had often had occasion to marvel at the Kaiser's truly religious spirit and his deep understanding of the significance of
religion. He shared the Kaiser's conviction, he added, that
religion alone is the foundation of obedience and hence of the
welfare of the peoples. Quite so! Any kaiser and sultan can
agree, though they be Christian and Moslem, on the value of
religion if they are allowed to dress religion in nationalistic
livery and make it their servant to further passive obedience.
God save us from such subservience of conscience in this
nation!

For one of the deepest needs of our nation is the very
opposite: men whose supreme allegience is to God and their
own consciences, and who, therefore, would never dream of
saying, "My country right or wrong," but always, "My
country right to keep her right, my country wrong to make
her right at whatever cost." There is the true patriot, not in
the puppet of the state which the dogma of nationalism would
produce. There is the hope of the people—not in one-hun-
dred-per-centers ready to jump in any direction when the
government cracks the whip, but in men of independent consciences, in time of peace or war, willing to defy the nation
in the interests of the nation.

Every Sunday in the navy the white flag of religion is

floated above the stars and stripes. It is the only flag that ever is floated above the national emblem. It is the symbol of what ought perpetually to be true about our consciences.

In the third place, this developed dogma of nationalism not only spoils monotheism and enslaves the Christian conscience, but it reduces Christianity to a harmless myth and keeps it from being a program of real action. How easy it is to reduce Christianity to a myth! A preëxistent, divine Being, virgin-born into the world, who died an expiatory death, rose in the body on the third day, ascended in the body to the skies and thence straightway will return to set up his millennial government on earth—how easy it is to reduce the Christian gospel to its mythological framework! But what that Being said when he was on earth, the kind of life he lived, the principles of individual and social life he taught—how easy it is to neglect that! And when a man refuses to neglect that, when he finds there the very nub of the whole matter, he comes into irrepressible conflict with the dogma of nationalism.

For one thing, the dogma of nationalism means anarchy. If I should say this morning that I am an anarchist, that would cause a stir. But what is an anarchist if not one who says that each individual is a sovereign unit with no coöperative control over him to represent the interests of the community? And what is nationalism but that very doctrine that each nation is a sovereign unit, that if it wishes to make war it may make war, that if it wishes to build a great army and navy it is at liberty to do so, that, being sovereign in war or peace, it may do what it will so long as it is strong enough to get away with it. My friends, let us call things by their right names. That is anarchy. That is where we are now—in international anarchy. That is where we will be as long as the dogma of nationalism obtains.

This dogma loves to make itself respectable. It arrays itself in the panoply of patriotism. It moves in good society. But, for all that, it is sheer, shameless anarchy, and, because it is anarchy, it means war. While the forces of war are organized, those of peace are not, and the dogma of nationalism does not want them to be. This is the gist of the whole matter: nationalism long since organized the forces of war and now it is fighting with determination against every endeavor to organize the forces of peace. This dogma of nationalism therefore, involving anarchy in theory, involves war in fact.

And such war! There are people yet who think that you can clip this tiger's claws while the wild beast still is at large. They credulously believe that, knowing how to drop bombs on villages, we may be persuaded not to do it in war time; that, poison gases being in our control, so easy to make, so tremendous in effect, we may outlaw them from actual employment when war's passion bursts; that, having within reach the technique of infecting enemy populations with pestilential bacteria, we may be beguiled into not doing it when we need it most. How credulous people are in spite of all the lessons of history! Believe in any superstition you will— believe in witchcraft, believe in demoniacal possession, believe that an eclipse is caused by a dragon swallowing the sun —but how can one believe that when war comes enemies will fail to employ any agency of destruction they can lay their hands to? As each new instrument of death, from the days of bows and arrows to the days of gunpowder, has been ruthlessly employed in spite of all the cries of horror that have been lifted at its introduction, so nothing will prevent the use of any agency of ruin when war bursts.

We face, then, the conclusion that the dogma of nationalism, involving anarchy in theory and war in fact, must work out to its climax: that, as long as that dogma obtains, it will repeatedly happen that one nation will conscript its Christians and another nation will conscript its Christians, and the two nations will hurl their Christians at one another's throats. Those Christians will drop bombs on one another's villages, murder one another's mothers and babies, consolidate vast blockades and starve one another by millions, poison one another with gas, and slaughter one another with pestilences.

Do you seriously think there can be any compromise or

accommodation between this dogma of nationalism on the one side and the spirit of Christ on the other?

Nationalism at its best can be beautiful. At its best it is one of the unifying forces of the world. Here in this country it takes folk of every tribe, tongue, people, and nation and braids them together. It is stronger than creed, stronger than class, stronger than race. It takes diverse multitudes and makes them one, weaving America, like Joseph's coat, of many colors and yet unified. But just because we feel so deeply the beautiful meanings of nationalism when it is at its best, we hate the more this new dogma of nationalism that rips our one God into tribal gods, tramples on the sacred heritage of a free conscience, and makes of our Christianity an idle myth instead of a program of serious social action. Ah, men of Philippi, not all dead yet, who, facing Christ, say still about his gospel: "not lawful for us to receive, or to observe, being Romans"!

Christianity More than Duty—Not Weight but Wings

OUR thought starts with the fact that many modern people have been reducing their religion to ever simpler and simpler terms until it consists of little more than trying to do their duty. They have found in the old beliefs so many incredible elements and in the old churches so many distasteful practices that in recent years the history of their Christian thinking has been progressive elimination. So far as quantity is concerned, at any rate, they have not nearly so much religion as they used to have. They have been "reducing" religiously. And some of them have reduced so much that one of them could say to me the other day, "Well, a man who keeps the Golden Rule is a good enough Christian for me."

In this regard how different the generations are! Some generations work for a maximum of faith. They enlarge the borders of their Christian thought and experience, enrich it with all the wealth they can discern, claim for it the art, the science, the philosophy of their time, so that the whole spirit of their generation seems to be saying, not How *little*? but How *much* can we believe? Our time, however, like others before it, notably the eighteenth century, is in a different mood. One of the commonest problems presented to any counselor of souls is the typical question, How little can a man believe and still be a Christian? Somehow to get by on a minimum, to pare, shave, and trim until we have this whole business of being Christian so reduced that one may sum it up as fidelity to the Golden Rule—that is characteristic of our time.

Moreover, the consequences also are becoming characteristic. At last we do get our Christianity reduced to a minimum. There is, let us say, very little left in it except a few ethical principles. Whether by downright disbelief or by neglect and sheer forgetfulness, we have eliminated one thing after another until nearly everything is gone except this final residuum: we try to do our duty. With this minimum for our religion, then, we go out into a generation like this— a terrific generation, on every side driving men and women into cynicism and despair, one of the most distracted and chaotic times in history so that even the wisest often feel like Gulliver when he landed in the country of the giants— and here we discover that a religion so reduced that it means little more than blowing on our hands and trying to do our duty is not ample and profound enough. You remember the saying of Isaiah, "The bed is shorter than that a man can stretch himself on it; and the covering narrower than that he can wrap himself in it." Many a modern man has reduced his Christian faith to the point where its inadequacy is like that.

In the membership of a single club in one of our American cities, there has been, we are told, one suicide after another this last year. In general we may take it for granted that those men were of high principle and that under ordinary circumstances we could have trusted them to try to do their duty. It is not enough, is it? Soon or late, life puts every one of us in a situation where we need something more than exhortation to duty: we need horizons around our life and profound spiritual meanings in it; we need reserves of inner power available for daily use and a philosophy which is to the dry channels of our courage what rain among the mountains is to the parched streams of the summertime. That is, we need some of the very things which many people have been eliminating from their Christianity.

This morning, therefore, what I say to you I say first to my own soul about a vital matter. Religious life, like economic life, moves in cycles—inflation and deflation. In this last generation we have been religiously deflating. It was absolutely necessary. There were so many incredible elements in popular Christianity that deflation was inevitable. Only the other day I had a letter from a man who thought it a great matter to believe that he could affect the weather by praying about it. What incredible things people do believe in the name of religion! The crude supernaturalisms of popular Christianity, our unbelievable theologies and mythologies, our magical sacramentarianisms and theories of Biblical or ecclesiastical infallibility, have made inevitable reduction, elimination, deflation. But, my friends, that never can be the final word about the spiritual life. When a man talks about music he does not say, How little music can I know and still be called musical? When a man thinks of friendship he does not say, How little a way can I venture into it and still be called friendly? When a man thinks of his family he does not say, How little of a father can I be? What a starved soul such parsimony would produce! Now, in its depths the Christian life is like music, friendship, and family. It is a rich realm concerning which a man ought to say, not How *little*? but How *much*?

Consider, then, some things which we would better not eliminate from our Christianity.

For one thing, a vital Christian faith is much more than doing our duty, in that it involves for those who understand it a deep sense of sacredness in our own lives. Once when this church was under construction, I came into the chancel to watch the workmen graving the stone and, seeing an especially beautiful piece of carving, I expressed appreciation. "Yes," said the workman, "that is lovely but you do not need to thank us for it. You never could know what it means to us to have a chance to do our work this way. Generally they tell us to hurry, that it is good enough as it is, but here we have a chance to do our work as beautifully as it can be done. No one can estimate what that means to us." I am right—am I not?—in thinking that after the chancel had been dedicated by that attitude of the workmen there was very little we could do to dedicate it further, that this spirit of the artist, loving to do his work as beautifully as it can be done, is one of the noblest things we know, and that as William Blake rightly said long ago, a man who is not an artist is not a Christian.

Now, when we think of that workman we feel at once

that around his doing of his duty, sustaining it, clarifying it, putting meaning into it, was a sense of sacredness in his life so that his work had to be handled as beautifully as it could be done. Do not say that is not religious. Wherever we touch the sense of sacredness we are dealing with religion. Religion always has been saying about *something* that it is sacred —this mountain, this temple, this altar—and the genius of Christianity is that with this sense of sacredness it steps inside a man's life and says about personality, You are sacred; you are a temple of the living God; now are you the son of God.

Many of us here would bear witness that whatever Christianity has done or left undone in our lives, the finest living of it that we ever saw in our homes or among our friends has brought this consequence, which we never will be able to shake off—the conviction that life is a trust, that we must not abuse it or waste it or desecrate it or throw it away, but use it as beautifully as can be done.

We never can understand Jesus without that. He did his duty. Indeed he did. But how little a thing that is to say of him! Look at all the unexplained remainder there,—his radiancy, his buoyancy, his reserves of power, his height of character,—the godlike in him which has fascinated the centuries. When you enter that realm you find at least this much over and above the doing of duty: life was sacred to him; it was a trust; the Eternal had committed it to him; it must be handled as beautifully as possible.

Do you think that we, in the active doing of our duty or in the bearing of those inevitable tragedies which, soon or late, life brings to every one of us, are likely to get on well if our inner souls become paganized and the sense of sacredness departs from them? A friend facing a terrific tragedy said to me once, "Life is a trust and no matter what happens to a man he must carry on with it finely to the end." That is a great religion—life is a trust. I beg of you, do not eliminate that from your Christianity.

Again, a vital Christian faith is much more than doing one's duty, in that it involves one's interior, spiritual companionships. You remember Marcus Aurelius' saying that our lives are dyed the color of our imaginations. That is to say, the good life is not simply blowing on one's hands and doing one's duty; the quality of life comes from the deep fountains of the imagination and the color of life is determined by the tincture of our thoughts.

True as this is in general about all our habitual thinking, it is especially true about our interior, personal companionships. Here in this city multitudes of people live who do not deeply affect our character. Outward, physical fellowships do not make the deep difference. Far inside our souls, however, some of us habitually live with persons who make all the difference in the world to our quality. To some of us solitude is not solitude. It is richly populous. We have lovely persons to live with. Some of them are still on earth; though divided by the miles, they live in us and make life beautiful. Some long since have passed from the seen into the unseen but still they dwell in us, inhabiting the mansions of memory and imagination. And some of them are the great souls of the race, the poets and singers and artists, the saints and the prophets.

My friends, the good life is not simply doing our duty; it is the interior richness that comes from living in great companionships. A poor German schoolmaster, we are told, who lived in a humble house in a small village, carved over his doorway this proud inscription: "Dante, Molière, and Goethe live here." That schoolmaster had learned the secret that the richness of life lies in one's spiritual companionships.

Turn, now, to a Christian like Paul and hear him say, "I live; yet not I, but Christ liveth in me." Unfortunately, we have frozen words like that into theology. We have stiffened them into dogma until the life has gone out of them. If a schoolmaster can say that Dante and Molière and Goethe live with him, why cannot a man say that Christ lives in him? Why must we dry the reality out of an experience which at first was so fresh, genuine, and transforming?

That experience is at the very center of the Christian life. Is somebody here still thinking that all there is to

[171]

Christianity is keeping the Golden Rule? My friends, keeping the Golden Rule is a very great matter, but alas for a man if he reduces his Christianity simply to that! We need also the inner richness of great companionships. Without them the bed is shorter than that a man can stretch himself on it; and the covering narrower than that he can wrap himself in it.

It is the people who forget this who keep saying that there is nothing in worship. Nothing in worship? Life all work and no worship? I can understand your saying that, if you mean that some elements in the stereotyped worship of the church have no value for you. To be sure, we can spoil anything by formality. But worship, worthship, the recognition of worth, the love of excellence, deliberate sensitiveness to the highest that we know, the hospitable opening of the soul's doors to the Divine, the welcoming of life's noblest companionships—how do you get on from day to day without that? The value of our life depends upon the quality of the things we are sensitive to. Take your dog for a walk through the woods and the difference between what you and the dog get out of it depends on the difference in the things you are sensitive to.

What, then, are the great hours of human life, the hours of elevation, emancipation, purification? They are the hours of worship, when the soul expands before something greater than itself. Many people do live by this but do not call it worship. Keats once read a new translation of Homer and, as everybody knows, sang afterwards that he felt

> . . . like some watcher of the skies
> When a new planet swims into his ken;
> Or like stout Cortez when with eagle eyes
> He stared at the Pacific—and all his men
> Look'd at each other with a wild surmise—
> Silent, upon a peak in Darien.

Was he not carried out of himself by something greater than himself, to which he gave himself? Indeed, some of us here today need that experience religiously as an habitual resource more than we need almost anything beside. We have tried to do our duty. Indeed we have. Sometimes we have desperately tried to do our duty, but a man can go on year after year trying to do his duty and still find life thin and poor, cold and parched. Life is something more than just blowing on your hands and trying to do your duty. We need elevation and liberation and purification, and that does not come from blowing on your hands.

> . . . I have felt
> A presence that disturbs me with the joy
> Of elevated thoughts.

Once more, a vital Christian faith is more than doing our duty because it confers on one who understands it resources of inner, spiritual power. Without that, trying to live the Christian life may well ruin a man. I mean that when a man gets the duty side of Christianity without the power side of it he is in an unhappy place. That can easily be seen. A few moments ago we quoted with approval the arresting idea of William Blake that a man who is not an artist is not a Christian. Now, one of the marks of a true artist always is that he has high, inner standards of excellence so that, no matter what the community in general may be saying about his work, he is utterly miserable if he is not living up to his own, inward demand upon himself. Everybody, then, who knows the biographies of great artists understands that it is anything but a peaceful experience to be one. Chopin used to pace the room, chew his quill pens to pieces, tear up his manuscripts, and live for days in torment. The trouble was not that Chopin could not write music good enough to please the public. That would have been easy. The trouble was that Chopin could not write music good enough to please himself.

The other day, in a new and revealing monograph on Shakespeare I ran across this: "Shakespeare, therefore, wrote to please his audience. But first and foremost and all the time, he wrote to please himself." That is always the mark of a great artist. As one of our fine critics recently put it, "The artist's conscience is a fearful thing." Well, a man who is not an artist is not a Christian. The Christian's conscience is a fearful thing. Let a man be trained in it in his home; from his youth let him have drawn upon his imagination the portraiture of a Christlike life so that, whatever he may do theologically, psychologically he cannot escape from that haunting ideal of what it means to live beautifully; let him so get the duty side of Christianity but miss the power side and he is an unhappy man. The offices of the psychiatrists and the confessional conferences of the ministers are littered up with such "conscience complexes,"—that is what they call it,—a high standard of duty and a low level of power. The bed is shorter than that a man can stretch himself on it; and the covering narrower than that he can wrap himself in it.

Matthew Arnold said once that conduct is, at the very lowest computation, three-fourths of life. I do not believe it. The older I grow the less I believe it. I know people who could not go on from one day to another if they did believe it. Granted that a man wants to do his duty, a large part of life is learning to tap resources of power to do it with. Some of you, tired out and whipped, turn to nature and like Wordsworth find there a presence divine. You come back with margins of reserve around your need to do your duty with. The other night after a long, hard day, I listened to a poet read his poetry and, unexpected miracle! although I started that hour from a sheer sense of duty, tired out, I came to the end of it reinvigorated and refreshed, like a new man in a new world.

Granted that a man wants to do his duty, most of life is tapping reserves of power to do it with. That is at the center of the Christian gospel. The New Testament rings with the note of power: "strengthened with power through his Spirit in the inward man." The places where men do their duty are often conspicuous where all can see. The cross on Calvary stands out against the sky. See, cry the centuries, what a deed was done there! But, my friends, behind every Calvary, where a magnificent deed is done, is always Gethsemane, where the doer in solitude taps the resources of inner power. No Gethsemane, no Calvary.

This, then, is the conclusion of the matter. Do not, I beg of you, eliminate God from your Christianity. Even though you have a thousand unanswered questions about him, do not reduce this amazing universe to accidental, purposeless matter. This last week I had a letter from one of my radio audience, obviously a thoughtful, intelligent man deeply devoted to personal duty and to social reform, and this in part was what he said: "I am an uneasy but conscientious materialist. My loss of faith, which I used to regard as an asset, is now so great a burden that I rarely dare even to think of it." Desperately trying to do his duty with a philosophy so devastating that he does not dare to think of it—the bed is shorter than that a man can stretch himself on it; and the covering narrower than that a man can wrap himself in it.

Religious Faith: Privilege or Problem?

WE COULD take our text almost at random this morning from the book of Psalms. "The Lord is my strength and song"—these words happen to come from the 118th Psalm, but they express a characteristic attitude of all genuine religion. We must recognize, however, that there are many people today deeply interested in religion, concerned about it and given to much thought upon it, who could not say that at all. What they would have to say would be very different—The Lord is my problem. How familiar that is! God is a problem; prayer is a problem; the church is a problem; the Bible is a problem; immortality is a problem. Everything about religion has become a problem, difficult to solve, much worried over, and long discussed.

On one of our college campuses there has been held for years the annual Week of Prayer. Recently they have changed the name. It now becomes the Annual Religious Forum, and with that charming candor which makes the younger generation famous, the editor of the college paper explains why. The editorial reads:

> . . . The venerable institution formerly called the Week of Prayer has at last been relieved of the weight of a misnomer. . . . With the thoroughly modern sounding name, "Annual Religious Forum," we feel that it ought to enjoy a new lease of life. . . .
> The word "forum" means a place where questions are thrown open to discussion. This word expresses perfectly the modern attitude towards religion. . . .
> Instead of furnishing an inexhaustible well of peace, religion has become a source of harassed confusion. The painful attempt to work out religious problems for ourselves has taken the place of acquiescence of authority.

There you have it. That is truth well put. There are few

things more typical of our contemporary religious situation than that. For multitudes of people religion has ceased being their strength and song, and has become a matter of discussion and debate. The characteristic symbol of much modern religion has become a discussion group. Surely, some of our religious dryness, our lack of spiritual spring and spontaneity, our dearth of joy and radiance goes back to that. Some generations are predominantly appreciative. They enjoy their religion. They make a festival of it. They create great music to celebrate it and build classic cathedrals to enshrine it. And other generations are predominantly critical. They ask questions, raise doubts, seek for reasons, analyze their faith. The first kind of generation instinctively cries, "The Lord is my strength and song," but the second finds the Lord a very difficult problem indeed.

There is, I take it, no doubt as to which kind of generation we are living in. One hears it commonly said that there never was a time when there was more interest in religion than now. That may be so. At a typical midnight session on a college campus one may be fairly sure that two subjects will be discussed: love and religion—but, mark it! it is religion as a matter of debate; it is religion being botanized, its stamens and pistils being classified and tabulated; it is not religion as a matter of joyful confidence and song.

Let us face frankly the disabilities of this situation, for, with all the advantages of it, a generation where the symbol of religion has become a discussion group has its disabilities. So we recall the familiar whimsy:

> A Centipede was happy quite,
>   Until a frog in fun
> Said, "Pray, which leg comes after which?"
> This raised her mind to such a pitch,
> She lay distracted in the ditch,
>   Considering how to run.

Multitudes of religious people are like that centipede. Once their religion was spontaneous. They took it for granted; they depended on it and lived by it. But now, with many questions raised concerning it, it has become a problem and they lie distracted in the ditch.

To all of this I can imagine some one saying: But religion *is* a problem, and nothing any one can say will stop its being that. Here on the one side we have an inherited faith, with imaginations of God and his relation to the universe at large and us within it formulated in prescientific ages, before men dreamed that the earth went about the sun; and on the other side all this new knowledge from Galileo to Einstein. Religion is a problem. What do you think of God? How do you imagine him? What do you make of prayer? How do you justify the idea that God is good in the presence of the miseries of men? How can you argue for the ultimate sacredness of personality, and how do you picture immortality? It is a problem. You may not like it that religion has ceased being for so many people a singing confidence by which they gladly live and has become a matter of debate, but it is a problem and no wishing will stop its being that.

To which I answer, Very well, it is all that to me. Once it was not. In my adolescent youth I took religion for granted, without question, and then one year in a storm the questions came. Since then religion has been a problem. It will be till I die. My life's vocation is to face religious problems. I have no use for an uncritical religion that is afraid of questions. But, for all that, I refuse to lie distracted in the ditch. Nature is a problem too. Ask the scientists and see—abyss after abyss of problems unsolved and questions unanswered there. If you approach it from that one angle, move up to it by that one road, concentrate your thought on that one aspect of it, nature can loom as a gigantic problem. That, however, is not the whole story. Nature is my strength and song. I love her. I love her mountains and her seas, her quiet moods and the grandeur of her storms. In wintertime, amid the cañons of these city streets, I comfort my soul with memories of her trees. I hunger for the lakes where the trout rise and for the dash of her sea spray on windy days. If, now, you say, You have no right so naively to enjoy nature when nature has become a tremendous problem with thousands of unanswered questions, I say, Starve your own soul if you will, but not mine.

> . . . How oft—
> In darkness and amid the many shapes
> Of joyless daylight; when the fretful stir
> Unprofitable, and the fever of the world,
> Have hung upon the beatings of my heart—
> How oft, in spirit, have I turned to thee,
> O sylvan Wye! thou wanderer through the woods,
> How often has my spirit turned to thee!

Problem or no problem, nature is my strength and song.

Or, again, the family is a problem too. Indeed it is. If religion has gotten over into the discussion-group class, what will one say about the family? Read some books about it, listen to some speeches on it, and one would suppose that the family was that alone. No theory as to family life is unquestioned and no practice is beyond doubt. That, however, is not the whole story. There are some of us yet to whom the family is our strength and song.

We of the older generation well remember Professor John Fiske of Harvard. Once he wrote a letter to his wife describing a visit with Herbert Spencer, the philosopher. He was being entertained in Mr. Spencer's English home, and when Mr. Spencer asked him about his family he showed him a picture of his wife and children. That night he wrote his wife about it: "I showed Spencer the little picture of our picnic-wagon with the children inside. When I realized how lonely he must be without any wife and babies of his own, and how solitary he is in all his greatness, I had to pity him. Then as I watched him studying that picture and gazing at our children's faces I said to myself, 'That wagon-load of youngsters is worth more than all the philosophy ever concocted, from Aristotle to Spencer inclusive!'"

So be it! If, now, one says, But you have no right so naively to enjoy the family when everybody knows that the family in modern thought has become a problem, I say, Starve your own soul if you will, but not mine. To some of us yet the home is the loveliest relationship on earth, our strength and joy.

Today we are claiming that exactly that same thing is true about religion. Every area of life is made up of two aspects, problem and privilege. If a man tries to monopolize the privilege alone and forget the problem, he becomes a sentimentalist. Granted that! That is a familiar emphasis today. But if a man becomes so obsessed with problems, holds them so closely to his eye that he can see nothing else, he becomes dry, sophisticated, unhappy, uncreative, futile. And particularly in religion he ceases having strength and song and has only a debate.

Consider, for example, the central matter of religion—God. Say that very word to some people today and their instinctive response is a puzzled awareness of difficulty. There have been generations when the thought of God brought back a singing answer:

> Holy, Holy, Holy, Lord God of Hosts!
> Heaven and earth are full of thy glory.

But today try the psychological test on many a casual Christian, saying, "God," and see what a stream of questions you start. Is there really a God? What is he like? How do you imagine him? How can you justify his ways with men? What a problem he is! Well, of course, he is a problem. Here we are with our little minds developing for a few millennia upon this midget planet in an immeasurable cosmos. Do we think that with our butterfly nets we can capture the sun at noon, that we expect with our wits to capture the blazing truth about the Power that made all things? The idea of God is the most august that ever allured the imagination of man. That is no reason, however, why we should lie distracted in the ditch. After all, what we are driving at when we think of God is not obscure. It can be clearly put.

There are two sides to us, the physical and the spiritual. There are two sets of faculties, not far off but here in us, the world of matter and the world of spiritual values—on the one side things that we can see, touch, weigh, and measure; on the other side, the invisible, the intangible, the love of goodness, truth, and beauty. On the one side is what we call body, on the other side what we call soul. When, now, we say that we believe in God, we mean that never can we adequately interpret the Power that made us in terms of the physical alone, that the spiritual life came from Spiritual Life, and that by the road that starts in us as spirit we must send our thought out toward God.

If that is true, we do not need to solve all the problems about God before we begin to enjoy him. Spiritual life is here. Here is where we first meet it and most practically deal with it—not far off, that we must climb the steeps to bring it down, but here. Wherever goodness, truth, beauty, love are, there is the Life Divine; there we most intimately know it and most practically handle it. There is the near end of God. And that Life Divine, loved and served, can be our strength and song.

How many problems there are about this envelope of atmosphere encompassing our globe! Men send up balloons and airplanes yet to find answers to unanswered questions about its extent, its density, its quality. Man, however, does not need to solve all the problems about the atmosphere before he begins to enjoy the air. That is here. We can breathe it, love it, live by it. There are times when man ought to puzzle his mind about the problems of the atmosphere, but there are other times when a man does well to say, Give me this northwest wind that blows the fog away; I love it.

Unless a man is a downright, dogmatic atheist, he can have that same kind of experience with God. We do not need to solve all the problems about God before we can begin to be enriched by him. As one listens to this contemporary debate one longs to speak one's mind. Discuss God, one would say; he is well worth discussion, and there are depths beyond depths in him that the longest plummets of your debate will never reach; but for your soul's sake enjoy him, depend on him, live by him, be true to him. When you say "God," you mean spiritual life projected to the very center of the universe. But that spiritual life which you are projecting to the center of the universe is also here. Here is where you start with it. Wherever goodness shines or love and beauty sing, there is the near end of God. Love him there; be true to him; be enriched by him.

One feels sure that some people present are in this line of fire. They are excessively problem-conscious. It is a familiar type of modern pathology. For there is nothing that cannot be reduced to a problem. English literature can and some of us have seen it done. There are problems historical about Shakespeare's plays, problems biographical about his life, problems concerning the derivation of his plots, problems of scansion and prosody, of diction and vocabulary. How Shakespeare can be reduced to a problem, and how some of us have seen it done in the classroom until we wanted to cry, Just for an hour let us declare a moratorium on problems and enjoy him!

> Wilt thou be gone? It is not yet near day.
> It was the nightingale, and not the lark,
> That pierced the fearful hollow of thine ear;
> Nightly she sings on yond pomegranate tree:
> Believe me, love, it was the nightingale.

To be sure, there are literary problems about Romeo and Juliet, but, after all, Romeo and Juliet are among the loveliest lovers in the world. Once in a while, at least, enjoy them. To be so obsessed with problems about Shakespeare that you lose Shakespeare—that is a pity. But there are multitudes to-day who so lose God.

There must be lives here that bear witness to the need of this emphasis. You have problems about Christ. Of course you do, problems about the ancient documents where his life was recorded, about the stories of his birth, the miracles attributed to him, the prescientific world-views he shared with his generation, the early church's theological interpretations of him—endless problems. And such is the capacity of the human mind to be obsessed with problems, even when dealing with something singularly beautiful, that there are many today who never get any nearer to Christ than that. He is a problem.

That is not simply a pity; that deserves to be called stupid. To be sure, to neglect the problems as though they were not there, so that, credulously uncritical, one writes a life of Christ such as Papini did, that is stupid too, sentimentally stupid. But, after all, my friends, the most significant thing that ever happens on this planet is the coming of great personality. In science or art or religion that is true. The whole world steps forward when great personality arrives. He breaks like a tremendous wave through sandbars that have barricaded us, letting us lesser waves flow in after him.

So came Christ to the world. Do we really mean that in his teachings of the good life we can see nothing but problems? In that luminous personality that incarnated them and made those teachings beautiful, so that across the centuries men like George Matheson have said, "Son of Man, whenever I doubt of life, I think of Thee," and men like George Tyrrell have said, "Again and again I have been tempted to give up the struggle, but always the figure of that strange Man hanging on the cross sends me back to my task again," do you see nothing but problems?

That is being pathologically problem-conscious. That is like taking a Beethoven sonata and seeing there nothing but a puzzle of date, composition, documentation, rendition, until the one thing is forgotten which is most worth remembering, that a Beethoven sonata is very beautiful and can enrich the spirit.

Be sure of this: anybody who finds in religion nothing but discussion never commends it to anybody. In any realm, be it science or art or religion, nobody commends anything to anybody unless he first enjoys it, glories in it, depends on it, and is enriched by it. Wanted, therefore, Christians fearless and honest, to be sure, in facing problems, but so deeply enriched by their religion, so practically living it, that they commend it as a subject well deserving to be discussed!

You have problems about prayer. Of course you have. Be honest with them. But, I beg of you, find some way of praying that is real to you. Do not let prayer stay merely a puzzle. A friend once said to me, "I do not pray the way you do." "Well," I said, "how do you pray?" And he answered, "On the piano." I have heard him doing it, improvising. From the too hectic fret of modern business he turned at times to another spiritual technique, opened himself, became responsive, and talked with the Divine in a language that steadied and enriched him. If you cannot pray as you would, then pray as you can, but do not leave that great realm involved in prayer and worship merely a problem.

Or you have problems about the Bible. I hold a chair in a theological seminary on that subject, so that when you have told all the problems about the Scripture that puzzle you, I ought to be able to go on and tell you others still, but that is no reason for lying distracted in the ditch. In this book are passages which poured up out of the souls of men in hours of insight and which have been remembered all these centuries because deep calleth unto deep still at the noise of their waterfalls. If you cannot understand all the Bible, make something worth while out of that much of it you can understand, but do not leave the greatest religious literature of mankind a mere problem.

This reduction of religion to a problem has become so familiar that some people today are using it as a defense-mechanism. They hide behind it. They push their problems to the front, like old savages who have been known to fight behind their women and children. Faced by the rich opportunities or the urgent duties of the Christian life, they erect an interrogation point and hide behind it. They have discovered that Christianity is easier to discuss than to live, and they are dodging the living of it behind the discussion of it. How much of that there is today!

I know well that I am dealing honestly with some one's conscience here when I say, Get out from behind that interrogation point! That is no place for a man to hide. Whatever problems there may be, there is positive and practical Christian living that you could undertake if you really wanted to.

As for some of you—and there are multitudes of you in

the world today—whose religion quite honestly has gotten over into the discussion-group class, remember that the deepest and loveliest experiences of life are never reached by discussion only. Discuss love; read all the books about it; inform yourself about every modern theory concerning it; hold your campus sessions on it; debate its history, physiology, psychology, codes and laws; but, however far you push your discussions of love, you will not reach love by that alone. Love is an adventure of the whole personality. One comes to understand it, not so much by discussing it as by giving oneself to it.

So is religion. Real religion, like real love, lies not at the end of a discussion, but at the end of the soul's adventure.

You are right—how many problems there are in religion! How much we wish we did have answers to some of our questions! Here in the church we would like to help you find them. We stand for the free discussion of religion. But if some of us are going to get to the heart of the matter, we must go deeper. We will have to take our souls in hand and say, O my soul, religion is like nature or music or the family, full of problems but with something deeper there—life, life that is life indeed, our strength and song!

Getting Out of Us the Best
That Is in Us

MANY people habitually wish that they could possess themselves of qualities which they lack. Cursed with bad temper, they want good temper; timid, they want courage; bothered by sensuality, they crave emotional peace. As they picture the situation, they commonly wonder where these desirable goods are to be obtained. Where does one get them? Sometimes they even shop around for them and if they pray about the matter they probably say, O God, give me—give me good temper, or courage, or peace.

Of all ways of imagining the situation this is the most false and discouraging. Nobody can put qualities into us from the outside. It ought, then, to be practically profitable for us to come at this common problem from another angle. These powers and virtues of the soul without which the good life is impossible are in us already. Indeed they are. They are in us already, undeveloped, imprisoned, but there—seeds that never have been watered and so have never grown, dynamic powers that have slumbered in our souls because the right prince never called their sleeping beauty to awake.

You remember the occasion when Jesus turned to Simon and said, "Thou art Peter." Now "Peter" means "rock" and if there was one thing that Simon visibly fell short of being, it was that. Vacillating, mercurial, temperamental, swift in emotion and uncertain in stability—in all that group he was about the last naturally to be called "rock." Yet Jesus said to him the stimulating word which we shall try to say to ourselves this morning. It is in you, he said; being a rock is in you; thou art Peter; the imprisoned splendor of a steadfast life is there and needs but to be released.

Surely, that way of looking at the situation is worth considering, and biography reveals the truth of it. Among the outstanding memories of my young manhood is the marvelous

ships, personalities that can release those hidden springs and elicit in us the self-expression of our best.

That is what we are pleading for, my friends, the much abused thing, self-expression. The sinners have tried to monopolize it. They have sadly messed up the world with their rendition of it. Come, they have said, let us be drunk and express ourselves; let us give free play to sensual indulgence and express ourselves. Then the Puritan mind, horrified by that, has risen in opposition, crying out against self-expression as though self-restraint were the ideal. We never will get anywhere by that route. The only way we can conquer self-expression is by self-expression. Come, let us get gloriously out of us the best that is in us—that is the answer.

If some one protests, saying, Yes, but that is not Christianity; Jesus said, "Deny yourself"; not self-expression but self-denial is Christianity; I say, Consider artists who deny themselves so seriously for their art's sake that one of our best critics writes that "art begins where freedom leaves off." Walk around that and take the full measure of its truth, all exponents of loose self-expression! Art begins where freedom leaves off. That is to say, real art begins where self-discipline and self-denial take possession of the soul. But why do artists so deny themselves? That they may express themselves.

So Jesus did say, "Deny yourself." He is saying it yet. But when he talks about the ultimate end for which such self-denial is indispensable, he rises into another kind of language altogether. "I came that they may have life, and may have it abundantly." Get gloriously out of yourself the best that is there. Self-denial is never anything but means. The end is self-expression. Lose yourself in something worth disciplining yourself to serve and, so losing yourself, you will find yourself. No, we cannot set what we are saying this morning over against the message of Jesus. Peter and James and John expressed themselves. Who ever would have thought that what Jesus got out of them was there?

This is Abraham Lincoln's birthday. You do not need from me a tribute to his elevated character. I am not going to talk about Lincoln—and yet I am talking about Lincoln. This sermon came in part from brooding over him. At first there seemed to be little in him. Those closest to him never dreamed what was there. It was not easy for the imprisoned splendor to escape. The very best in him never did come out until the end, when he rose magnificently to meet the terrific responsibilities of the presidency. In the fine phrase of Jeremiah, all his lifelong he kept bringing out the precious from the common. I wonder if there ever was a man in history who more amazingly got out of himself the best that was there.

My friends, that is about the least—is it not?—that any of us can try to do, and it is about the most also.

For a few moments let us ask ourselves some leading questions about those forces and influences which help a man thus to get the best out of himself.

For one thing, what about our religious faith? A vital religious faith, a deep conviction about God,—assurance, that is, that our human life has spiritual origin, spiritual backing, spiritual destiny, and that things unseen are real and eternal, —is one of the most powerful influences in the world in helping a man to bring out the best that is in him.

Did you see a recently published interview with Mr. Clarence Darrow? Mr. Darrow, I take it, is our foremost American atheist. Now in his seventy-sixth year, after an able, distinguished, and public-spirited career, he sends back his message to the younger generation coming up the slope behind him. This is what the newspapers report him as saying: "If I were a young man, with life ahead of me, I think I'd chuck it all, the way things are now. The odds are too great against you, and anyway, the world is all wrong nowadays." "I certainly have no encouragement for the young bloods that are just starting out looking for jobs. The sooner they jump out of windows, the sooner they'll find peace."

So that is the message of the foremost atheist of America to the younger generation!

To be sure, not all atheists would feel that way or say that thing and yet I do not see how one can read our modern atheistic literature, with its Menckens and Cabells, and not feel the abiding and constantly illustrated kinship between irreligion and cynicism. At any rate, Mr. Darrow says, "If I were a young man, with life ahead of me, I think I'd chuck it all." Well, I would not. You young people are going out into a world of difficulty. Some of you are all dressed up with education and nowhere to go. It is not a hospitable generation that invites you to live in it but I would not chuck it all. You are going to live through some of the most momentous days in human history. You are going to see changes in our economic and international life that will either make or break our Western civilization. If sometimes you have envied those who lived in the crucial days of ancient Greece or Rome, you can spare your envy now. These days ahead of us are going to be more exciting and more consequential. I would not chuck it all. If I could secure a job that would somehow keep body and soul together, I would interest myself in some cause of public welfare, would get hold of some handle and lift, would have some part, though only that of water-boy, in this game that humanity must play. I would not chuck it all.

That is not because I am a better man than Mr. Darrow. Mr. Darrow is an able and worth-while character. It is because I have another philosophy, a profound conviction about the ultimate meaning of life, which cannot chuck it all or jump out of windows to find peace, or even feel about humanity the cynicism of which such words are the exaggerated symbols. Through this turbulent generation God is marching still, as he has marched through many another like it in history, to ends beyond our picturing. "Wherefore we faint not; but though our outward man is decaying, yet our inward man is renewed day by day. . . . while we look not at the things which are seen, but at the things which are not seen: for the things which are seen are temporal; but the things which are not seen are eternal."

That kind of faith does make an immeasurable difference when a man endeavors to get out of himself the best that is there. There are days when difficulties come, when looming

deny the Lord thrice and go out to weep bitterly? It was not easy for Simon to believe that Peter was in him.

I well recall the day when a young man poured out a broken-hearted tale of moral dilapidation and defeat. When he was through, I said to him, "My friend, you are a fine-spirited, high-minded youth." I think I never was looked at with more startled eyes. "Yes," I said, "you are a clean, fine-spirited, high-minded youth. That integrity is in you. If that were not in you, you would not be feeling the way you do about what you have done. You are a fine boy." I can hear him yet as he bowed himself down and wept. You see, it was the old story over again: Simon, thou art Peter.

If, however, we are to believe that, if we are creatively to identify ourself with our best self until it becomes our real self, a friendly voice must say it to us. O Thou great Friend of all the sons of men, say it to some of us today! Tomorrow we are going out into a difficult world. Tomorrow we shall be impinged upon by a society that constantly appeals to our worst. Tomorrow we shall be tempted to think that we cannot get the best out of us amid the handicaps and hardships of this time. Tomorrow we are likely to forget that difficult days do two things to people: in some bring out the worst, in others bring out the best. There are personalities like Lincoln who never get out of themselves the best that is there until they face terrific difficulty. Tomorrow that test is going to fall on some of us. Therefore today, O God, give us a listening ear: Simon, Simon, thou art Rock!

The Fine Art of Making
Goodness Attractive

OUR thought today, however far afield it may ultimately carry us, starts close at home in the simple and familiar fact that nothing so much helps us to live a good life as somebody who makes goodness attractive. We are not forced into goodness nor exhorted into it nor legislated into it; we are allured into it. Concerning any genuine goodness in any one of us today, we may be sure that sometime somebody made that kind of goodness attractive.

We need not be surprised, then, to discover that in the New Testament there is a verse which reads: "Adorn the doctrine of God our Saviour in all things." The verse is found in the letter to Titus in a passage describing the virtues of the good life, rising to a climax in which the writer says that Christians ought to show "all good fidelity; that they may adorn the doctrine of God our Saviour in all things."

It is as though the author were saying to that early church: This teaching of yours about the meaning of life, about the God behind it and the hopes ahead of it—you must do more than believe it, more than argue it; you must adorn it. Make your lives an ornament of it. Dress it in the garments of captivating character. O Church of Christ, small in opportunity and despised in power, going out into the Roman Empire, if you are to win the world, make your goodness attractive.

This morning I present to you that old appeal as one of the most necessary messages that we moderns can attend to. That the appeal in general is valid seems clear. In every realm doctrine—teaching, that is, a true idea of the matter in hand—is basic. A Gothic cathedral is founded upon architectural doctrine. Every step in architectural evolution, from the mud hut up, depends on an advance in architectural doctrine.

But when for the first time some of us stood in a cathedral and fairly wept for joy because we thought we heard the angels singing, "Holy, holy, holy" among its aisles and arches, it was not the doctrine that fascinated us but the way it had been adorned in the expanded spaces and elevated altitudes of the house of God. So if you hold that the basic Christian ideas of life are true in comparison, let us say, with materialism or atheism, I agree. But, my friends, the doctrines by themselves will not win their way. O Church of Christ, going out into this modern world, if you are to be victorious, adorn your teaching by attractive lives.

This is the more important just now because for a decade and more we have been dealing with a bear market in goodness. Our basic morality has sadly slumped in private character and in public life, from sex to citizenship.

A Spanish story has it that a Gypsy once went to confession and the priest asked him if he knew the Ten Commandments of the Law of God, to which the Gypsy answered, "Well, Father, it's this way. I *was* going to learn them but I heard talk that they were going to do away with them." One suspects that many today have not learned the commands of God because there has been much talk about doing away with them.

Be sure that I am not thinking now of little things, of external changes in codes, of new manners and customs, of fresh freedom in word and action. There is too much at stake which concerns the very substance of morals to grow hot and bothered over lesser things. Is there some one here worried over what some people call the waywardness of the younger generation? Listen to this, then! "Young women of today live in a perpetual round of amusement. They go about, by day and night, in perfect freedom. Their sole occupation is to walk, and drive, and amuse themselves with dancing. They read the most improper books, and the foam of a poisonous philosophy falls from their lips." Does some one say, Just so! Well, that is a quotation from *The Ladies' Magazine* in 1800. We are not dealing, then, this morning with fussiness about small matters. There has been a serious slump in our basic morality with such consequences in private character and public life that every good man and woman that I know is worried. Never in my lifetime have low-minded and cynical men been so openly contemptuous of decent standards of public and private life as these last ten years. Never have lofty ideals of personal character and public service been more difficult to maintain, so that sometimes I think I hear again the cry which our early Christian forefathers heard in the disillusioned Roman Empire but which we have not heard for many a long year, "What must we do to be saved?"

For this immorality of ours has not worked out well anywhere. Some of you will recall how in the old country school the teacher sometimes was called from the room and, with the restraint gone, we boys broke loose, went wild, kicked our heels, thumbed our noses, stood on our heads, enjoying our liberty. Something like that has been going on in wide areas of our population. The restraints were off, the codes were gone, the watchword was "Liberty!" But in the long run any generation discovers that liberty which exhibits itself chiefly in thumbing one's nose and standing on one's head is not permanently desirable. It does not get one anywhere, so that even if we may not want the old teacher back again we want some teacher to bring order, to give security to social life, to conquer pandemonium with intelligent purpose, to encourage socially minded self-discipline and make it possible for a good man to hold up his head again. I suspect that that desire is coming back once more.

What we are saying, then, is simply, Capitalize that returning desire! We never will force our generation into the good life or exhort them into it or legislate them into it: now is the time for all good men to make goodness attractive.

Let us begin the investigation of our truth close at home in the family circle. We have said that there has been a serious slump in character, and yet the solid elements of genuine goodness among our people are wide-spread, deep-seated, and dependable. A man cannot handle this generation, the younger portion of it in particular, without seeing that he is dealing not with sleazy cheesecloth, that pulls easily apart, but with strong material that could be used to make almost anything worth while. And if you ask now where these solid elements in our national character come from, the answer is easy. For the most part they have been grown in homes where goodness was adorned and made attractive. O my soul! ask yourself whence came your own goodness, such of it as you may have!

Some boys are like Henry M. Stanley, a fatherless child brought up in a workhouse, subjected to such dour discipline in his school that at thirteen years of age in despair he ran away, yet rising at last to high stature. How can a boy overcome obstacles like that? But as for us, if we have any personal decency or public usefulness, we know where it came from. Somebody in a beautiful home made that kind of living attractive.

Who of us is wise enough to discern what goes on in the imagination of our children? Jane Welsh, who afterwards was Mrs. Thomas Carlyle, tells us that when she was nine years old she idealized the Romans. Reading about them in her Latin book, she fell in love with them and elevated in her imagination their heroic and masterful qualities. "Would I prevent myself," she wrote afterwards, "from doing a selfish or cowardly thing, I didn't say to myself, 'You mustn't; *if you do* you will go to Hell hereafter'; nor yet, '*If you do, you will be whipt here*'; but I said to myself simply and grandly, '*A Roman wouldn't have done it.*'" "That," she adds, "sufficed under ordinary temptations." Once, she tells us, when in her early childhood an angry gander hissed at her and instead of running away she bravely seized the gander by the neck and turned him right about, she went all that day with a high head saying to herself that she had "deserved well of the Republic." Such is one main source of character— a family where a child becomes possessed by ideals, with whatever names she calls them, that make strong and courageous living attractive.

In days like these, when the problems of the world's life, gigantic in extent and complex in detail, often weigh upon our consciences, how often we feel too small to do anything about them! What contribution can we make to such Titanic matters? But, my friends, behind this angry clash of politics, this surge and thunder of economic restlessness, the basic business in any moral restoration this world will ever know is being done in families where boys and girls are not being dragooned into goodness or frightened into it or even exhorted and disciplined into it, but attracted into it. The tragedy of much American family life is that there are so many homes where goodness is not attractive but repellent, or where the goodness that is made attractive is of so narrow and individualistic a kind that it does not fit the needs of this tremendous day. Let nobody in a home with children say that he or she can do nothing. That is the elemental place in which to adorn the doctrine.

If our truth does so obviously apply in this intimate, domestic group, let us leave that for a while and swing out on a wider circumference.

Some here are primarily interested in our political chaos. What a mess our American municipal government is! Or when one thinks of the national Congress, how all too mediocre the quality of mind and character! Moreover, how easy it is to pick out individual scapegoats on whom to lay the blame for our political estate! One could name them in this city, the men whose shameless use of political power for private graft, whose obsequious surrender to a political machine, egregiously sinning against light and opportunity, justly awakens the indignation of the better citizens. Only, my friends, here as everywhere, seeking out individual scapegoats does not go to the heart of the matter. The heart of the matter is that we, the American people as a whole, have not made public office attractive to our best minds and characters. Indeed we have not. Do you remember what the word "ambition" comes from? It is derived from the Latin word "ambitio," which means "going around," and it recalls old days in the Roman Republic when politicians ran around to get votes. Well, there is plenty of ambition in this country. And, because so many politicians are willing to run around and get votes, we are deceived into thinking that public office is a desirable estate. No, it is not, not for men and women of the best brains and the finest character. How many, do you think, of our finest citizens in this town would want to be mayor?

They do this thing better in England. Winston Churchill told us that on his last visit. While some things England might learn from us, there are things we might learn from England—a high tradition of public service; the ablest men from the great families or from Cambridge and Oxford proud to go into politics; men who have been prime ministers gladly sitting in the House of Commons now as an honorable place of public ministry; the whole sphere of statecraft elevated into a dignified and honorable profession, crowned by prestige, assured of economic competence, and regarded as a public duty and a public trust. Why is it, upon the contrary, that when a man in this country like Mr. Dwight Morrow does go into politics, we think it a miracle? Search not for individual scapegoats. We, the people, are to blame. We need men of good citizenship who will devote to the preservation and progress of the country something of the intelligence and character which our forefathers gave to its creation, and so make public office an honorable and dignified estate and claim for it the best of our brains and character.

In any realm where we look, the moral conflict simmers down pretty much to this question: Which of the two, good or evil, is making its mode of behavior the more attractive? "Satan," says Paul, falling back on an old first-century way of expressing a weighty matter, "Satan fashioneth himself into an angel of light." Indeed he does. That is his game. He adorns himself. He makes himself attractive. He dresses war in pomp of uniform, sets it moving to martial music, calls it by high names of patriotism and loyal sacrifice. He dresses drunkenness in gaiety, makes it seductive with good fellowship, the clink of glasses, and the lilt of song. He dresses licentiousness in the appearance of liberty, adventure, and gay self-expression. He makes economic greed alluring. In these days one can fairly fancy the devil, as Milton or Paul would have done, using an economic system based on private profit for its major motive to make greed infinitely attractive until it deceives the very elect. He is a great strategist. He does not mainly force men into evil nor exhort them into it nor legislate them into it. He attracts them into it. And the chief reason why the so-called forces of righteousness—what a name, *forces* of righteousness!—and the church in particular are such inadequate competitors is that, so often, far from making goodness attractive we make it repellent.

You know yourselves that there are some kinds of good people whom you would walk blocks to avoid meeting. There are the conventionally good who, through a long lifetime having observed little rules of respectability, immoderately admire themselves in consequence, like the Pharisee in Jesus' parable: "I fast twice in the week; I give tithes of all that I get." There are the negatively good whose goodness consists in having kept the lid clamped tightly down on their insurgent badness so that they are repressed and dried up and sour. How dreadful they are! There are the censoriously good whose morality is all for export, who in endless interferences with other people's business try to do us good. There are the narrowly good, who make an infinite to-do about infinitesimal matters of behavior which do not matter much and who never get their eyes on the great ethical issues of their day, on economic justice and international peace.

My friends, the chief enemy of real goodness is not badness but our repellent caricatures of goodness. Listen to this from a representative of intelligent youth. "The church has unwittingly committed itself to a policy of repression which has made goodness so *repellent* as virtually to keep thousands away who otherwise would be drawn to its services." Aye, that is a shot between wind and water, so that we Christians who are interested in the influence of Christianity in this modern world had better say to ourselves, Adorn the doctrine; challenge the strength of this new generation with a courageous, adventurous, socially minded goodness from whose claim, once they have felt it, they cannot escape.

To the achievement of this end I suggest that we have in our possession two instruments of ready use.

In the first place, our share, however small, in the creation of public opinion. I beg of you as Christians not to treat that lightly. Lincoln was right: the sources of power in the nation are not so much with those who make its laws as with those who shape its public opinion. Sometimes, when I grow weary with preaching, that tones me up. The Christian churches of America, with so many millions in their membership, could do something important through public opinion if they were once aroused. For example, in our economic life today, just as in politics, we are tempted to blame our calamitous estate on individual scapegoats. Men like the Insulls occupy the front page. Granted that if they have done anything illegal it would be a salutary thing to punish them! Never forget, however, that the materialistic successes which they sought, the methods which they used, the speculative greed regardless of public welfare which they practiced, have for long years been crowned with popular applause. We, the people, have made such disregard for public welfare attractive. We have salaamed and kotowed to selfish success. We have woven for it inward garlands and bestowed upon it public praise. We have even feebly surrendered to the mad idea that that is what an economic system is for, to serve the interests of private greed rather than the interests of public welfare. *Mea culpa,* let the public say: My fault! For the things which we secretly have admired and popularly have praised have now calamitously befallen us. You and I do have something to say about public opinion. There is some group where what we think has weight. What are we making attractive—good citizenship, social-mindedness, public service, or the winning of a greedy game?

Finally, and more intimately, we have at our disposal, in making goodness attractive, our personal lives. That is the gist of the matter. It is people, radiant, attractive people who make goodness alluring, and to be that kind of person is to render to the world its most essential service. Does not every one know in these times how easy it is to be tempted to disillusionment and even cowardice? Is there any one of us who does not fall into low moods like that which Hamlet described to his friends: "I have of late—but wherefore I know not—lost all my mirth, forgone all custom of exercises; and indeed it goes so heavily with my disposition that this goodly frame, the earth, seems to me a sterile promontory; this most excellent canopy, the air, look you, this brave o'erhanging firmament, this majestical roof fretted with golden fire,—why, it appears no other thing to me than a foul and pestilent congregation of vapours." When you are in a mood like that, what pulls you up? Not an argument,—oh, never an argument!—a person. Even in a book to meet a man like Robert Louis Stevenson, sick but singing, cast down but not dismayed, kindles in us by contagion the courage that had gone out and makes the good life both alluring and possible again. Ah, my soul! how some people do take the heart of goodness out of us and how some people do put it back again!

Who has been the most influential character in Western history? Jesus of Nazareth. By what method, then, did he achieve such influence? "I, if I be lifted up," said Jesus, "will draw"—attract, allure, fascinate, draw—"all men unto myself." What is it, then, to be a Christian? Adorn the doctrine in a life that, lifted up in the circle of your friends, will draw.

Being Good without Trying

MULTITUDES of people are very tired of trying to be good. They often wish they were good but it requires such strenuous endeavor that they cannot stand the strain. If only there were some way of being spontaneously at one's best as water runs down hill! Upon the contrary, this world seems to be built upon another principle altogether. If as farmers we spontaneously let ourselves go we get weeds, but if we want wheat we have to work so hard and often under such discouraging difficulties that even in a naturally fertile land like this the agricultural problem is acute. So moral excellence is all too rare, not so much because folk question its desirability as because they keenly feel its difficulty—easy to get moral weeds, hard to get moral wheat! The result is that many pulpit arguments in favor of the good life, however intellectually convincing they may be, roll off our minds like water from slate.

We argue, for example, that whatever the good life costs is worth spending. We have to deny ourselves *something*, we say. If we do not deny ourselves the bad life for the sake of the good life, then we are denying ourselves the good life for the sake of the bad life. We get self-denial going or coming. The question is simply which we will deny, the low life for the high or the high for the low, diamonds for dust or dust for diamonds. Since, therefore, self-denial is inevitable, far better to give up promiscuous relations for the sake of a lovely home than to give up a lovely home for the sake of promiscuous relations; far better to give up bad temper for the sake of having friends than to give up friends for the sake of having bad temper; far better to surrender shady practices in business to keep honor and peace of mind than to surrender honor and peace of mind in favor of shady practices in business. Surely, that is reasonable. There is no theoretical argument against it. But we all know the practical argument. Life seems to be built, not only physically but morally, with the gravitation downward. It is easy to slip, it is hard to climb up; and many people are tired trying to be good.

Or we argue in the pulpit that much of the current talk about the danger of repressing primitive instincts is one-sided. We have to restrain *something*, we say. We cannot let everything in us go helter-skelter. The result of that would be like the corner of Broadway and Forty-second Street without traffic regulations. If we are to have any freedom of movement, we must hold something back in order to let something through. If a man insists that he will not restrain his violent temper, he inevitably will restrain his friendly feelings. If a man insists that he will not restrain his wilder passions, he will restrain his nobler, spiritual loves. However much we may dislike restraint and repression, one cannot avoid the fact that inevitably every life adopts a scale of values and controls some things in order to give others liberty.

Said one of our better psychologists, "Conscience is the voice of the repressed good." That might well be written by airplanes in smoke on the sky over every American city: "Conscience is the voice of the repressed good." There are other things in life dangerous to repress beside our primitive instincts. Our higher instincts are dangerous to repress. Conscience is the voice of them. Therefore we argue: Do not subject the high to the low; subject the low to the high; do not repress your good.

That, too, is reasonable. There is no theoretical answer to it. But we all know the practical answer. It is hard work doing that. Drifting down stream is easy, rowing up stream is strenuous; and many become very weary trying to be good.

In answer, I suggest that we remember two kinds of good people whom we know. Some labor painfully at being good. Like a singer who strains his voice so distressingly that his audience travails with him, so are some people with their goodness. They toil at it. They observe rules. They are obsessed with the things they ought not to do. They belabor their wills. But we must have known some whose goodness was not like that. They did not seem to work at it. It was spontaneous; it overflowed. It shone out like light. Joy and radiance were in it as when a master plays a violin and one loses the consciousness that he is working at all. Effortless ease made it beautiful as though the life were good by nature and could do no more than be itself.

Some of us had mothers like that, and some of us for many years have had a Christ like that, who never seemed to try to be good because he *was* good and would have had to try to be anything else. What if there were a secret of being good without trying?

There is a secret, and one of the worthiest expressions of it in all literature you will find in the third chapter of Paul's second letter to the Corinthians: "We all, with unveiled face reflecting as a mirror the glory of the Lord, are transformed into the same image from glory to glory." "Are transformed," you see, not "transform ourselves," not "strive and struggle." We Christians are supposed to live in spiritual relationships that change us, so that inevitably out of them comes a consequence and spontaneously we are transformed. As Henry Drummond paraphrased that passage, "We all reflecting as a mirror the character of Christ are transformed into the same Image from character to character." What if that is true? Of course, there never can be any kind of goodness without some trying in it, but what if this thing Paul says is true and there are spiritual relationships, living in which brings an inevitable and beautiful consequence so that we are changed?

Note, in the first place, that the principle on which this idea rests is true in our experience. Did it seem incredible at first that there could be such a thing as goodness without trying? Upon the contrary, none of the finest things in our characters today came, I suspect, by effort. We caught them from somebody. In one of the European galleries is an old Greek statue of Apollo, a beautiful figure of physical perfection. It is interesting to stand aside and watch the crowds of casual visitors pass by. If anybody stands long enough before that statue, almost invariably he begins to straighten up. He is not trying. He is not even conscious of what he does. He is revealing the instinctive basis for a great law of life: we grow like what we live with. Indeed we do! That law is revealed in many a home where two folk who profoundly love each other have lived together for many years until their kinship of thought and taste and feeling is the strongest influence in their lives. When we care about them, we grow like those we live with.

Put on one side the virtues we possess that can be attributed to the sheer strain of our volition, and put on the other side whatever fineness we possess because we had good homes and because in those first intimate days, when all the doors and windows of our lives were open, our fathers and mothers shone upon us with their very souls. In those days we were not trying; we did not know how to try; we did not have integrated wills purposefully to try with. But what the psychologists tell us today we know to be true: the most important influences of our lives were playing on us then. We were living in a spiritual relationship and were being changed.

A young friend of mine, a boy ten years old, was run over by a truck in front of his own home and cruelly hurt—for weeks we did not know whether he ever would walk again. They picked up his broken body and carried it into the house and while they were waiting for the physicians his mother sat beside his bed. He was badly scared. By and by he said, "Mother, are you frightened?" She pulled herself together, looked at him steadily, and said, "No, I am not frightened." "Well, then," he said, "I will not be either." His courage did not come from trying. He caught it from somebody. How many of the finest things in our lives have so come by contagion!

Do not suppose that, because our first illustration of this truth comes from home life, it is primarily a matter of sentiment. Our psychologists are teaching us that it is not our wills that make us so much as it is our mental images, our interior, spiritual companionships. If we hang beautiful pictures on the walls of our souls, mental images that establish us in the habitual companionship of the highest that we know, and live with them long enough, we cannot will evil. Our wills are powerless in the face of the accumulating influence of beautiful imaginings and inward, spiritual fellowships. Free will? Thank heaven, some of us are not free!—not free to lie, to steal, to slander. We could not will such things. We are not free because we have lived so long with mental images of another sort that the accumulated consequence is more powerful than any stroke of our volition. Or on the other hand, if we hang on the soul's walls unlovely pictures, unworthy mental images bespeaking a vain, shallow, unclean, selfish life, and live with them long enough, we cannot will good. No use, then, urging us to flog our volition. Our wills are the slaves of the accumulated influence of our interior companionships. What we can do is to get new mental images. We can do that. We can move out into better spiritual relationships until we are changed.

Suppose, then, in some future heaven a presumptuous fellow stepping up to Paul and saying: "What a will you have! You started a persecutor and you ended by writing the most glorious passage on love in the world's literature! Changed life, tremendous achievements, what a will!" How shallow that would be in comparison with the sort of answer Paul would give. "It was not my will," he would say. "I lived with Christ. I had an inner fellowship with him. I kept him in my imagination. There were hard and evil days but always in my imagination's eye I saw him. Never a day passed when I did not for at least a little while reëstablish my fellowship with him. All that was finest in my life came from that. With unveiled face reflecting as a mirror the character of Christ, I was changed from character to character."

Note, in the second place, that not only is this principle true to our experience but it is reasonable. In no realm today, when we want results, do we primarily blow on our hands and put our wills into it. First of all, we back away from our problem and put our intelligence into it. We ask what conditions ought to be fulfilled in order to get the consequence we wish. We desire, for example, giant power in industry and we are going to get it, but we shall not get it by simply putting our wills into it. Our wills by themselves are not one whit better than Nebuchadnezzar's. He had a strong will. But there is one thing we know that Nebuchadnezzar did not—how to ask and answer questions as to what conditions ought to be fulfilled in streams and waterfalls to get power. The whole strategy of modern science is to want something away off *here* and then to go away off *there*, fulfil the conditions, and get it. We may fulfil conditions at Niagara Falls to get power hundreds of miles away. That is not, first of all, putting your will into it; that is putting your intelligence into it.

One of the early indications, they say, that Napoleon gave of his amazing strategical skill in military affairs was at the siege of Toulon. The Jacobins had been attacking the Royalist city of Toulon in vain and then Napoleon, a lieutenant of artillery, came, put his finger on the map at a place outside Toulon altogether and said to the war council, "There is the key of Toulon." Quite so! All the great Toulons of life are captured, not by direct assaults of the volition but by knowing the strategical places somewhere else, where, if you fulfil conditions, you will get Toulon.

If you carry a symptom to a physician, he does not merely attack the symptom. He may go a long way from the symptom and ask what conditions need to be fulfilled elsewhere that health may come and the symptom disappear. When we want results anywhere we raise this prior question: What conditions are to be fulfilled to achieve the consequence?

If men desire to be good, however, we say to them, Try! But have you not watched them try until it almost broke your heart to see their struggle? Tell a man that he ought to be Christlike and should try, as though by any stroke of his volition he could lift himself to such spiritual quality! Paul was a scientist in building character before the other scientists arrived. He knew that greatness of spiritual quality depends on fulfilled conditions. In what spiritual relationships are we so intimately living that we inwardly are changed from character to character? That is the deepest question in the problem of goodness.

Of course, the men of religion are not alone in seeing it. The novelists have seen it. Read Hawthorne's *Marble Faun*. It is the story of a man who grew like what he lived with. Read George Eliot's *Silas Marner*. The old miser was not transformed because he willed it. He did not even wish to be transformed. Some one came into his life, a child left at his threshold, who lured him out of himself, bewitched him away from his sordidness, opened doors in his soul that he had not dreamed were there, unshuttered windows and let sunshine into rooms where it had never come. He lived in a new companionship and was changed.

As for our psychologists, you should hear them talk! How they blame us, the moralists, because we so misuse the will, as though a kitten tangled in a skein of yarn were likely to escape merely by kicking harder. How they hate also the advertisers who promise almost overnight to give us new wills so that, no longer the loose-lipped, sad-eyed weaklings vividly portrayed before us on the printed page, we shall become instead this paragon of virile resolution, firm-jawed, tight-lipped, clear-eyed—"Fill in and mail the coupon now!" Nonsense! If you and I are in any real moral and emotional difficulty, the trouble lies far in the hinterland of our souls. Not by one chance in a thousand can we escape merely by trying. Indeed, like a man in quicksand, the harder we try the deeper we may sink. When, however, under wise guidance a man goes back into his soul to discover the thoughts he has been living with, the faiths he has been living by, the mental images he has been cherishing, the habitual things he has been saying to himself in his interior conversations, the spiritual relationships he has been clinging to, and changes some of these, the results do often seem miraculous.

We have two things to rely on for goodness: first, our wills—they are important but they do not go far; second, our capacity to be inspired—how amazing it is! From a boy who was not frightened, though he was crushed half to death, because he caught courage from his mother, to Paul living under the spell of Christ until he surpassed himself and was raised from weakness to strength, how amazing is the capacity of the human soul to be inspired by great books, great music, great art, by the beauty of nature and by human friendship, by high faiths, by lofty ideals, by the interior fellowship of the Unseen Friend! The finest qualities of our characters do not come from trying but from that mysterious and yet most effective capacity to be inspired.

Under what kind of inspiration, then, are you and I living? Be sure, the world will find out in the end. Judas did not betray his Lord all of a sudden, because he willed it. He had been living with some mental images for a long time and his sin, slowly accumulating, like an avalanche all unsuspected, in a crisis broke. His will was powerless. And Paul did not of a sudden write the thirteenth chapter of First Corinthians, because he willed it. Over many a year he had lived with some one and the accumulating consequence of that inward fellowship with "Love divine, all love excelling" one day overflowed in spontaneous utterance. He could not have willed it.

Sometimes when a man who understands human nature speaks to a congregation on such a theme, he feels the solemnity of this fact. According to all statistical probabilities, there are some people in this congregation who within a few years will crash in moral ruin, obvious, public, and irretrievable. Men will say your wills were weak. That will not be the real cause. You are living now with inward faiths, imaginations, fellowships, whose accumulating consequence like a tidal wave some day will oversweep the resistance of your will. Live on low inspirations and the world will find it out at last. Live on high inspirations and there are some of us here concerning whom our friends may some day think: Reflecting as a mirror the character of Jesus, he was changed into the same likeness from character to character.

Finally, consider not only how true this is to our experience and how reasonable, but what a fascinating kind of goodness it produces. Goodness is not all of one quality. Some is very painful. Goodness in this regard is like courtesy. Some courtesy can be stiff and formal. A man who really is not fine and kindly can by the deliberate stroke of his volition use the outward forms of politeness. He is polite but he is working at it and it is not attractive. In what sharp contrast does a man stand whose courtesy is a matter of his nature and not simply of his will. Some one has defined a gentleman as a man who never unintentionally offends any one. Intentionally he may offend some one. When the occasion requires he may intentionally be severe and stern, but unintentionally, when his will is off guard, when his nature, unrestrained, is overflowing its banks, he never offends anybody. His courtesy is like sunshine, like water running from a spring, like the laughter of little children; it is spontaneous. He *is* a gentleman.

That is the kind of goodness that Jesus loved. He hated legalism, the morality that never gets beyond the restrained and regimented will. Jesus said, "Consider the lilies of the field, how they grow; they toil not"—they do not work at it; they have gotten into true relationship with the sun and the earth and something beautiful is spontaneously coming in consequence; their loveliness grows up from within. "They toil not, neither do they spin: yet I say unto you, that even Solomon in all his glory was not arrayed like one of these." Jesus always pushed back behind the goodness that is a mere matter of volition to the goodness that is a matter of one's nature. "A good tree cannot bring forth evil fruit, neither can a corrupt tree bring forth good fruit." You see, that is what we have been saying all this morning.

Some one, to be sure, may rise in protest. He says this truth does not make goodness easier but harder. Goodness without trying—what nonsense is this that a man can get a new nature, be what Paul called "a new creature," without trying? Well, my friend, you may be sure of this: you never will get a new nature *by trying*. That is certain. Recall Dr. Keate, the old terror of the Eton schoolboys, whose sermon on purity of heart has long been famous. "It's your

we surrender the case, in advance of argument, to a materialistic philosophy. Not by our intellects, my friends, are we
made materialists but by our imaginations, that picture solid,
brutal facts against insubstantial, beautiful ideals.

Consider then! Herod does represent fact. In his cynicism,
in his cruelty, in his willingness to do anything rather than
surrender his greed of power he does represent appalling and
terrific fact. But the Christ Child also was a fact. Ah, my
soul! whoever could have dreamed how prodigious a fact he
would turn out to be!

At Christmastime few things should mean more to us
than this simple, basic matter: Jesus was a fact. In a world
where there are so many other kinds of facts he was a fact
too. Out of the womb of the universe from which all facts
come he came also. We call him an ideal. Yes, but we can
make either Christ or Herod our ideal. That depends on us.
One thing we may not do is to deny that either of them is a
solid and substantial fact.

See, then, how inadequate was our first statement of this
matter! We do not face solid, brutal facts versus insubstantial, beautiful ideals. We face two kinds of solid facts, both
tremendously real, standing in clear conflict, with the question rising on which side we are casting in our lot.

Beware how we deceive ourselves with that dangerous
word "ideal." We call courage, for example, an ideal. Yes,
but do you not remember how Captain Scott died in his little
tent amid the terrific tempests of the Antarctic wilderness
writing that unforgetably brave message to his friends?
Ideal? That is a fact.

We call lovely motherhood an ideal. Yes, but why is it
that at Christmastime the memories of Mary and her babe
are so strangely moving if not that we too have known lovely
motherhood? Ideal? That is a fact.

We call social progress an ideal. Yes, but two hundred
years ago multitudes believed in witchcraft, used magic
charms, were frightened at the portent of comets, made fantastic medicine out of excrements, had pock-marked faces,
had not dreamed yet even in theory that government could

exist for the sake of the governed, so that for all the sinister evils that surround us now, not for the world would we go back two centuries. Progress ideal? Yes, but those are facts.

We do not face substantial, brutal facts versus insubstantial, beautiful ideals. We face two kinds of solid facts and the conflict between them sometimes seems to run to the very center of the universe. At least, so the great religions have said.

Hinduism called it a combat between reality and illusion. Zoroastrianism called it a combat between Ahura Mazdah, the good God, and Angra Mainyu, the God of evil. Judaism and Christianity said it was a struggle between Jehovah and Satan. Plato said it was the contrast between spirit and matter. How many symbols there have been of these two orders of conflicting facts!

For myself, my personal faith in God, then, is no neat affair, all finished off and proved, with a Q.E.D. appended. My faith in God is a militant business, a staking of life on the triumph of the facts revealed in Christ over the facts revealed in Herod. For there are solid facts to be taken into account by any one who in this modern world is tempted to get rid of God. Order, symmetry, beauty, law-abiding regularity in nature—a cosmos not a chaos here—that is a fact. Constructive forces also that have produced personality and sustained social progress, great music, great art, great characters—facts, my friends, as solid as they are beautiful. Christ against Herod! He who believes that Christ can win because there is something eternal at the heart of the universe upon his side, and who stakes his life on his faith, has taken hold upon the real God.

It is a conflict, however, as at Bethlehem. Foolish sentimentalists that we have been, remembering angels and shepherds and forgetting Herod and the slaughter of the Innocents! No Christ child ever yet was born without Herod waiting. Herod would not have minded Christ as a baby if he had stayed a baby. But he would not have him grow up. Ah, Herod, you are using the same old strategy still and you are right about it. Kill them young, these Christ children, these new-born hopes of peace and brotherhood and economic justice and high character. Catch them young and stab them with the swords of your cynicism. You see what happened because you missed him at Bethlehem. Another Herod tried to make good at Calvary what you failed to do at the manger. Too late! Your youngest son, Antipas, had a hand in the cross of this Christ Child now grown up. Too late! Not at the cross, Herod. You never can stop any Christ at the cross. At the cradle, if you could catch him there!

You see what I mean. So many new-born hopes, so many old, hard, cynical Herods determined they shall not grow up —two kinds of facts. And we on one side or the other.

Consider, in the second place, how we come out, not simply when we reëxamine our use of the word "fact," but when we reëxamine our use of the word "ideal." How flimsy that word often sounds! What will-o'-the-wisps these angels seem that sing over our Bethlehems! Very well, then, let us look at that word again and see what it means.

An ideal is simply a possibility that somebody perceives in the actual facts. That is the sum of it. Ideals are possibilities resident in actual facts. An ideal, then, is about the most hard-headed and creative thing that mankind handles. We all know the story of Mr. Edison's long-drawn-out work on the electric light. The creative, driving, motive power behind such arduous labor and achievement is always an ideal. Mr. Edison looked so deeply into the actual facts that he saw a possibility. Ideals flimsy? They are the most creative forces in the world.

To be sure, any power of man such as this capacity to frame ideals is bound to be abused. Men do take this ideal-framing power and with it build fictitious and fantastic worlds of make-believe. The uses of this capacity are as far apart in quality as the work of a hard-headed scientist like Edison at one end of the line and at the other the delusions of an insane man who thinks himself the angel Gabriel. So always the perversion of the best is the worst.

Moreover, it is true that this capacity to frame ideals is peculiarly abused in religion. So Mrs. Thomas Carlyle came home from church one Sunday and wrote to a friend of hers that she had been "all stewed into mush" by a popular preacher. What fictitious and sentimental worlds here and hereafter has religion built!

Since, when, however, has it been sensible to discard great affairs because they can be caricatured? A little while ago this church in which we worship was an ideal. That bridge over the Hudson was at first an ideal. A few years ago the aircraft that cleave the sky were incredible ideals. Beethoven's symphonies and Shakespeare's plays are facts now but once they were ideals. Ideals are the most creative powers that mankind handles. They are the possibilities resident in the facts. Let all hard-headed realists take notice: no fact is the whole of itself; its possibilities are the rest of it.

Turn back, now, with this in mind and see how inadequate was our first statement of the matter—with reference to international peace, let us say. Hard-headed realists making war, soft-headed idealists dreaming peace—no strategy of the militarists is much more effective than that way of painting the picture. The fact is, however, that on this modern earth with its economic interdependencies it is the war-makers who live in the land of fantasy. International peace is an ideal only in the sense that it is a possibility resident in the actual facts and absolutely demanded by them. So far is it from being flimsy that Professor Shotwell, of the Department of History at Columbia, says that in all the past no reform has ever gone so far in so short a time as our modern peace-movement.

Well, if the possibilities are there, we had better line ourselves up strongly on that side. For Herod is at work. Long ago in Homer we read the horror of the ancient Greeks at poison on arrows and now we modern Christians, disciples of Jesus, have become accustomed to poison gas. Herod is at work. He thinks he is hard headed. Is it not, rather, the very summit of fantasm in this modern world to rely on competitive armaments and war for national defense? I load; you load; I load more; you surpass me at the game. We gather all the armament we can amass dollars to buy, and then, some spark setting us off, we blaze away at each other, and afterwards sit down for a quarter of a century amid the appalling economic havoc which we mutually have caused, winners and losers alike mired in the same hopeless pit—and the hard-headed realists call *that* national defense! Ah, Herod, Christ will beat you yet at your own game of hard-headedness! The only adequate national defense in this modern, factual world is organized goodwill. It is that or nothing. It is that or perish. We have tried your way, Herod, now for centuries, and see us still, the miserable victims of the economic catastrophe consequent upon your wars. You will discover yet that Christ, so long despised as an idealist, is the realist. Civilization will travel his path or else stop being civilization at all.

Ideals flimsy? Public education was an ideal. Freedom of scientific research was an ideal. Religious liberty was an ideal. Equality before the law was an ideal. Every decent thing on earth emerged as an ideal. They all were little children once and over their slight and lovely promise terrific Herod loomed. Still, somehow,—how could it be in a world where there was nothing but matter going it blind?—somehow they escaped him, not nipped in the bud. Somehow they did get from Bethlehem to Calvary and so into the heart of the world.

Well, Christ stands against Herod. Where stand we? After the attempt to climb Mount Everest in 1922, the qualities necessary for such an enterprise were set down by the participants: experience in mountain climbing, "perfect physical fitness," "singleness of aim," but, beyond that, "unswerving faith in the possibility of its achievement." So Christ challenges the world in the face of Herod and seems to say to every one of us this Christmastime, Have you faith enough in me to help give me a chance to grow up?

Crucified by Stupidity*

FROM New Testament days until our own, the cross of Jesus has been closely associated with the problem of sin. It was because of sin that Jesus had to be crucified, it was by sin that he was crucified—such has been the familiar teaching. Today, on the threshold of another Holy Week, at the center of whose memories the crucifixion stands, we are not minded to deny that long association between the cross and sin, but we would set beside it another association. Jesus was put to death not simply by sin but by stupidity. It was stupidity that cried, "Crucify him." It was stupidity that nailed the Son of man between two thieves.

Indeed, the Master himself said that. "Father, forgive them; for they know not what they do"—numberless times those words from the cross have been repeated and yet how little have we seen into their depths! Generally we have interpreted them as an expression of Jesus' magnanimity. In happier days, by word of mouth he had taught his followers to love their enemies and to forgive seventy times seven, and now on Calvary forgiveness rose to heights that words alone can never reach and he pardoned those who slew him. He even made excuse for them, blamed their deed upon their ignorance, asked that they might be forgiven because they knew not what they did. So we have understood those words.

That interpretation clearly is true, but I ask you to look at the words again, not now from the standpoint of the Master's magnanimity but from the standpoint of the men who crucified him. So seen, the words take on another aspect. They change their hue. They cease their gentleness and become accusative. Those angry men before Pilate, crying "Crucify him!" did not know what they did. What a tragedy! Those people by the roadside jeering at the staggering figure under his heavy cross did not know what they did. How ter-

* A Palm Sunday sermon.

rific a thing stupidity can be! Pilate and Herod and Caiaphas and all the rest who went to bed that night content, thinking that everything now was well done and Jesus finished, did not know what they had done. How appalling an accusation that is! Looked at from the standpoint of Jesus, those words mean one thing; looked at from our standpoint, there is little comfort in them. To crucify Christ stupidly, when we know not what we do,—that is an epitome of the most terrific tragedies of individual experience and human history.

Surely, this thing needs to be said, especially in the churches. In a scientific laboratory, an electrical power-house, a responsible business position, everybody knows that stupidity is ruinous. To say of a man there that he is conscientious and means well, important though that is, does not cover the ground. He must not be stupid. But how often in the churches have we heard men talk as though to be kind-hearted and well-intentioned would solve the spiritual problems of mankind! To see that this will not do, one needs only look in history at those things of which mankind always will be ashamed. The Athenians who made Socrates drink the hemlock, far from being bad, were among the most earnest, conscientious, religious people of their day. But they stupidly thought Socrates an atheist because his idea of God was so much greater than the popular opinion. They stupidly thought that Socrates was misleading the youth of Athens, he who now, like the Parthenon, is one of the glories of the ancient Greeks. So, in intention, the crusades were not so much wicked as stupid; the people who threatened Galileo with torture were not wicked but stupid; the judges at the trial of Joan of Arc were not bad but senseless, and over the most shameful tragedies of history, as over the cross of Christ, the judgment stands: "They know not what they do."

When one looks not at history but at our contemporaneous public life, one sees the same fact. The men who cry up war and all its noble consequence are not wicked but stupid. The people who think our economic system can go on without deep-seated changes in the interests of all the people are not wicked but stupid. Look at the record of the United States Senate since the Great War. Part of the trouble may be badness but most of it is stupidity, dangerous stupidity, when wisdom is critically needed. The imposition of the Versailles Treaty on the conquered Germans, binding them and unborn generations to economic servitude, was stupid, and now the Hitlerite reaction against the servitude, with its anti-Semitism, has, as good friends of Germany well may fear, stupidly stolen from that nation a great deal of what it has been regaining in fifteen years.

Look anywhere and see the cruel crosses lifted by stupidity! So Anatole France quotes a confrère as saying that fools are more redoubtable than knaves because knaves take a little rest sometimes but fools never do.

We cannot, however, stop with history or with contemporaneous public life. This road leads straight into a man's own soul. Let a man in some hour of honest penitence face those things about which he is most sorry and ashamed, and of what does he accuse himself? Is it not of folly? I can answer for only one man. Always in retrospect the things of which I am most ashamed wring from me the cry, "O Lord, be merciful to me, a fool!"

To many people this way of putting it does not seem especially Christian. Christian teaching has been so absorbed with the problem of sin that in the churches' imagination men have been divided into good and bad, righteous and sinners, rather than into wise and foolish. Listen to Jesus, however. Some people called sinners he called sinners too. They were bad. Others called sinners he called sick. "They that are whole have no need of a physician, but they that are sick." And many more called sinners he called foolish, stupid, blind. "Every one that heareth these words of mine, and doeth them not, shall be likened unto a foolish man, who built his house upon the sand." "Thou blind Pharisee, cleanse first the inside of the cup." "The hour cometh, that whosoever killeth you shall think that he offereth service unto God." "They are blind guides. And if the blind guide the blind, both shall fall into a pit." "Then shall the kingdom of heaven be likened unto ten virgins, who took their lamps, and went forth to meet the bridegroom. And five of them were foolish, and five were wise." "And he said, This will I do: I will pull down my barns, and build greater; and there will I bestow all my grain and my goods. And I will say to my soul, Soul, thou hast much goods laid up for many years; take thine ease, eat, drink, be merry. But God said unto him, Thou foolish one, this night is thy soul required of thee."

You see, what Jesus said from the cross was not a solitary judgment. Throughout his ministry, the tragedy of his life came from people who knew not what they did.

Let us test this truth on our pulses by applying it to daily life.

For one thing, there is the familiar stupidity of the small, closed mind. That is what crucified Jesus. The Pharisees, with whom from the beginning he had his major difficulties, far from being bad people, were about the best people of their day, strict moralists, earnest religionists, men of profound conscientiousness. The very word "Pharisee" means Puritan. Indeed, looking back on them now, one feels sorry to see so much devoted goodness going to waste, losing its reputation and becoming a byword. Going to waste, did I say? Far worse than that. It was precisely this goodness which crucified Jesus. For, mark it! it was not so much badness that nailed Jesus to the cross; it was goodness, determined conscientiousness, driven by small, closed minds.

That is not ancient history. Take goodness anywhere,—determined, devoted conscientiousness,—put it at the disposal of small, closed minds, and you have about the most dangerous force that ever has been let loose into the world.

One can see that even in families. Most parents are not bad, but many of them are stupid. Ask the psychiatrists, then, what ruins children, twists their plastic lives, imposes on them inner handicaps which the finest skill often cannot remove, and they will say it is not so much bad parents—they are not so frequent—as stupid parents. And the crux of the matter lies here: they did not need to be stupid; there was plenty of information available if they had counted it as serious a part of their obligation to be intelligent as to be kind. They knew they ought to be kind. All the moral voices that ever spoke to them about parenthood told them to be kind. Nature herself said that. But not enough voices have told us that to love children without being intelligent about it can damn them as utterly as brutality can. How many little children are being crucified today by conscientious stupidity!

One sees our truth evidenced in the churches. Narrow, sectarian Christians with small, closed minds are not bad people. Upon the contrary, they are often very good people, but they are something else which is just as ruinous to the cause of Christ as being bad—they are stupid. As Paul said long ago concerning those who fought against his life work,—an inclusive Christian church that would take Gentiles in,—"I bear them witness that they have a zeal for God, but not according to knowledge." That is ruinous. So good people, facing the profound spiritual needs of this generation with minds closed to new truth, blind to great issues, obstinate against new methods, are crucifying Christ afresh in his church, not by wickedness but by stupidity.

Indeed, if our American democracy as a whole should go to pieces, do you think sin chiefly would be the guilty conspirator? That would not be half the story. Nothing can destroy our American democracy except our own stupidity—but that can.

One suspects a certain discouragement in some as they face this way of putting the matter, as though they would say, If we were only bad we might improve ourselves and do better, but if one is stupid what can one do about that? Such an attitude shows how neglected this theme has been. We do not need to be so stupid as we are. We are needlessly stupid because we have not been taught to count it a serious part of our moral obligation to be intelligent as parents, as churchmen, as patriots, as citizens of the world. A salesgirl in a small shop said recently to my friend: "This world crisis has waked me up. I never before had thought or read about public affairs; I never even bothered about how I voted. But now I see that we are all sunk unless we all think. Believe me,

I am reading and thinking now." Just so! We do not need to be so stupid as we are.

If we are to call ourselves Christians, we had better not be stupid. Who was it said that his disciples were to be as wise as serpents and as harmless as doves? Jesus. To many people that does not sound like Jesus at all—"wise as serpents." But it sounds like him to those who know him. "Harmless as doves," that is, men of goodwill, his followers were to be, but also wise as serpents. I wonder if, when Jesus said that, he foresaw that one day he would be crucified by men who knew not what they did.

Again, there is the stupidity, not only of small, closed minds, but of false choices. Jerusalem that last week, like all the rest of us all the time, was confused by competing interests—the financial interests of the money-changers, the orthodox interests of the Pharisees, the concern of the Sadducees to keep on the right side of Rome, the fanaticism of the Zealots against Rome, and then Jesus himself, apparently at odds with all of them. Something had to be eliminated. Some of those interests had to be sacrificed to others. So they dropped Christ. And at last, at the most dramatic moment in Pilate's court, they found themselves choosing between a murderer and Jesus, and saying, "Release unto us Barabbas." Wicked? Yes, but stupid.

Nevertheless, let any man here look deep into his own soul and regard those things which shame him most and see if they are not associated with such choices. To have some Christ in our experience where we might have welcomed him and stupidly to choose some Barabbas instead, and then, when it is too late, to wake up to see what fools we have made of ourselves—that is a familiar tragedy.

Indeed, one thinks of that today, not simply as a Christian but as a citizen. How can one look on this current American scene and not see the imminent danger of our loss from stupid choices? To start with a mere detail, we Americans are letting ourselves be shot up on every side by criminal gangs with machine guns. The big business of the gangs is carried off with machine guns. Couldn't we stop that? Of course we could. Machine guns are manufactured in definite places and sold through definite channels and everybody knows that no private citizen has any legitimate business with a machine gun, so that there is no conceivable excuse for their being obtainable by private individuals. One effort after another has been made to put a stop to this. All efforts have failed. One wonders if the manufacturers of munitions have been too powerful. So we go on being shot up by machine guns. Wicked? Yes, but stupid!

Or consider a larger matter in the spectacle which we are making of ourselves with reference to the return of liquor. Sometimes one wishes that one could get all the "wets" together, now that they are in power, and talk sense to them, something like this:

We agree that prohibition has broken down. Some of us did not want it in the first place. But we call your attention to the fact that the ultimate responsibility for prohibition was not the prohibitionists but the saloon. That was the dirtiest, most disreputable element in our society. It became at last so intolerable that the whole nation rose up and cast it out. And now that prohibition has failed as a method of dealing with the liquor traffic, which always has been dangerous, lawless, and corrupt, see what you "wets" are doing. Apparently you have learned nothing. You are up to the old game again. Here in this state you are trying once more to establish corrupt relationships between politics and the liquor traffic. You who so solemnly swore you did not want the saloon back again are doing everything within your power to get it back again. Wicked? Yes, but stupid! We in this country who care not for prohibition but for temperance are not all dead yet, not by a long sea-mile! We want decent laws, laws that will shut out the old saloon, laws that will divorce the liquor traffic from politics, laws that will keep the private profit motive from debauching the appetite of youth to make saloonkeepers and brewers rich. We want decent laws and if you, the "wets," now being in power, will not give them to us, you are not half so much bad as foolish, because as sure as consequence follows cause, the inevitable Nemesis will fall on you like a thunderbolt.

You see what we are trying to say. There are many things

in life which we call wicked, which we might get rid of if we had sense enough to see that they are stupid. Who can look at war in this modern world and not see that it is stupid? Who can look on economic methods doing to us what our economic methods have been doing and not see their stupidity? As for personal character, I beg leave to speak for a moment especially to you young people. I plead with you— dare I say it?—not so much against wickedness as against stupidity. You have a great chance. How many older ones there are in this congregation who wish they had again the chance that you have now! Your reputations are not smirched. Your character is still sound. You have not yet said, Release unto me Barabbas! You have not yet crucified your Christ. I pray you, stay your hand if you are tempted to. To build a strong character, to live a high life, to undergird your soul with great faiths, to dedicate your life to noble ends, to keep your Christ and let Barabbas go—that is not simply being good, that is being intelligent. "Every one therefore that heareth these words of mine, and doeth them, shall be likened unto a wise man, who built his house upon the rock."

Once more, there is the stupidity of the short look. The essence not only of character but of intelligence is involved in a man's ability to sacrifice an immediate gratification for the sake of an ultimate satisfaction. What calamity falls upon us because of our stupid refusal to do that! You remember how the Master put it on that Palm Sunday long ago, when he had heard Hosannas from the crowd but, looking on the Holy City, saw clearly the shadow of his cross upon it: "If thou hadst known . . . the things which belong unto thy peace!" One often says *that* when a man comes to him for confession, after trouble has taken possession of the field— If you had known what belongs unto your peace! Of course, we all feel the lure of the immediate. Immediate sensation, immediate gain, immediate explosion of emotion—from a youngster eating green apples to an old fool whose green apples take on a more mature form, every son of man knows the terrific lure of the immediate. Probably it is the chiefest single cause of human folly.

I wish I could help some one here, especially some young person, to take a long look. Dealing as I habitually do with the intimate affairs of young persons, I find myself constantly saying to them, not "Don't be bad"—they are not bad—but "Don't make fools of yourselves." And never until I started to preach this sermon did I realize how Scriptural that counsel is.

Far back in the 1840's a Mediterranean immigrant landed in Australia, bearing as a memento of his home a flower pot with a prickly pear. Who could have guessed what would come of that? For the prickly pear is now one of the important affairs of the Australian government, the fight against the prickly pear one of the considerable items in its budget, and, despite all that they can do, the prickly pear steadily gains each year over a square kilometre more of ground. If they had known what belonged unto their peace!

What is your prickly pear? My young friend, this is a law-abiding universe. You cannot get away with anything. Says the New Testament, "Be not deceived,"—that is, Don't fool yourself,—"God is not mocked: for whatsoever a man soweth, that shall he also reap."

At any rate, Jesus was right about those men who crucified him, was he not? Indeed they did not know what they did. Nearly two thousand years have passed since Calvary and he who hung there has become to millions of us the Lord of life.

I wish I could for a moment make you see that cross. When Lincoln's body was brought from Washington to Illinois it passed through Albany and, as it was carried through the street, they say a colored woman stood upon the curb and lifted her little son as far as she could reach above the heads of the crowd and was heard to say to him, "Take a long look, honey. He died for you." So, if I could, I would lift up your spirit to see Calvary. Take a long look. He died for you. But with all our gratitude, there is warning there. He was nailed on that cross by human stupidity. They knew not what they did.

The Soul's Invincible Surmise*

EVERY one of us has an intimate, personal concern with the Easter message. We all have had relatives and friends who have gone down into the experience of death and have disappeared into the invisible. We ourselves face that same experience—we have a rendezvous with death —when we too shall disappear into the unseen. And facing this universal fact of death it is difficult, I think, for any man altogether to escape, at least at times, "the soul's invincible surmise"—to use Santayana's phrase—about that unseen world.

Doubtless we all have passed through many moods about the matter.

Sometimes we have tried to be nonchalant, have said that death is natural, to be taken for granted, and that what lies on the other side, if there be anything at all, will care for itself without our bothering. But then death touched upon the shoulder some one concerning whose companionship we felt as Carlyle did about his wife's—it was "the rainbow of my poor dripping day,"—and, lo! our nonchalance went all to pieces and we wondered with an invincible surmise about the unseen world.

Sometimes we have seen death fall when it was so welcome that it came like a mother to put a tired soul to rest and we were content to say of our dead, "After life's fitful fever, he sleeps well." But at other times we have seen death fall as on Shelley in his youth—drowned in the careless sea, when his song was just beginning to spread its wings—and it has seemed intolerable that God should make personality with such possibilities only to snuff them out with their imprisoned splendors unrevealed. So the old invincible surmise about that unseen world has risen again.

* An Easter sermon.

[231]

Sometimes we have tried to take the agnostic attitude. We do not know anything, we have said, concerning the yonder side of death. We cannot gather data or make inductions or establish proof. One world at a time, therefore, must be enough for us. But in thoughtful hours, under the stars at night, or in a home where death has come, we have found ourselves thinking what Mark Twain said once: "I have never seen what to me seemed an atom of proof that there is a future life. And yet—I am strongly inclined to expect one." How strong the soul's invincible surmise about the unseen world!

This Easter morning we approach the clarifying of that surmise by remarking that the real difficulty which most of us experience in holding a vital faith in immortality lies not so much in our intellects with their arguments as in our imaginations. We cannot picture immortal life. That is the trouble. Indeed, consider the language which today we already have been using about death. Our friends disappear, we say, into the invisible. Just so! And, alas, we are creatures in bondage to our eyes. We live in a world of things where reality to us consists in the fact that they are visible. Here is the test and touchstone—is it not?—of anything's being real, that we can see it. Seeing is believing, we say; and then, out of this world of the seen, our friends disappear into the unseen. No wonder that life beyond death is not real to us; we cannot visualize it.

To be sure, mythology has always tried to make good that lack. It has pictured the unseen world, sometimes with Dante and Milton, in majestic symbolism; sometimes in cheap and tawdry drawings of heaven's glory for the populace; sometimes in tender, wistful poetry as in Rossetti's "Blessed Damozel"; sometimes with ugly literalness, as when the old preacher portrayed Christ protecting his chosen ones from "the hail that shall eternally lash the howling millions of the damned." But such pictures, I take it, are known to us for what they are. They are mythology. To take them seriously is to make a bad matter worse and to render immortal life more incredible. Immortal life is an unseen world. Our friends do disappear into the invisible. How, then, can we make it real to ourselves?

There is, I suspect, only one answer to that: we must perceive that now, not after death alone but today, we really live in an invisible world.

You recall the verse in the Epistle to the Hebrews where it is said of Moses that "he endured, as seeing him who is invisible." When did he do that? After death? Upon the contrary, here in a very difficult, earthly life. Surely, Moses lived efficiently in this visible world. He saw Pharaoh. He saw those Hebrew slaves. For years he saw the tragedy of circumstance and the tyranny of things. No one can make of him a mystical recluse. But, says the New Testament writer, the strength of the man and the sources of his power came from the unseen. The real world in which he lived, even here, was not this external system of things. "He endured, as seeing him who is invisible."

My friends, even apart from religion, every one of us has to do something like that. Consider the reality of the invisible.

For one thing, we ourselves are invisible. Our bodies can be seen but not our personalities. Personality is self-conscious being with powers of intellect, purpose, and goodwill. We cannot see that. Self-conscious being, mind, purpose, love— their effects are visible and their embodiments our eyes can see but they themselves, the creative realities behind the visible, are invisible forever.

Say it to yourselves this Easter morning, that we ourselves are now invisible, inhabitants of an unseen world—thoughts, ideas, purposes, loves, insights, devotions. All the creative realities with which inwardly you deal and by which you live are now invisible.

No mirror is so bright and polished that it can ever show us to ourselves. Photographic plates are made by which pictures can be taken in the dark but no photographic plate ever will take the picture of a personality. No, not of one idea in the mind or one aspiration in the spirit. We are essentially invisible.

Indeed, consider that, everywhere we look, creative forces

spring from the unseen. This church building is visible but
not the forces which produced it. The inner spiritual needs
that wanted it, the faiths expressed in it, the intellectual ability of the architects who planned it, the mechanical skill of
the engineers who reared it—the creative forces behind it are
all essentially invisible. New York City at first sight looks
like a staring argument for materialism. Is it not a vast salmagundi of external things? Yet all the creative forces which
produced it, from subway to skyscraper, have risen from the
invisible: needs and hopes, ideas and skill, which, as the New
Testament says about God himself, no man hath seen at any
time. Everything we look at is like a book—it is visible but
what created it is not.

If the reality of the invisible is thus illustrated even in a
city, how much more inside our lives! Coleridge once defined
art as being the subjection of matter to spirit so as to be
transformed into a symbol, in and through which the spirit
reveals itself. That is a glorious description of art. A great
painting or symphony, what is it but invisible spirit subjecting visible matter to itself so that it is transformed into a
symbol in and through which spirit reveals itself? Yes, but
all great human living is that also. Our realest life now
springs from a spiritual world invisible.

Ideas, for example. We never have seen an idea but we
often have observed a man completely transformed by having a new one take possession of him. As John Eglinton put
it: "Without an idea man is frivolous, anarchic, dissatisfied,
despicable. With an idea, the long-hoarded initiatives of his
nature are liberated, he strains forward to new consum-
mations."

Or love. We can see love's expressions and value its physical aspects; we may even agree with Browning that soul does
not help body more now than body helps soul; but love itself
we have never seen. Yet how powerful a force it is! I am not
thinking, most of all, of you young people now. You do not
know what love means as some of us older people do. So
Stephen Phillips put it on the lips of Marpessa:

And though the first sweet sting of love be past,
The sweet that almost venom is; though youth,
With tender and extravagant delight,
The first and secret kiss by twilight hedge,
The insane farewell repeated o'er and o'er,
Pass off; there shall succeed a faithful peace;
Beautiful friendship tried by sun and wind,
Durable from the daily dust of life.
And though with sadder, still with kinder eyes,
We shall behold all frailties, we shall haste
To pardon, and with mellowing minds to bless.
Then though we must grow old, we shall grow old
Together.

Such love belongs now in the world invisible.

Or hope. We never saw hope, yet what is life without it?
Let visible things fall on our lives like plenteous rain until
the sight of our eyes is gratified, yet what man lacking hope
would not lift a cry of utter poverty, as indeed one man did
lift the cry, "All that life has to offer except an incentive
to live!" But incentives to live, meanings in life, motives that
glorify it, rise from the world invisible.

Or faith, undergirding, empowering, and directing life—
we never saw it. We can see David Livingstone going to
Africa but not the faith that impelled him. We can see Dar-
win in his English garden but not the faith in his hypothesis
which sustained him. Yes, in many ordinary people we can
see their gracious, steadfast, courageous, outward living,
but not the faith that makes it possible. Out of the Unseen
springs that quality in even common folk which made Bayard
Taylor say,

> . . . The healing of the world
> Is in its nameless saints. Each separate star
> Seems nothing, but a myriad scattered stars
> Break up the Night, and make it beautiful.

My friends, I do not know whether or not you are accustomed to think of that invisible world of which we have been
speaking, in terms of God. For a moment I am not concerned
about the name. But this is certain that, in so far as you

[235]

have risen into those higher altitudes which are the distinction of humanity, your real life and the sources of your deepest power are now in a realm unseen and unseeable. You do endure, you must endure, if you endure at all, as seeing what is invisible.

Indeed, let us carry our statement of the reality of the invisible one step further. Do we not see now the basic reason why not only we Christians, but the profoundest philosophers, cannot believe that materialism and atheism are the last word? Everywhere we look we see the visible created by the invisible. Is not that true also in the universe at large? Science itself cannot stop with the visible. On the awe-inspiring edge of everything that eyes can see, science stands today looking out into the unseen, saying with Jeans, the physicist, that "the universe seems to be nearer to a great thought than to a great machine," or with Haldane, the biologist of Oxford, that the only real world is the spiritual world, or with Russell, the astronomer of Princeton, that even physical science, in seeking the ultimate nature of the material universe, faces at last an invisible series of mathematical relationships, or with Balfour, the philosopher, "We now know too much about matter to be materialists." Once in a while the most modern scientists say things that sound extraordinarily like the New Testament, and this is one case: "By faith we understand that the worlds have been framed by the word of God, so that what is seen hath not been made out of things which appear."

If such is the reality of the invisible everywhere, not after death alone but here and now, does not that support the soul's invincible surmise about our friends who disappear into the unseen? What is the difference, indeed, between life and death? Yesterday my friend was alive; today the physicians say that he is dead—what has happened? The visible is here. Something invisible has gone. Life itself is invisible. All the realest forces in the world are invisible. Everything that we can see is only a shadow cast by something that we cannot see. "The things which are seen are temporal; but the things which are not seen are eternal."

Having so endeavored to perceive everywhere the reality of the invisible, let us carry our truth up into our thought of immortal life and consider its consequence. For one thing it does support and clarify our faith in life eternal. Probably the major difficulty about believing in immortality lies in our obsession with the visible body, as though the body were a noun and the spirit its adjective, so that should the noun go the adjective would have nothing left to modify. How many people think that!

You and I have friends who say to us about this matter:

Be realistic; quit your romancing about life beyond death; it is all wishful thinking; you do not want to die and stay dead and so you concoct all sorts of reasons for believing that you don't. Be realistic; look with your eyes and see; you do die; you *are* your body, and when that goes you are gone.

To which I answer, Being realistic is precisely what we are driving at and realistically we are not simply our bodies. The visible is only the surface of us, and even here and now deep beyond deep lies behind that in the world invisible. Indeed, being realistic in the sense of using only our eyes has been the curse even of physical science. Men saw apples fall for ages and, stopping with that visual surface, perceived no important truth at all, until a man looked at a falling apple not with his eyes alone, but with his mind, and, lo! an invisible force that holds the stars together! We had indeed better be realistic. And when we look at the visual surface only which our physical bodies present in this visible world, we are not being realistic. The creative forces of personality are now invisible.

To be sure, everybody knows how natural it is to feel that life beyond death is too mysterious, too marvelous, too good, it may be, to be true. But, my friends, consider. The real mystery is not thus post-mortem; the mystery is here and now. We are inhabitants today of the world invisible; that is the mystery. Sometimes when one ponders it—how everywhere the visible world is but a door which, when we push it open, ushers us into a world invisible—one bows in awe unspeakable. There is not a mystery about the unseen world beyond death that is not essentially here now.

Indeed, this, I think, would be the mystery, that this universe should produce personality with its amazing possibilities of knowing, creating, loving—imprisoned splendors, such as exist in all the cosmos nowhere except in personality—and then, having produced the spiritual world invisible, should snuff it out like a guttering candle as though it did not matter. That would be a mystery.

And this, too, would be a mystery, that the invisible world in which today we do most truly live should have arisen by accident, with no eternal reality to call it forth. Why, nothing similar can be found anywhere beside! If we have eyes it is because there first was light. If we have lungs it is because there first was air. Always what is in us was called into being by some reality. And now men say that personality, the invisible being that we really are, came by fortuity, correspondent to nothing, an unwanted by-product of an accidental process that did not care. Would not that be an incredible mystery? No, I tell you, the invisible world, now and forever, is the real world—

> On the earth the broken arcs; in the
> heaven, a perfect round.

Again this appeal to the soul's invincible surmise makes life immortal more homelike. To be sure, countless questions about our friends who have disappeared into the unseen we cannot answer. We had better be agnostic about details. Only charlatans pretend to know them. This, however, is true, that, when a soul that long has dwelt in the unseen disappears into the invisible, it must be like going home. On that day, long ago, when Jesus passed into the "house not made with hands, eternal, in the heavens," do you think it seemed strange to him? Had he not always lived in the unseen, from it drawn his power, to it given his devotion, for it laid down his life? Was not disappearing into the unseen for him like going home?

Consider, indeed, the serious ethical consequence of our

thought: the sense of reality in life eternal comes not so much from our intellectual arguments as from living now in the eternal world. Here, this morning, if one wishes assurance of eternal life, one may well crave not so much a new argument as a fresh, compelling, transforming experience of the invisible. Some of you, for example, love Francis Thompson's poetry, especially his "Hound of Heaven." Remember, however, that for years he was an ineffective soul, failing professionally, enslaved by the drug habit, even calling cabs and holding the bridles of horses on the curbs of London streets to get a few pence. He was elevated out of his obscurity and failure into a singer of immortal beauty by his mystic sense of the reality of the unseen world. He was singing of the realm most real to him when he wrote:

> O world invisible, we view thee,
> O world intangible, we touch thee,
> O world unknowable, we know thee,
> Inapprehensible, we clutch thee!

> Does the fish soar to find the ocean,
> The eagle plunge to find the air—
> That we ask of the stars in motion
> If they have rumour of thee there?

> . . . .

> Yea, in the night, my Soul, my daughter,
> Cry,—clinging Heaven by the hems;
> And lo, Christ walking on the water
> Not of Gennesareth, but Thames!

A man who thus could see the invisible now would find immortal life like going home.

Go out, then, on this Easter day, with a song of triumph. The invisible is real. Say it to yourselves. Let it be a rallying cry to your souls when days are difficult and endurance hard, when death befalls your friends or, like a "dark mother always gliding near with soft feet," comes to your own doorsill. The invisible is real. Let it challenge your conscience also, when carnal things loom too vivid and spiritual values

[239]

seem too dim. The invisible is real. Let it usher you now into life eternal so that when the great change comes it may be for you, whose real life long has been in the unseen, like going home. For this is the root of all great religion, this is the meaning of all faith in God, this is the basis of immortal hope, this is the radiance of the Easter morning, that we endure as seeing him who is—aye, and those who are—invisible.